HEALING POWER:
THE WORKBOOK

PAIN-METHOD-QUALITY

Philip Shapiro, MD, MPH

authorHOUSE®

AuthorHouse™
1663 Liberty Drive
Bloomington, IN 47403
www.authorhouse.com
Phone: 1 (800) 839-8640

Published by AuthorHouse 01/18/2016

ISBN: 978-1-5049-6836-2 (sc)
ISBN: 978-1-5049-6835-5 (e)

Library of Congress Control Number: 2015920944

Print information available on the last page.

To the triumph of love over pain

Praise for the Book

My clients and I love *Healing Power: The Workbook*, the companion manual to Dr. Shapiro's original book, *Healing Power: Ten Steps to Pain and Spiritual Evolution Revised, 2010*. Rich universal spiritual principles are made accessible, not just to scholars, but to all who suffer and seek relief. Here you will find a practical approach to spirituality. Every sentence is a pearl of love wisdom that heals. Kelly Fitzpatrick, Mental Health and Addictions Counselor

Although both spiritual traditions and mental health techniques offer ways of alleviating suffering, they remain largely separate. As a psychiatrist and spiritual seeker, Dr. Shapiro is able to integrate self-healing techniques from the great spiritual traditions with those of modern mental health treatment. This workbook represents a major step forward by presenting an integrated model for alleviating suffering which bridges these traditions. Dr. Phil Bolton, Psychiatrist

I use Dr. Shapiro's Healing Power principles in my personal life and professional work as a mental health counselor. The Ten Steps to Pain Management bypass the constraints of diagnosis and educational level to speak to the core human experience of pain and healing. With this Healing Power Workbook, readers have direct access to the principles, approaches, and pearls of wisdom that guide an individual on a personal and spiritual path of recovery. Megan Chaloupka LPC, CADC-1, Clinical Manager, Central City Concern

The very best of Central City Concern has been the work of Dr. Philip Shapiro, specifically a wellness class based on his model, *Healing Power*. Prior to engaging with this group, I spent too much time either ruminating about things that happened thirty years ago that I cannot change, or worrying about the future. By practicing mindfulness, I have learned to live in the here and now, and to face my demons, to go through the fire much as a piece of coal does to become a diamond. Practicing healing qualities on a daily basis replaces negative thoughts and feelings with hope. Samm McCrary, Intern, Central City Concern

This workbook contains a map for spiritual evolution. Each part contains the whole. Dr. Shapiro invites and urges the reader to roll The Universal Healing Wheel, to practice the methods and incorporate the healing qualities into our consciousness and actions. This is an experiential approach. It can be used by people of all educational levels, utilizing any belief system, or indeed, open skepticism. The proof is in the practice. I have used it with clients who suffer from trauma, mental illness, and addiction. I have been amazed and gratified at how they engage with the material, and embrace and benefit from the concepts. I use this model myself to address challenges and problems that arise in my own life. I now understand painful problems are a launching pad for spiritual development. Seiza de Tarr, LCSW, CADC II

For six plus years, we have used *Healing Power* to guide our innovative Living Room program at our Federally Qualified Health Center. Over this time, we have developed a closely connected community in that room based on "Healing Power" principles, no easy feat in a center whose work is based on serving persons with severe and persistent mental illness, addiction, and medical problems. However genius the original is, though, a workbook is definitely needed to help our members access this heart-led work more easily. We welcome *Healing Power: The Workbook* as an essential tool for strength-based recovery! (The Living Room is a drop in center with groups and classes) Shauna Hahn, Psychiatric Nurse Practitioner

I have suffered from rheumatoid arthritis for 75 years. Thanks to Dr. Shapiro's healing model, the pain is gone for the first time. Tone Kristiansen

The Universal Healing Wheel helps people manage a wide variety of painful problems. Dr. Shapiro presents effective ways for anyone to invoke their own healing system to manage pain not responsive to traditional medical interventions. As a professional, I am gratified to have a sound, practical set of spiritual tools added to the toolbox of integrative healthcare. John R. Turner, PhD, CPRP (Retired)

The potential for healing this compilation of wisdom represents cannot be overstated. Dr. Shapiro brings together the essential pieces of mind-body-spirit medicine in a way that meets any individual exactly where they are. It is a bountiful set of tools for everyone, from those new to alternative forms of healing, as well as practiced spiritual seekers. It provides structure, inspiration, and hope for those seeking to reduce mental, emotional, and physical pain. E.B. Ferdig, E-RYT500, Co-creator, Unfold Studios, Yoga therapist, specializing in anxiety and mental health

One of the most moving and marvelous gifts I received from Dr. Shapiro's book is the beauty of the one hundred healing qualities he identifies as part of the Universal Healing Wheel. The qualities are the heart and soul of this work. I remember the joy, awe, and wonder I felt when I realized we all carry within us, every one of these qualities. The qualities, once discovered and strengthened through the practice of the fifteen methods described in the workbook, are more powerful than any pain we may encounter, no matter how devastating. For me, the result of discovering Dr. Shapiro's model through his amazing books, is that I now, in the second half of my life, have found a road map to follow with a direction and goals true to my most sacred values of minimizing suffering, and increasing the love, compassion, and joy I find within and bring to the life around me. Gila Iris Aron

Contents

Illustrations and Text Boxes

Acknowledgments

I have been blessed with profound support from family, friends, teachers, colleagues, patients, and editors. I would like to express my deepest gratitude to the following. Without their help, there would be no book.

My beloved parents, Edward and Dorothy Shapiro and sister Suzanne, who taught me goodness, empathy, and purity of heart.

My patients, who teach me forbearance, courage, humility, and sweetness every day

The lineage of spiritual masters of Self-Realization Fellowship, represented by Paramahansa Yogananda

Jesus, Buddha, Krishna, Rumi, and all of the saints, sages, gurus, teachers, and masters of the great faith traditions whose wisdom permeates this work

Amy Livingstone, for her wonderful illustrations, Dr. Phil Bolton for his review of this manuscript, and Bill Johnson and Steve Roberts for their wise counsel.

My dear friend and spiritual brother, Corbett Monica for his love, strength, humor, and inspiration

The members of my spirituality and healing groups, my students, and all of my colleagues and clients at Central City Concern for their invaluable commentary on how the ten-step healing model works in their lives. A special thank you to Robin Roberson, Kealy Slaughter, Cathy Kennedy, Tim Casebeer, Miles Richmond, Seiza DeTarr, Shauna Hahn, Kelly Fitzpatrick, Geoff Sittler, Nicole Randt, Moira Ryan, Ed Blackburn, Rebecca Birenbaum, Dr. Rachel Solotaroff, Kathleen Roy, Dr. John Bischof, Megan Chaloupka, and Erika Armsbury.

My sons, Jon and David, daughter-in-law, Siobhan, and grandchildren for their love and support --Taylor, Michael, Collin, Kiley, and Bec.

My phenomenal wife, Sharon Whitney. She knows things. She is the Goddess of Culture. She is my muse. She can change my direction with a glance or a word. She makes my laugh. She is my rock.

I bow to you all.

Foreword

In *Healing Power: Ten Steps to Pain Management and Spiritual Evolution, Revised* (2010), Dr. Shapiro distills the wisdom from the world's great spiritual traditions into principles, steps, methods, and tools that help us overcome not only daily hassles and challenges, but also life's tragic and most painful experiences. In this book, *Healing Power: The Workbook*, Dr. Shapiro expands the teachings and provides greater opportunities for deeper healing.

Healing Power unlocks a form of knowledge that nourishes the mind, body, heart, and spirit. Dr. Shapiro speaks to the inevitable suffering of life, the painful realities we must all face. Suffering and pain can come from life events out of our control, like loss or the death of a loved one. Sometimes pain is an indicator of difficult changes we must make to get back on the right course and be happy. For example, we may be forced to deal with betrayal, to end a hurtful relationship, or to overcome bad habits that are harming others or ourselves. Other times, pain is a natural part of the process of personal growth.

Through Dr. Shapiro's Universal Healing Wheel, or Pain, Method, Quality (PMQ), you learn effective ways to deal with any type of pain that life throws at you and transform that pain into healing qualities. PMQ is accessible. In ten steps, using fifteen methods, you can achieve one hundred healing qualities.

Dr. Shapiro provides detailed instruction on how to use healing methods such as meditation, affirmation, and forgiveness to open the power and presence of love and spirit. Applying these methods, you can break free from the chains of a negative past and the destructive patterns of behavior, thought, and beliefs that perpetuate pain. The helpful suggestions, points to remember, affirmations, and exercises offer opportunities to examine the pain you are experiencing now, identify what you can learn from this pain, and move through and past the pain to healing.

I was first introduced to Dr. Shapiro and to *Healing Power* in 2013 when I was visiting the Assertive Community Treatment (ACT) program at Central City Concern, where Dr. Shapiro serves as the psychiatrist for the ACT team that provides comprehensive mental health services and support to individuals with serious mental illness. As I interviewed Dr. Shapiro regarding his role as the psychiatrist for the ACT team, it was immediately clear that his vision and insight regarding the healing process went well beyond the Western medical model, yet he didn't mention his book in the interview. It was the team leader for the ACT team who discussed the central role that *Healing Power* served in their work with individuals struggling with mental illness. She provided me with a copy of *Healing Power* and couldn't say enough about how it had transformed not only their approach to working with clients, but also how they had incorporated some of the methods into their daily team meetings and practice of self-care for staff members of the ACT team.

In 2015, I invited Dr. Shapiro to be a keynote speaker at the annual Oregon Center of Excellence for Assertive Community Treatment conference and to provide a workshop based on *Healing Power.* The impact on the conference participants was profound. They described the workshop and presentation as "moving," "inspirational," and "a healing process at the heart level." Mental health practitioners highly valued the methods offered in the workshop to address spiritual healing as an important dimension of their work. Conference participants also appreciated the focus on holistic health, mind-body-spirit, and the framework for how to discuss spirituality in a workplace setting safely and effectively.

It is extremely hard to break free from the ongoing drama of everyday life. Dr. Shapiro describes the dynamic process of how pain often stimulates a reactive response. When we recover from pain, we are not only recovering from the painful event itself, but also reducing our reactivity to the pain. Understanding the "pain and reactivity to pain" process enables us to increase our awareness and reduce our own reactivity. We can't control events, but we can control our response to events. *Healing Power* offers methods to become skillful pain managers, reduce our reactivity to negative life events, and live a deeper, more meaningful, and spiritually-centered daily life.

Dr. Shapiro's *Healing Power* is now a central resource in my daily practice of wellness. I continue to keep the book by my bedside and nightly read a sentence, paragraph, or chapter. With each reading, I benefit from an even deeper understanding of how to develop my loving and healing qualities. I turn to *Healing Power* when I am faced with a new life challenge or when I am embroiled in a deeply painful life experience. The methods help me remember I possess the skills to overcome pain and that I can use my pain to stimulate healing qualities such as peace, love, and joy and thereby become a successful pain manager.

Two of the methods I was introduced to in these books, yoga and the power of forgiveness, have transformed my life. The body is a magnificent instrument, a powerful tool, a compass designed to tell you if you are on the right path. But to manifest this power, we must learn to listen, perceive, and assimilate information offered by the body, mind, and spirit. We need to listen to our essential selves through nonverbal cues that signal when we are following our true paths. In *Healing Power,* Dr. Shapiro describes how the practice of yoga allows the body to become an instrument for receiving the spirit and achieving higher consciousness.

Dr. Shapiro provides a framework for understanding the healing power of forgiveness. Forgiveness is one of the hardest lessons people must learn, especially when betrayal is severe. I find the process of forgiveness offered by Dr. Shapiro to be a powerful healing tool. The method of spiritualizing the story is profoundly and deeply restorative. Practicing self-forgiveness—as well as the forgiveness of others—brings peace, strength, and a renewed trust in our inherent goodness.

Using these methods in real time as a painful event is in process takes time and practice, maybe a lifetime of practice. *Healing Power* and *Healing Power: The Workbook* provide the resources we need and can draw on again and again. The pearls revealed in these teachings instruct us how to use methods to manifest our highest good. We learn to transform painful life experiences into self-knowledge to become our highest selves where there is an abundance of peace, grace, and emotional and spiritual well-being. Imagine if each of us were able to manifest our highest good and give it back to each other in our families and our communities. Imagine how we could make the world a better place.

Heidi Herinckx, 2015

Part 1
Introduction

Prologue

If you are still in pain when you finish with your doctor, this workbook is for you. This is a self-help, self-healing model designed to help health care professionals and consumers skillfully manage the pain the medical model cannot fix. Here you will find fifteen methods and one hundred qualities you can use to contain, reduce, or eliminate your suffering and skillfully guide you through what is left. These methods and qualities are a composite of the wisdom of the ages from the sages. If we follow their advice, we can expand our healing power, become ever-increasingly skillful pain managers, and evolve. If you have finally had enough suffering, if you have a passionate desire to change, and if you are ready to do some work, this model answers the call.

Chapter 1

Skillful Pain Management

- This is a companion workbook to *Healing Power: Ten Steps to Pain Management and Spiritual Evolution, Revised* (2010). Here you will find a summary of that work with some additional principles and tools. Ideally, one would read *Healing Power, Revised* first, but this is not a must. These two books can be used separately or together. The goal is the same: skillful pain management, expansion of healing power, and spiritual evolution.

- This is a pain management workbook. Life is painful. Pain is complex, tricky, and difficult to master. We need all the help we can get. In this workbook, we will study the complexities of pain, see how it works, and offer a variety of methods and qualities to help us respond skillfully.

- Here you will find a composite of healing principles extracted from the great wisdom traditions and organized into steps and tools designed to help you turn the table on your pain, so it becomes your ally rather than your enemy. You will learn how to make your pain work for rather than against you. You will learn how to be a more skillful pain manager. You will learn how to *make medicine out of your pain*.

- Our pain can be physical, mental, emotional, interpersonal, or spiritual—in any combination and sometimes all at once. It can be overwhelming. Everyone gets a turn. No one is immune. We all suffer.

- Painful problems of body, mind, and soul take over and steal the peace. We find ourselves caught in a web of pain. We don't know how we got there and we don't know how to get out.

- At some point in our lives, most of us turn to short-term remedies that provide temporary relief but ultimately add to our pain—alcohol, drugs, food, sex, materialism, power, gambling, and the like. Because we manage our pain unskillfully, we find ourselves in more trouble; poorly handled problems are a source of untold difficulty.

- If only there were a way to reduce our suffering rather than compounding it. There is. We can learn how to become more skillful pain managers. Here's how:

- Pain is comprised of two layers:

  1. The inevitable suffering of life
  2. Our reaction to it

- We cannot control the inevitable suffering of life, but we can control how we respond to it. We are afraid of suffering, disease, disability, change, the unknown, and death. This mental distress slows down the healing process and makes the pain worse. When disease persists, we can learn how to slow down and relax so we stay in charge and get our lives back.

> Every painful problem has a mental component, because it must pass through the mind. The mind can make the problem worse by responding with one of its negative habit patterns, or it can help contain, reduce, and sometimes completely eliminate the problem. The methods taught here help us restructure the mind's habitual negative responses into positive healing qualities. We learn how to control pain so pain does not control us.

- This workbook recommends active practice of a variety of spiritually-oriented methods we turn to when our doctors and other health care professionals are unable to solve our problems and relieve our pain entirely. They are intended to supplement—not replace—existing components of our treatment regimen, such as medication, acupuncture, massage, diet, exercise, herbs, vitamins, counseling, psychotherapy, and so forth.

- The methods do not require professional attention. They are self-help, self-healing methods. We practice them on our own or with like-minded peers. This workbook will show you how to use these methods to nurture healing qualities that activate the mind-body connection and produce palpable changes in your response to your pain.

- *How you manage your pain will determine whether you move forward, backward, or stay stuck in this life.* By reading this workbook and putting its exercises into practice, you will learn what to do and what not to do to more skillfully manage your reaction to pain.

- This is more than just a pain management workbook. Throughout this work, you will learn about the intimate relationship between pain and love. Skillful pain management inevitably leads to expansion of healing power and spiritual evolution. That is to say, if you learn to be a more skillful pain manager, you are going to love more. You will feel better. You will become a better person. And you may even experience higher states of consciousness.

- If you have finally had enough suffering, if you have a passionate desire to change, and if you are ready to do some work, this model answers the call.

- Read on and you will find:

  - a host of profoundly important universal spiritual principles, methods, and qualities you can use for full recovery and deep healing.

  - fifteen proven methods—from ancient wisdom and modern science—designed to help you crack open the shell of religion to release its pearls of wisdom, hidden secrets, and soothing healing powers.

  - an arsenal of one hundred healing qualities that add up to Love. I capitalize the word *love* here to emphasize its divine nature. You can use these qualities for protection, guidance, and wisdom. The qualities will help you manage any pain or problem. With the cultivation of these qualities, you will be ready for anything that life throws at you, even the most brutal realities.

Summary

- This workbook addresses the inevitable suffering of life that cannot be eliminated by the medical model.

- We look at every domain of pain: physical, mental, emotional, interpersonal, and spiritual and offer a host of techniques to manage that pain skillfully.

- The supreme goal is to become an ever-increasingly skillful pain manager and expand our love until it is unconditional, one day at a time and for the rest of our lives.

- Here you will find a host of tools you can use when the going gets rough. The rest is up to you. You can take it as far as you wish. The payoff is as big as you want it to be.

Chapter 2

Personal Spiritual History

"Two Wolves"

An old Cherokee Indian was teaching his grandson about life.

"A fight is going on inside me," he said to the boy. "It is a terrible fight between two wolves. One is evil—he is anger, envy, sorrow, regret, greed, arrogance, self-pity, guilt, resentment, inferiority, lies, false pride, superiority, and ego.

The other is good—he is joy, peace, love, hope, serenity, humility, kindness, benevolence, empathy, generosity, truth, compassion, and faith.

This same fight is going on inside you—and inside every other person, too."

The grandson thought about it for a long minute and then asked his grandfather, "Which wolf will win?"

The old Cherokee simply replied,

"The one you feed."

When I was a young man, I had a lot of problems.

You might say the bad wolf had too much power.

To say this in another way, problems occur in five zones: (1) physical, (2) mental, (3) emotional, (4) interpersonal, and (5) spiritual. I had difficulty in four of these five. I have been blessed with good physical health, but I got hit pretty hard in the other four zones. My sister was very sick and died young. I lost my religion of origin. There was a lot of addiction in my family. And I had my fair share of character defects.

My problems added up, overlapped, and overwhelmed my best defense. If I were a quarterback, it would be like getting sacked too many times in the game, sacked by my own emotions. I didn't know how I got into all of this suffering, and I most certainly didn't know how to get out.

I needed help. I needed to learn how to heal my pain and how to more skillfully manage the pain that would not go away.

I went into traditional counseling. It helped a lot, but it wasn't enough. My pain was still too intense. So I became a spiritual seeker. I studied with the sages, saints, gurus, teachers, and masters of the great faith traditions, searching their models with a fine-tooth comb, looking for elements that strengthen the healing process.

The masters offered a simple, threefold prescription for my pain.

1. Love everybody, all the time, no matter what.

2. Knowing this was a tall order, they gave me techniques to help carry it out—breathwork, affirmations, meditation, mindfulness, the presence of God, yoga, transformation of emotion, contemplation, prayer, and a few more.

3. To further move the process along, they gave me a pill called LSG: *love, serve,* and *give.* They wanted me to take this pill four times a day: morning, afternoon, evening, and nighttime, and they told me I could take as many additional pills (PRNs) as I wanted because there were no side effects, no toxicity, no insurance, no managed care, no doctor, and no therapist. This pill is free and completely safe. (PRN is a medical abbreviation for taking a pill as needed only.)

I thought, *How simple, elegant, profound, and beautiful—unconditional love and service with some techniques to back it up. But does it work?* I didn't know. But what did I know? The one thing I knew for sure was that my life wasn't working. I decided to give this a try.

I studied and practiced their teachings. Slowly, three things happened:

1. I started to feel better.
2. I became a better person.
3. I began experiencing the superconscious states I was reading about in sacred spiritual books: the peace that surpasses understanding, pure love, ecstatic joy, bliss, nirvana, or God. It doesn't matter what I called it: it was gorgeous.

You might say the saints showed me how to feed the good wolf. And that good wolf started to take over.

I continue the same prescription to this day. I tell people I'm on the pill—the *love pill.* On this pill:

1. I have come a long way.
2. I continue to slowly improve.
3. I have a lot of work to do.

Both wolves are still here, but I've changed the ratio.

All of this would have remained a private experience if not for the advent of mind-body-spirit medicine, which now has ample scientific evidence that people with an active faith system have better outcomes in medicine, surgery, mental health, and addiction.

In other words, what goes on in the mind counts a lot. When we find the system that works for us, something in the mind clicks and sends something down into the factory of the cells, into the machine that facilitates healing.

If we can define that something—I call it the essential healing principle of religion—and transfer that principle safely to healthcare, we can bring more healing power to our clinical work for ourselves, our patients, and the organizations we serve.

I have tried to define this essential healing principle in the book I wrote in 2005, revised in 2010, and elaborate in this edition.

This is a self-help, self-healing model. I use it myself, and I teach it to staff, patients, and students if they are interested.

The model is my seventy-two-year story translated into principles, steps, tools, and exercises that may be of use to you and the people you serve.

In the next chapter, you will find some suggestions on how to start and maintain a successful spiritual practice.

Chapter 3

Getting Started

In *Healing Power, Revised*, Chapter 11, Getting Started, (pp. 161–80), you will find some suggestions for starting a successful spiritual practice. You may want to review these now. Topics in that chapter include:

1. Goal: cultivate healing qualities.
2. Support: get a support network of like-minded people.
3. Solitude: learn how to be alone.
4. Self-reform: change the world by changing yourself.
5. Ego reduction: reduce your ego to expand your soul qualities.
6. Spiritual healing: recognize the difference between physical and spiritual healing.
7. Self-acceptance: accept where you are while striving to improve.
8. Discipline: suffering is a stimulant for the cultivation of spiritual power.
9. Expectations: spiritual rewards occur on their own timetable.
10. Calm concentration: the best practice position.
11. Stay in the present: minutes and moments.
12. Start slow: one step at a time.
13. Continuous practice: there is always work to do.
14. Pace yourself: it's a long climb.
15. Do your best: leave the rest.
16. A balanced healing program: fifteen pain management options.
17. The scientific method in metaphysics: direct personal experience.

Following are some additional topics that may help you start and maintain your practice.

1. Simplicity and complexity
2. Deepest suffering and deepest healing
3. Design your own program
4. Stages of learning
5. Wisdom pearls
6. Role of medication
7. Risk and benefit

8.   Group guidelines

9.   What to expect: the work-pain-joy cycle

10. Right attitude

Simplicity and Complexity

- Healing Power is a complex model with a lot of working pieces. It can be overwhelming. However, if you continue your study, you will see the model is as simple or complex as you want it to be. Here is how this works.

- The entire story of religion contracts to a single word: love. Love expands to PMQ (pain, method, quality). PMQ branches out into any pain, fifteen methods and one hundred qualities with traction devices. (See illustration, next page.)

Story of Religion

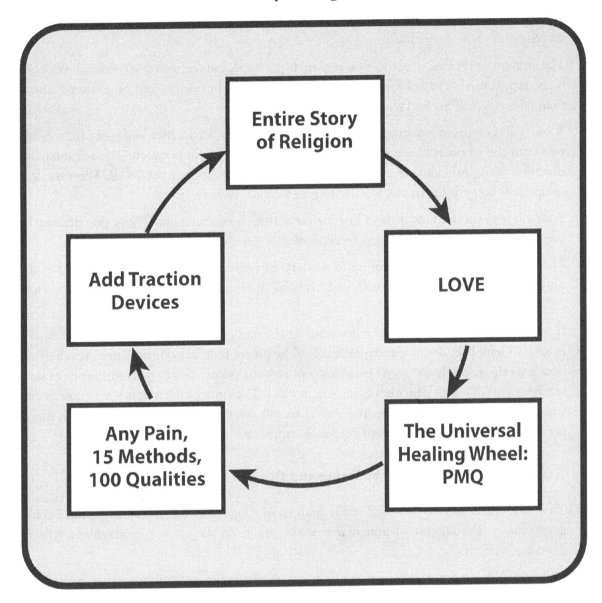

- Start with the entire story of religion. This is obviously complex.

- We can reduce this down to a single word: love. Love is the elegant essence of religion. This is as simple as it gets.

- Love is expressed through the *universal healing wheel* or PMQ.

- PMQ expands to any problem, fifteen methods, and one hundred qualities.

- Add back the traction devices from the stuff of religion, and we are back where we started: the entire story of religion.

- The universal wheel with traction devices captures the entire story of religion while offering a cafeteria of options. You choose the degree of complexity and structure that works for you.

- You can be atheist, agnostic, religious, or spiritual.

- Your belief system can be simple or complex, fixed or opened.

- Your practice can be as simple as breathwork and a few loving-kindness affirmations to full on religion.

- The amount or type of structure you require is personal, but the universal goal is love. Love is the report card. The vehicle is not important. Ethical humanists can be more advanced than religious persons and vice versa.

- Some will want just a few nuggets to chew on for months before they add more later. Some will want the whole package. Others will choose something in between. The advantage of this is obvious: individuality, flexibility, and choice. One size does not fit all. There are lots of options. You create as you go according to your needs at the time.

- Your job is to choose how little or how much of this you want or need. Your practice can be one minute twice a day all the way to *one continuous sacred ritual*.

- The path laid out is from beginning to mastery. Mastery is beyond us but is included as the ultimate vision achieved by others and available with sustained long-term practice. How deep do you want to go?

- If you are overwhelmed with the complexity of the model at this point, hang in there. Study, think, contemplate, discuss, and practice. Put the pieces together one at a time. You will see how it works. Complexity won't be a problem at some point. The elegant simplicity of it all emerges as PMQ with or without traction devices. The only problem left is whether or not you will practice. If you do, then and only then can you unpack this wisdom through direct personal experience. And you will keep it as simple or complex as you wish.

Deepest Suffering and Deepest Healing

- This model takes more time and study than most, but if you put in the time, the benefit is enormous. The biggest advantage is that you are given the tools to manage any type or degree of suffering.

- The pain addressed in this model can be physical, mental, emotional, social, or spiritual.

- The problem can be tiny, small, medium, large, or huge, all the way to the most brutal reality—the cave of darkness, the dark night of the soul, or a personal ground zero where there is nothing but death, pain and suffering, and the unknown. I don't have answers to that, but the great wisdom traditions do.

- This work presents that wisdom of the ages, the teachings of saints, teachers, gurus, and masters. I transfer their wisdom and float it as options: healing principles, methods, and qualities that are more powerful than any pain or problem, even the most brutal of realities.

- The teachings of the great spiritual teachers can help us meet, match, and transcend any barrier we face. This model highlights key universal healing principles, fifteen powerful methods, and one hundred healing qualities. You choose as you go.

- It is very difficult to go deep. We want to squash our anxiety with a quick answer or quick fix. This model supports us to enter where we want and control the speed and depth of the work.

- You can discover which methods and qualities you need for problems of different sizes and shapes. You can take it as far as you wish.

- The deepest suffering requires the deepest healing. Which methods and qualities will work best for you when your pain gets too intense?

Design Your Own Program

- In this model, there is no universal prescription for length or type of practice. The healing ball is in your court. You design your own program. There is no set way to practice.

- With any pain, fifteen methods, and one hundred qualities, you can individualize your program to suit your needs.

Design Your Own Program

- You determine which problem you want to work on.
- You determine which method you want to practice.
- You determine which quality you want to cultivate.
- You determine which traction device you want to use.
- You determine which wisdom pearl you want to affirm.
- You determine where, when, how often, and how long you will practice.

- This is different from other models for which you might be advised to practice a method such as mindfulness or meditation thirty minutes twice a day.

- With this model, you can practice for a few minutes and expand as time and circumstance allow.

- You can also change problems, methods, and qualities to suit your needs at the time.

- This flexibility has its advantages. It appeals to the differences between individuals and allows for the natural changes that occur in our schedules and life circumstances.

- Every one has PMQ, but *you* decide which problem, method, and quality you want to work with and add traction devices as needed.

- You may practice one or two exercises for a few minutes and build from there to a continuous practice of one or more methods and qualities throughout the day.

- Medical students and young couples with children may be too busy to meditate, but one can always practice breathwork, affirmations, and mindfulness.

- How much or what type of structure do you want?

- What works best for you?

- For more information on how to design your own program, see the chapter on methods in this workbook on p. 59

Stages of Learning

- Some go to a lecture or read a book about healing and think that's enough. This is a good start, but no change can occur without work and practice.

- Without practice, we cannot change a current long-term brain groove carrying a negative pattern to a new groove carrying positive methods and qualities.

- This is a practice model. The following steps summarize the learning process we need to start and maintain a self-healing practice:

> **Stages of Learning**
> 1. Read
> 2. Contemplate
> 3. Discuss
> 4. Practice
> 5. Experience
> 6. Repeat steps 1–5

1. Read
- Read this or a similar book on self-healing. Go through the material to see what is there. This is like looking at a map to get the lay of the land.

2. Contemplate
- If you're not familiar with this practice, you might review Contemplation in chapter 16, (p. 237) in Healing *Power, Revised* and chapter 24 on p. 176 in this workbook.

- With contemplation, we stop reading and sit quietly with a paragraph, sentence, or even a single word and let the material go deep.

- We crack open the shell of a pearl of wisdom to reveal its hidden secrets and release its soothing healing powers.

- We convert the great ideas embedded in wisdom texts from shallow words in our heads to real healing vibrations that permeate consciousness and action.

- With this study method, our understanding of the healing process gets a little bit deeper every day.

3. **Discuss**
   - You will inevitably run into barriers and have questions. Bring these issues to your group. Discuss the material with fellow students and teachers. Get feedback and clarification.

4. **Practice**
   - At some point, we have to stop talking and thinking and get to work. We need to begin practicing the methods: mindfulness, meditation, breathwork, affirmations, and more.
   - In this stage, we are working directly with our body, consciousness, energy, mind, will, emotions, desires, decisions, and actions.

5. **Experience**
   - You will notice a slow but sure growth of peace, compassion, understanding, strength, courage, wisdom, forgiveness, humor, and other wonderful healing qualities. You feel better, you become a more skillful pain manager, and you may even experience higher states of consciousness.

6. **Repeat**
   a. Repeat steps 1–5.
   b. Where are you in the process?
   c. Are you ready to do the work?

Wisdom Pearls

- Throughout this work, you will find a host of wisdom pearls.

- A wisdom pearl is not just a positive thought but also a super-positive deep thought with the potential power to help us heal—not just in the moment but also over the course of a lifetime. Wisdom pearls have the potential to help us in every domain of life, but it takes time to understand them. A deep wisdom pearl can grow throughout our lives and even then not be fully understood.

- An example of a wisdom pearl central to this work is "Love is the great healer." This sounds simple, and it is. But at the same time, this simple truth is profound, deep, complex, subtle, and nuanced. There is no limit to the power and variety of its manifestations, how it can work its way into our lives to help us untie knots and dissolve problems, how it can help us manage our pain skillfully, and how it can help us evolve.

- Each of the one hundred qualities recommended in this work is a wisdom pearl. As we apply these qualities to our problems—even our most serious problems—we can see over the years how much power they have to help us heal.

- You will find a variety of wisdom pearls throughout this work. Let the story unfold, spiritualize the story, deep healing in the *room of stillness*, Higher Power options such as omniscience, omnipotence, omnipresence, and much more.

17

Healing with Wisdom Pearls

In this work, you will learn how to:

1. Drop wisdom pearls into the center of your consciousness.
2. Let the pearl sink in, absorb, digest, and expand.
3. Apply wisdom pearls to the circumstances of your daily life.
4. Practice in the moments, days, weeks, months, years, and lifetimes.

- When we do this work, we become that wisdom a little bit more every day for the rest of our lives. The healing we get is profound.

The Role of Medication

- How does medication fit into the picture? Following are some general rules. There are always exceptions.

- On a scale of 1–10, symptoms can be mild (1–3), moderate (4–6), severe (7–9), or extreme (10).

- We can practice the methods when symptoms are mild to moderate. It's very difficult or impossible to practice the methods when symptoms are severe or extreme.

- Mild (1–3): We can practice the methods. Medication is not required.

- Moderate (4–6): We can practice the methods. Medication is an option.

- Severe (7–9): There is possible danger to self or others. It is very difficult or impossible to practice the methods. Most need medication.

- Extreme (10): There is danger to self or others. Medication is indicated. Cannot practice the methods.

Risk and Benefit

- Before we get started, a word about reactivity. Recall that pain has two levels: the inevitable suffering of life and our reaction to it. When we practice the recommended methods, we reduce unnecessary reactivity. This is to be distinguished from the heightened emotions and sensitivities resulting from major mental illnesses: schizophrenia, bipolar disorder, PTSD (posttraumatic stress disorder), anxiety and depressive disorders, traumatic brain injury, and more. In these instances, there is a biological and/or genetic contribution to heightened reactivity that may or may not respond to the techniques recommended here.

- In addition, some techniques—like meditation, transformation of emotion, and forgiveness—may cause our pain to get worse before it gets better. Opening a dialogue with emotional pain can be frightening, requiring a dive into uncharted territory and facing the unknown. When we stand alone and ride the pain waves, there is likely to be considerable resistance. We should never underestimate how frightful this may be. We should never push anybody into such a process.

- Some cannot and should not engage in exploring their pain in such a manner without seeking professional help; it might flood their defenses, causing alarm or panic. If you feel your pain is too intense when you practice any method, please avoid it at that point and consult with a professional counselor.

Guidelines for Groups and Classes

- Please review the following guidelines. If we follow these suggestions, we can extract the essential healing principle from religion and apply it to healthcare safely, efficiently, and effectively.

- We use these guidelines for groups and classes. It works. We have enjoyable, educational discussions without getting into destructive debate.

- The model is a composite of universal healing principles from the great wisdom traditions. It does not push religion. It does try to equip persons of all persuasions with the essential healing principle embedded within religion.

- We do not promote a particular religion. We do promote your individual approach to spirituality.

- We have respect and tolerance for the great variety of ways to understand and practice spirituality.

- The model is for any person: atheist, agnostic, spiritual, or religious.

- The model is for any problem: physical, mental, emotional, interpersonal, or spiritual.

- The methods can be practiced anywhere and anytime—at home, at work, or at play.

- There is a cafeteria of options. You can add these options to your current belief system or build your own program.

- Take what you need and leave the rest.

- The term *Higher Power* is used to describe the God of your understanding, our higher self, higher states of consciousness, or your higher meaning and purpose.

- One person's traction device is the next person's gag reflex. Don't let language stop you. For some people, even the word *spirituality* is a problem. Nuke offensive language and substitute your own. For example, you might substitute Higher Power for God, higher self for soul, healing qualities for spiritual qualities, or cognitive behavioral practice for spiritual practice.

- Some chapters in this book speak to those who believe in a God of love. Other chapters are more universal. If you don't believe in God, let alone God as love, substitute with words like spiritual qualities, healing qualities, qualities, The Tao, The Way, The Great Spirit, Creator, compassion, or any other term that gives you traction. The universal goal is to become a more skillful pain manager, expand healing power, and evolve. As you proceed, use whatever term is most acceptable to you.

- Stay in your own lane.

- Reform yourself and not others. We are not here to change others. We are here to change ourselves.

- We do not proselytize. (convert others to our point of view.)

- We engage in discussion without debate.

- We are here to listen and share, learn and grow, study and practice.

- Although active participation is encouraged, it is perfectly okay to remain silent throughout the meeting.

- During the class, we take turns reading. If you don't wish to read, you are welcome to pass.

- The group lasts sixty minutes. Each person reads a paragraph followed by a discussion and contemplation of the material.

- We avoid giving advice or trying to fix other people's problems. We focus on our personal experience using the spiritual methods for cultivating healing qualities in response to life's problems.

- When we finish the book, we return to the beginning and read it again.

- This is an open group. You can come and go as you please.

- We begin and end each class with a period of silent meditation for two minutes. The best meditation position is with the eyes closed, focused on the point just above and between the eyebrows, feet flat on the floor, hands resting in your lap with palms upward, spine straight, and slightly bent as a bow. You may repeat your focus word, mantra, or a favorite affirmation. You might also just focus on your breath.

What to Expect
The Work-Pain-Joy Cycle

- Spiritual belief systems make many grandiose, idealistic promises: eternal peace, unconditional love, and abundant joy. In the beginning, the hope for such experiences gets many people involved in the rigorous discipline of the spiritual path. After doing the work, it is a natural human tendency to expect the promised rewards. However, there will be times when there seems to be nothing but work, effort, and pain—without compensation. Progress toward healing, pain relief, and higher states of consciousness can be very slow or seem nonexistent.

- It's best to have no expectations; if our demands are not met, we might stop doing the work. If we are patient and try not to imagine how fast our growth should be, we can persevere and stay on our chosen path. Though results are often slower than we would like, progress occurs if we make the effort. Everything gets better slowly with practice, a lot of practice— but not on our schedule.

- Effort is progress. When we roll the universal healing wheel or practice PMQ, we are moving forward, even if we can't tell we are. The change is too subtle to pick up. New brain grooves that hold the qualities are forming, but they are not strong enough to manifest.

- The new brain grooves remain even when you backslide. Just get back to your practice as soon as possible. It's very important to remember this, as one can become demoralized when there is only work and pain—and sometimes even backsliding—with no apparent forward movement.

- When you are deeply immersed in spiritual work and experience no change, always remember that you are making progress even if it's invisible. The qualities are growing even when you can't feel it. The reward comes on its own schedule.

- It's worth working and waiting for ever-increasing peace, love, joy, power, wisdom, and a host of other healing qualities. You will feel better, become a better person, and may even experience higher states of consciousness. Tell yourself the qualities are growing even when you can't feel it. This helps keep you in the game.

- Following is the work-pain-joy cycle in five steps:

The Work-Pain-Joy Cycle

1. Work and pain without apparent change
2. Feel better and become a better person
3. Superconsciousness
4. Repeat
5. Mastery

---

1. Work and Pain without Apparent Change

- We are in pain. We do the work. We roll the wheel. We practice PMQ. The qualities are growing but not enough to feel. In this stage, there is work, struggle, and discipline without immediate reward.

- The length of this stage is determined by the extent of the problem. Some problems require just a few minutes of work. Others take longer. Deeply embedded severe problems may take years of work. The schedule is not up to us. Our job is to do the work. Relief comes on its own terms.

- Many quit here as they are looking for immediate gratification. If you are not ready for work and pain without immediate results, you will likely give up. If you persevere, you will feel better.

2. Feel Better and Become a Better Person

- The qualities are growing. You feel the change. There is a tangible experience of ever-increasing peace, love, strength, courage, joy, and other healing qualities. You feel better and become a better person.

- Keep going. You may experience a transformation of consciousness described in the next step.

3. Superconsciousness

- There is an unmistakable shift in consciousness: the peace that surpasses understanding, pure love, ecstatic joy, intuitive wisdom, a feeling of oneness with everything, and more. These experiences last for a few minutes or hours to several days, but there is inevitably a return to ordinary consciousness. There is more work to do.

4. Repeat

- Repeat steps 1–3.

5. Mastery

- There is a sustained state of superconsciousness. This is very advanced and requires decades if not lifetimes of work and discipline.

- With unceasing daily practice, the qualities become so strong that no external drama or condition of the body can dislodge them. We remain peaceful, positive, and poised no matter what life brings. We experience the soul connected to the Spirit as a durable love born of ever-expanding compassion, understanding, wisdom, and joy. We know we are the immutable peace of the soul connected to Spirit, eternally safe and protected. We know our love is greater than any pain or problem. We can get through any barrier, no matter how insurmountable it appears. Nothing can stop us. Nothing can touch us. We are awake, aware, and ready for anything. Serene and compassionate service to humanity is the natural outcome of this state of consciousness.

Right Attitude

A positive attitude is essential for recovery and healing every step of the way. We need this to get started, stay in the game, reduce unnecessary reactivity, and stay calm no matter the circumstance.

Following are some exercises to help you cultivate right attitude. You may find these helpful or create your own.

1. Pain Has a Purpose

- Pain and tests have a purpose: the cultivation of healing qualities and higher states of consciousness.

- Turn the table on the pain and make it work for rather than against you.

- When pain comes, the student affirms:

  a. Life is school.
  b. Pain is the teacher if I open to its lessons.
  c. The lessons always have to do with the cultivation of healing qualities.

- The student asks the pain:

  a. Why are you here?
  b. What are the lessons I need to learn?

    c. What do I need to do?

    d. What healing qualities do I need to be working on now?

- Respond to tests with healing qualities.

- Align your thoughts, feelings, desires, decisions, and actions with the qualities.

2. Little Steps, Little Victories

- We want perfect unconditional love and associated qualities, but we cannot achieve this due to our imperfections. Make peace with your imperfections, and keep that shining goal before you.

- Growth is slow, painful, and difficult, but it's inevitable if we make the necessary effort.

- The way is paved with little steps and little victories.

- When we fall down, we get up. We persevere.

- With work, effort, little steps, and little victories, we move past our current level—no matter that level—to a place beyond our imagination.

- Effort is progress. One, two, three, four--little steps, little victories.

3. Affirmations for Right Attitude

- I am positive, calm, focused, awake, and alert.

- I am willing, cheerful, and enthusiastic.

- I am always willing to change.

- I am ready to do the work.

- My intent is strong.

- My will is strong.

- I can overcome any barrier.

- I will overcome any barrier.

- I am ready for anything.

- Nothing can stop me.

- Nothing can ruffle me.

- Courage, perseverance, and faith pave the way.

- Positive thought paves the way.

- No defeat. Only will power.

- No discouragement. Only enthusiasm.

- No failure. Only positive action steps.

- Little steps, little victories.

- Slow, steady, this step, this action.

- I respond to tests with healing qualities.

- Knots untie. Problems melt. Balance and harmony result.

- It's not about the role I play but how I play it. I permeate every action with love.

- I do not try to escape a trial but rather endure it with the right attitude.

- I rise above by cultivating the qualities.

- Strength, courage, and perseverance get me through.

- Positive thought and healing qualities get me through.

- When all else fails, I endure and rise above.

- Effort is progress.

- I do my best and leave the rest.

4. Watch the state of your spirit. How would you describe it?
5. Are you down and out, about to throw in the towel? Or are you up and ready for the fight?
6. What are the ingredients for your right attitude?
7. What is going to keep you going no matter what happens?

Points to Remember

This work describes fifteen powerful healing methods. Practice these methods in the daily grind of ordinary activities, in the minutes and moments of your life, when things are good, when things are bad, and when you are in crisis. You will see that they work. Results are subtle, but they accumulate minute-by-minute, thought-by-thought, and breath-by-breath. Use every circumstance and every moment as an opportunity to practice.

- Spiritual work is difficult. It requires discipline, hard work, a long time, and it often hurts. However, if you persist, it gets easier—and the reward is great: expanded healing qualities and superconscious experience. If you persevere with courage and heart, you will learn, grow, and transform. Never, never, never give up.

- None of this works without practice, and practice occurs without immediate results. Many quit for lack of an immediate response, but if we persist when the going gets rough and we don't feel better, at some point we will. Then we see how the healing process works. We feel better and become better people. Then we trust the process.

- Wisdom pearls take time to grasp. Lots of time. A lifetime! Chew on a bite-sized piece. Digest it. Integrate it. Then another piece.

- You may have a little or a lot of time to do this work. A little is good. More is better. You can expand your practice or not, as you wish.

The next chapter has some information on how to use this workbook.

Chapter 4

How to Use This Workbook

This workbook is divided into five parts.

Part 1, Introduction: Chapters 1–7 introduce the principles of skillful pain management, personal spiritual history, ideas for starting a successful spiritual practice, how to use this workbook, mind-body-spirit medicine, key definitions, and a brief review of the ten steps.

Part 2, The Universal Healing Wheel: Chapters 8–15 describe the dynamics of the universal healing wheel.

Chapter 8, Setting the Stage to Roll The Wheel, outlines the conditions needed to start and maintain your practice.

Chapter 9, The Universal Healing Wheel, briefly introduces the basic principles of how PMQ (pain, method, quality) work together to help us manage our pain and heal.

Chapter 10, Pain, elaborates on important points we need to know about pain in order to manage it skillfully.

Chapter 11, Methods, gives a brief introduction to each of the fifteen recommended methods and some suggestions and exercises designed to help you practice the methods.

Chapter 12, Qualities, outlines important points about qualities and how to make them grow.

Chapter 13, Rolling The Universal Healing Wheel, describes the dynamics of how pain, method, and quality or PMQ work together in greater detail.

Chapter 14, The Universal Healing Wheel with Traction Devices, defines how traction devices for the wheel add more power to the healing equation.

Chapter 15, The Foundation, outlines key principles that underlie the workings of the wheel.

Part 3, The Methods: You will find an introduction to the fifteen recommended methods in *Healing Power, Revised, pp. 183-357*. Chapters 16–31 in this workbook review the fifteen methods in greater detail. Here you will find some additional principles and techniques.

In chapter 32, A Balanced Healing Program, you will find a brief review of the methods, suggestions for creating a balanced healing program, and some exercises designed to help you work on your most challenging and severe problems.

Part 4, The Qualities: Chapters 33–42 review ten qualities in detail.

Chapter 43, Fill Your Brain With Wisdom: 100 Healing Quality Pearls, elaborates on pearls of wisdom for each of the one hundred recommended healing qualities. This is a favorite of many and can be used as a prompt or discussion point for groups, classes, and individual therapy sessions.

Part 5, Miscellaneous: Chapters 44–55 cover a variety of topics.

Chapters 44–47 describe the house, the movie, school, and the car—metaphors that help us understand and practice self-healing.

Chapter 48 describes a universal healing method that includes will and grace. We can use this ten-step method to spiritualize any problem.

Chapter 49 reviews the serenity prayer—how to balance will and acceptance.

Chapter 50 documents the complexities of the ego and how it influences the healing process.

Chapter 51 defines the ultimate spiritual battle between Omniscient Love and terror at the abyss.

Chapter 52 is a collection of inspirational quotes.

Chapter 53 stages disease and recovery using the fifteen recommended methods and five levels. You will study *spin, float, integrate,* and *liberate.*

Chapter 54 outlines some frequently asked questions.

In the next chapter, you will find an introduction to mind-body-spirit medicine.

Chapter 5

Mind-Body-Spirit Medicine

- The medical model alone often leaves the patient with unmanageable pain from persisting illness. The healthcare practitioner and the patient need to know how to heal and manage that pain in the psychosocial and spiritual realm. There is evidence that healing takes place in each of these domains; enter the field of mind-body-spirit medicine.

- The scientific validation of mind-body-spirit-medicine allows us to combine the healing elements of spirituality and medicine. The next step is to find and transfer *the essential healing principle* from religion to medicine safely and without controversy. *Healing Power: Ten Steps to Pain Management and Spiritual Evolution, Revised* attempts to do that. This workbook is a companion piece to that book.

- To take advantage of the healing principles embedded in the religions, we need to solve the problem of confusing dogma, toxic language, and traumatic religious history. There is a way to do this. We can design healing models that serve people of all persuasions: Baptists, Sufis, ethical humanists, scientific atheists, true believers, and true non-believers. All of us have the same magnificent healing power in every cell of our bodies, and we know how to make it grow. This workbook is written for atheists, agnostics, religious, or spiritual persons. Anyone can play in the expanded field of healing power.

- This work is not about religion. It is about the healing principle extracted from religion, which we can apply in health care. Here you will find the essential healing principles of the great faith traditions translated into the universal language of mind-body-spirit practices.

- This model does not declare answers to life's big questions, such as why we are born, why there is so much suffering and evil, whether there is a God, and where we go after death. However, we can apply the wealth of healing wisdom in the great faith traditions to help us manage our pain and heal. In this work, you will find a cafeteria of options. You decide what works for you.

- In this chapter, we will review healing in three dimensions and review healing power's unique contribution to the field of mind-body-spirit medicine.

Three-Dimensional Healing

- Three levels of healing work together for optimal benefit. These three compliment each other. We need all three for deepest healing.

> ## Three-Dimensional Healing
>
> 1. The Body: The body heals itself.
>
> 2. Health Care Interventions: We get help from physicians and other health care professionals.
>
> 3. Self-Help: We can heal ourselves.

- To understand how this works, let's start with the intelligent power that operates every cell in the body and see how that relates to current medical practice.

The Body

- The body's power to heal itself is unfathomable! To contemplate even a tiny aspect of its inherent healing wisdom inspires awe and respect. Reflect on its brilliance. A cut heals. In response to bacteria or viruses, the body creates precisely-designed antibodies which hunt down and destroy the invaders. The body knows how to transform food into energy and building materials needed for the repair of our damaged cells. Individual cells assume specialized tasks as if they are construction workers—some build, some tear down, some transport, and others eliminate debris. (Suggested reading: *The Hidden Face of God* by Gerald Schroeder.)

- Every cell in the body produces two thousand proteins per second and sends these proteins where they need to go. The human body has seventy-five trillion such cells organized into tissues, organs, and systems working together in near perfect harmony so we can walk, think, decide, see, hear, touch, taste, smell, feel, play, enjoy beauty, give and receive love, and help others.

- When there is an imbalance disrupting any of these functions, the body's inherent healing wisdom springs into action. This intelligent power goes to work to fix any injury and illness and does so brilliantly. The body can and wants to be healthy. It heals itself automatically. At some point, however, the incomparably wise healing power needs our help.

Healthcare Interventions

- The wisdom of the body, however intelligent, cannot fix everything on its own. Some pain or problem gets past the body's inherent brilliant protections and breaks through as a symptom that won't go away.

- A new lump, a feeling of unfamiliar pain, or lingering discomfort sets off an alarm and disturbs our feeling of safety. Anxiety rears it head. We begin to worry. We think, *This could be serious! Is this the big one? Am I looking at a lifetime of suffering or disability? Am I going to die?* Fear of the unknown is a completely understandable reaction, and these types of worries are among the most common reasons for visits to primary care physicians.

- With symptoms and associated fear in hand, we go to the doctor. The doctor makes a diagnosis and treatment plan, which most often involves the use of medication or surgery.

These interventions in some way help the healing power do its work. If it works completely, the symptom, pain, and associated fear are gone. Back in our comfort zone, we feel safe and move on.

- But what happens when symptoms persist? We return to the doctor. More tests are run. More blood is taken. We may undergo X-rays, PET, MRI, or CT scans. More prescriptions are written. But even with our highly trained and skilled health care professionals and the advances of modern medicine, some illnesses resist treatment and become chronic.

- This is stressful and frustrating for both doctor and patient. Well-intentioned doctors and patients, looking together for pain relief and healing, often get caught up in unhealthy polypharmacy—the use of multiple medications. Alternatively, the physician knows the limitations of the medical model and does not continue to prescribe medications.

- You may be reading this workbook because you have been treated by a medical doctor or other health care professional, yet you continue to experience symptoms and pain. This can be a frustrating and sometimes terrifying place to be. The thought of being at the mercy of chronic pain can be overwhelming.

- Left to our own devices, many of us in this situation understandably begin self-medicating with anything that dulls the pain: substance abuse, unhealthy personal relationships, and a variety of other maladaptive behaviors that only make a bad situation worse. This is where integrative and mind-body-spirit-medicine can be of use.

Self-Healing

- Biological medicine is increasingly sophisticated and effective but remains reductionist, focusing on symptom management to the exclusion of all else. The aim of integrative medicine, on the other hand, is to treat injury and disease by making biological considerations only one piece of a larger puzzle that also affirms the psychological, social, and spiritual aspects of our beings and acknowledges that these combine to form our overall state of wellness. When you have reached the limits of biological medicine, you may need to step through the door to integrative medicine.

- With this holistic approach, you—the patient—play a much larger role in your health care. You will still go to the doctor and may take medication, but the responsibility for creating your state of wellness is now largely yours, especially when it comes to your psychological, social, and spiritual life.

- There are four evidence-based cornerstones of integrative medicine. We need comprehensive treatment planning with interventions in all four zones.

  1. Biological: The goal is a healthy body free of illness, injury, and pain. (This includes traditional, complementary, and alternative medicine.)

  2. Psychological: Strive to have a strong, positive, calm, focused, and resilient mind that finds meaning in the world and is ready for life's challenges.

3. Social: We are in this thing together. We recognize that we are complete only when we give and receive love. We engage in constructive, meaningful activities and serve others in need of support.

4. Spiritual belief systems: Meaning and purpose are often found in expression of our higher selves through devotion to a power greater than ourselves.

- *You already have the power you need to do this work.* But you may not know how to bring this power out and use it. This workbook teaches fifteen self-help methods for your psychological, social, and spiritual healing. By practicing these methods, you will learn how to expand healing power and skillfully manage the pain that your doctor cannot take away. The field of study you are about to enter is called integrative or mind-body-spirit medicine. Here, you are the healer.

Mind-Body-Spirit Medicine
Belief Systems Impact Disease and Healing

- Recent studies in the field of mind-body-spirit medicine have shown us that people with an active faith system have better health care outcomes in medicine, surgery, mental health, and addiction. These studies include patients with cancer, heart disease, strokes, high blood pressure, asthma, mental illness, addiction, and other health problems.

- The data demonstrates the essential principle that there is no separation between mind and body. The mind is connected to every cell in the body through electromagnetic and chemical waves. Thoughts have leverage in the inner workings of certain cells that affect disease and healing in the body. Although we don't know the mechanism, this provides us an entry point into our own process of healing.

- Mind-body-spirit medicine teaches us how to apply the power of belief to healing. The discipline is emerging as a major force in health care. The burgeoning appeal of mind-body-spirit medicine is due to its scientific validity as well as its cost effectiveness; it is ultimately a self-help program. In his book, *Timeless Healing: The Power and Biology of Belief,* Dr. Herbert Benson estimates that mind-body techniques are the treatments of choice in 60–90 percent of all doctor visits and have positive effects no matter the illness.

- Mind-body-spirit medicine is now established as part of modern medical practice. It is scientifically grounded and evidence based. What goes on in the mind counts a lot in health care outcomes. Beliefs impact disease and healing.

- There is an essential healing principle secreted in the religions. If we can define it, extract it, and transfer it to medical practice, we can positively affect disease, pain, and stress management. But this is no easy task. Bringing spiritual healing to traditional medical practice is not without controversy.

- Spirituality is a very confusing, complex, and contentious topic. Many people have been hurt or offended by religion. Some react strongly against spiritual or religious language in any context. Most protect their belief system, whether spiritual or secular, with fierce feelings and defensiveness.

- To transfer essential healing principles from religion to medicine safely, efficiently, and effectively, we need:

  1. A common language: the use of a respectful and common language that enables us to talk about these deeply personal and important matters without causing offense.

  2. Universal healing principles: we need to extract universal and inclusive healing principles, methods, and qualities that can work for atheists, agnostics, spiritual and religious people alike.

  3. Respect for individuality: recognition of the rights of those from different belief systems to practice according to the dictates of their faith, to deepen such convictions, or to build their own system of belief from scratch.

  4. A cafeteria of options: we need the widest possible range of options, combined with the right for people to take what they need and leave the rest.

- To accomplish these goals, the model described in this workbook was created in four stages:

  1. Deconstruct religion into discrete pieces.

  2. Eliminate theology, dogma, ritual, and other nonessentials.

  3. Extract essential healing principles we can use in health care.

  4. Organize the resulting principles into doable, practical steps and tools for self-healing.

- The model has ten steps, fifteen methods, and one hundred qualities expressed in a simple format called the universal healing wheel (UHW).

Healing Power's Unique Contribution to Transpersonal Psychiatry and Mind-Body-Spirit Medicine

- While modern high-tech medicine has great power on the physical plane, it ignores the world of spiritual healing. Mind-body-spirit medicine and transpersonal psychiatry try to change that by integrating medical science with the insights of various spiritual disciplines, including the role of contemplative practices for self-transcendence, superconscious states, and mystical experiences. *Healing power* contributes to this field in the following ways.

- It defines good mental health and demonstrates how it relates to higher consciousness.

- **Mental Health Definition**: The mind is calm, positive, focused, strong, and resilient. It is awake, alert, and ready for problem solving, creative intelligence, shaping meaning, goal accomplishment, pain management, and the creation of health, success, harmony, and joy.

- **Superconsciousness**: Healing power adds consciousness to good mental health. With the practice of techniques recommended in this model one not only feels better, but also may experience higher states of consciousness: the peace that surpasses understanding, pure love, ecstatic joy, bliss, nirvana, and God.

- **Soul and Spirit**: Gives a definition to soul and spirit and includes such options in health care for interested clinicians and patients.

- **The Universal Healing Wheel**: Reduces the entire story of religion to a single word—*love*—operationalizes that into PMQ, then adds back the stuff of religion as optional traction devices to add more power to the healing equation.

- **Love and Medicine**: Brings love to medical practice. It gives love a definition of one hundred healing qualities and a way to make it grow: rolling the universal healing wheel is expressed simply in four steps: stop, breathe, get in the present moment, and reframe.

- **Unlimited Creative Power**: The universal healing wheel with traction devices has unlimited creative power; with any problem, fifteen methods, one hundred qualities, and traction devices representing the stuff of religion, there are essentially unlimited options to choose from.

- **Cafeteria of Options**: Offers a cafeteria of options with individual control over speed, complexity, and depth.

- **Deepest Suffering and Deepest Healing:** Goes to the deepest root cause of our pain, including the gap-abyss, cave of darkness, and dark night of the soul and offers corresponding deep healing solutions. The individual chooses his or her pain and healing depth.

- **Horizontal and Vertical Axis**: Defines horizontal and vertical axis methods with the goal of moving the locus of control from outside to inside as the qualities become unconditional, spontaneous, and automatic.

- **Pain and Love:** Defines the dynamic relationship between pain and love.

- **Reactivity**: Defines in detail the importance of reducing unnecessary and destructive reactivity for skillful pain management.

- **Beginning to Mastery:** Outlines a path from beginning to mastery.

- **Unconditional Love:** Defines the importance of unconditional love in the healing process.

- **Ego**: Defines the ego in detail with exercises on how to build it up or reduce it, depending on the circumstances.

- **Will and Grace:** Defines the dynamic relationship between will and grace in the healing process.

- **Let the Story Unfold and Spiritualize the Story**: Defines the importance of letting the story unfold and spiritualizing the story, two key elements in the healing process.

- **Belief Systems**: Supports full on religion or deconstruction all the way down to PMQ without traction devices. Unconditional love is the goal in any case.

- **A Classification System**: Spin → Float → Integrate → Liberate with level 1–5, from no options to liberation.

- **Wisdom of the Ages:** Brings the wisdom of the ages and the sages to health care and the street.

Giving the Practice of Medicine a Story and a Soul

Here are things we like the most about adding spiritual healing to our work:

- It lights a fire of hope and possibility under traditional medical practice.

- It allows us to function under the umbrella of a great idea: bringing the wisdom of the ages to health care.

- It addresses the big questions of life without getting into trouble through the mechanism of a cafeteria of options.

- It embraces the interface between medical practice and the inevitable suffering of life.

- It goes to the root cause of our deepest suffering and offers corresponding healing solutions.

- It channels the wisdom of the saints and sages to universal methods for health care.

- It spiritualizes the practice of medicine by infusing it with a story and a soul.

- It offers a host of additional healing tools for healthcare professionals, patients, and consumers who can take it as far as they wish.

- It improves health care outcomes.

Points to Remember

- With the advent of mind-body-spirit medicine, it's now possible to combine the healing principles of both medicine and spirituality.

- To this end, I have designed a self-help, self-healing model I use myself and teach my patients.

- If we receive our medication, surgery, or natural remedy and are still in pain, there are a variety of psychosocial and spiritual methods that can help us manage that pain skillfully.

- This model has fifteen methods. The methods are the best of the best—a highlight reel of sorts—extracted from great spiritual books, teachers, and masters and translated into spiritually-oriented cognitive behavioral therapy (CBT), mindfulness, and meditative practices.

- When we practice these methods, we become more skillful pain managers, we expand healing power, and we evolve.

- The model is for health care professionals to heal themselves first and then support their patients in the same process.

- Patients can use this workbook directly, without a health care professional.

- Ideally, both professional and patient will practice the recommended methods.

The next chapter provides a list of definitions of key concepts used in this workbook. I suggest you review these definitions before you proceed.

Chapter 6

Definitions

Big Love and little love: Little love is human, conditional love expressed on the horizontal axis in our relationships with relatives, friends, and colleagues. Big Love is the pure, unconditional, unlimited love we cultivate with vertical axis methods. With sustained long-term practice of the recommended methods, little love expands until Big Love is all there is.

Brutal reality: Death, pain and suffering, and the unknown. Referred to as *reality*, because on the physical plane, suffering is unavoidable and death wins in the end. Brutal reality ultimately replaces the illusion of safety, security, and immortality defined below. Brutal reality is the painful side of duality.

Cave of darkness: A place of severe pain where we face the unknown, death, and/or evil without immediate answers to our questions. This is sometimes referred to as the dark night of the soul.

Duality: The law of polar opposites: pleasure and pain, good and evil, joy and sadness, love and hate, likes and dislikes, success and failure, anger and peace, life and death, and more.

Ego: The positive side of the ego helps us establish our place in the world of people and activities. The negative side of the ego separates us from others, the creation, and the Creator. This leads to selfishness—I, me, my, mine, territoriality, self-importance, and a host of other problems described throughout this work.

The Field: A singular power inhabits all space, unifying and harmonizing everything in the universe. This power is pure, formless conscious energy. It is at once the source of everything and the link that connects all. It cannot be born, confined, limited, divided, or broken. It is eternal, immortal, changeless, and one. It is inside, outside, everywhere, extending forever in every direction, unifying all things and people. We do not enter this field. We are already in it. It is already in us. There is no separation. All is one. We live in this infinite ocean as a fish swims in water. The *water* is always right here, offering peace, love, joy, wisdom, and safety. When we realize our oneness with the ocean, we know we are immortal, indivisible, and connected to all. (The *field* is also referred to as the big space or the ocean.)

Gap-abyss: The feeling of anxiety-panic we encounter when we introspect to find and work on our problems. Fear is the number one barrier to self-healing. Even making little changes can create a panicky feeling that we might unravel to the abyss. For deep healing, we must learn how to manage the feelings in the gap-abyss.

Grace: We have access to a vast intelligent healing power within and around us. We can tap into this power and get help with any type of suffering through work and grace. When we do our part at maximum effort, ask for help, and endure the problem as long as it is there, grace follows. Grace opens the gate to the unified field of omnipotent healing energy. We have no control over the gate. The Keeper of the gate, a mysterious intelligent force or law, opens the gate for us. The gate may or may not open for elimination of disease, disability or other painful problems. However, if we do the work, the gate will always open to allow expansion of healing qualities such as peace, love, strength, courage, wisdom, and joy.

Healing power: The magnificently intelligent healing power that operates every cell in the body. It knows what to do. It is incomparably brilliant.

Healing qualities: A list of one hundred qualities also referred to as the spiritual alphabet. These qualities are the attributes of love and reflect the character of the higher self, true self, or soul.

Higher Power: The God of your understanding, higher consciousness, higher self, or higher meaning and purpose.

Higher self: True self or soul, a composite of the one hundred qualities listed in the spiritual alphabet.

Horizontal axis: External action on the physical plane involving people, activities, places, things, and events. Used in conjunction with the vertical axis, which is internal action involving practice of spiritual methods described in this work. A balanced healing program includes work in both domains.

Illusion of safety, security, and immortality: There is no such thing as permanent or absolute safety on the physical plane. The best we can do on the physical plane is to create a feeling of safety based on the sense that we have more time. Referred to as an illusion as it is temporary, limited, and ultimately replaced by brutal reality.

Inevitable suffering of life: Life is difficult and painful for everyone. There is no way around it. All of us have to face the minor irritations of routine daily living and major life problems such as disease, disability, loss, change, the unknown, and death. This is the inevitable suffering of life. Reactivity is the suffering we add to the inevitable suffering of life. Reactivity is reversible. The inevitable suffering of life is not reversible.

Let the story unfold—the pain story: Allowing painful emotions to surface so they can tell their story, a very important first step in healing. For the second phase, see *spiritualizing the story*.

Liberation: Freedom from suffering through transcendence of body and mind to the pure consciousness and pure awareness of the soul connected to Spirit: a state reserved for masters after long periods of sustained spiritual practice.

Love: A combination of one hundred qualities defined in step 7. For our purposes, each time you read the word *love*, you can consider that as one or a combination of these qualities. If you don't favor the word love, you are encouraged to use one of the following names or any label that gives you inspiration: truth, power, wisdom, self-knowledge, higher self, true self, soul, the Buddha, Atman, the image of God, spiritual qualities, spiritual alphabet, healing alphabet, spiritual properties, qualities, healing qualities, or the attributes of love. It doesn't matter what you call it. What does matter is the recognition that at the very core of your being exists a host of healing qualities that can help you manage any painful problem.

Maya: The power inherent in ordinary consciousness that makes us think we are separate from the Creator, creation, and other creatures. Under the influence of maya, we experience the division, separation, limitation, impermanence, and suffering of ordinary or worldly consciousness.

Mental health: The mind is calm, positive, focused, strong, and resilient. It is awake, alert, and ready for problem solving, creative intelligence, shaping meaning, goal accomplishment, pain management, and the creation of health, success, harmony, and joy.

Mind-body-spirit medicine (MBSM): A field of study, research, and practice dedicated to the understanding that health care outcomes depend on the state of our body, mind, and soul.

One continuous sacred ritual: The act of spiritualizing and making every thought, feeling, and action sacred. The student is always practicing a method and quality.

Pain or suffering: In this work, the words *pain* and *suffering* are used interchangeably. Pain refers to any discomfort: physical, mental, emotional, interpersonal, or spiritual.

Prana: The intelligent energy or life force that permeates and operates every cell, tissue, organ, and system of the body.

Pranayama: Yoga techniques used to bring the life force or prana under control and direct it toward Spirit.

Reactivity: Reactivity is defined in step 5: Tools Become Barriers. The restless mind, high emotional reactivity, excessive material desire, the body, hyperactivity, and egotism add an additional layer of suffering to the inevitable suffering of life. This is called reactivity. Reactivity is reversible.

Recovery: Getting our social, recreational, vocational, and spiritual life back, no matter our disease or disability.

Roll the wheel: Roll the wheel or *roll the universal healing wheel* means practicing pain, method, quality (PMQ) in response to any pain or problem. See the definition of *universal healing wheel*.

Room of stillness: There is a place inside that is always still, quiet, spacious, and serene. This calm center is in the deepest part of our being. It is always there, no matter how turbulent or chaotic our lives. We can go there for refuge, comfort, and rejuvenation. Healing qualities and healing powers abound in the room of stillness. This is the place of deepest healing and the springboard for superconscious states.

School: Life is school. Pain is the teacher if we are open to the lessons. The lessons always have to do with the cultivation of healing qualities or love.

Skillful pain management: There are two layers of pain: the inevitable suffering of life and our reaction to it. We cannot control the former, but we can control the latter. When you practice the techniques described in this book, you reduce reactivity, the add-ons to the inevitable suffering of life. You cultivate strength and peace, no matter what your body or the world throws at you. You become a more skillful pain manager, and your quality of life improves accordingly. Skillful pain management is love itself.

Spiritual alphabet: The one hundred qualities defined in step 7, also referred to as healing qualities, qualities, the attributes of love, or love.

Spiritual evolution: When the qualities listed in the spiritual alphabet—such as peace, strength, courage, love, compassion, understanding and forgiveness—grow. You will feel better, become a better person, and experience higher states of consciousness.

Spiritual practice: Practicing any one or a combination of the fifteen methods described in this work.

Spirituality: Religious elements include story, metaphor, parable, concepts, images, aspects, sacred texts, rituals, traditional worship, social gatherings, committee work, attending services, music, architecture, and listening to sermons. Spirituality is the healing qualities and higher states of consciousness that permeate these elements. Religion is the structure and platform that creates spiritual qualities and higher states of consciousness.

Spiritualize the story—the healing story: The first phase of healing is to let the story unfold. (See definition above.) Spiritualizing the story is the second phase of healing in which painful emotions are reduced and replaced by strength, courage, endurance, compassion, understanding, peace, harmony, and a host of other qualities. The healing story trumps the pain story, takes over the dominant position in consciousness, and determines our true identity as peace, love, joy, power, and wisdom manifested as serene and compassionate service to humanity. Healing qualities are the spiritual solution to any pain, problem, conflict, symptom, disease, or disability.

Superconsciousness: An unmistakable shift in consciousness sometimes described as the peace that surpasses understanding, pure love, ecstatic joy, unfathomable stillness, intuitive wisdom, a feeling of oneness with everything, and other wonderful expressions of spirit. These experiences may last from a few minutes or hours to several days, but there is inevitably a return to ordinary consciousness unless one is a spiritual master.

Traction device: What gives the inspiration to do the work. Traction devices for the universal healing wheel are any of the elements from the great wisdom traditions: concepts, images, aspects, rituals, story, sermons, music, art, or metaphor. May include God, the God of love, the masters, mystery, karma, reincarnation, and much more.

Transpersonal psychology-psychiatry: the branch of psychiatry-psychology that attempts to integrate the science of psychology-psychiatry with the insights of various spiritual disciplines— including the role of superconscious states, mystical experiences, and contemplative practices for self-transcendence.

Universal healing wheel (the wheel): pain, method, quality or PMQ.

1. Pain: any physical, mental, emotional, interpersonal, or spiritual problem

2. Method: any one or a combination of fifteen practice methods described in this work

3. Quality: any one or a combination of one hundred healing qualities

PMQ is the essential healing principle of any wisdom tradition. It is the e = mc2 of psychosocial and spiritual healing. It is necessary and sufficient. This is all you need.

(*Roll the wheel* or *roll the universal healing wheel* means practicing PMQ in response to any pain or problem. See definitions above.)

USA (unconditional, spontaneous, automatic): At mastery, when a spiritual quality is fully developed, it is USA, or unconditional, spontaneous, and automatic. The greatest example of this is Jesus on the cross proclaiming, "Forgive them for they know not what they do." Jesus expressed unconditional, spontaneous, and automatic forgiveness, signaling his status as a grand spiritual master.

Vertical axis: Internal action involving the practice of spiritual methods described in this work. It is used in conjunction with *horizontal axis*, which is external action on the physical plane involving people, activities, things, events, and places. A balanced healing program includes work in both domains.

Will: Will is composed of two elements: free will and willpower. Free will is our ability to choose. It determines our direction. Willpower is the degree of intensity and passion given to our choices. As with physical muscles, willpower expands or atrophies depending on how much exercise it gets.

Wisdom tradition: All of the great religions, spiritual teachings, and other psychosocial healing models such as the twelve-step programs, DBT (dialectical behavior therapy), mindfulness based cognitive-behavioral therapy, mindfulness based stress reduction, and many more.

Yoga: Merging the soul with Spirit through love, service, wisdom, and stillness. Mental yoga is keeping our needle of attention on love, service, wisdom, and stillness in both meditation and activity.

Yo-yo effect: When we practice meditation, mindfulness, and other methods that involve calm concentration on a single point, the mind wanders. We bring it back to our point of focus, but it wanders again. This yo-yo back and forth movement between calm concentration and the wandering mind will go on for years. It is a part of the natural process of the methods described in this work. The yo-yo effect is the route to full power and deep healing.

The next chapter describes the ten-step model. You will learn how to use the inevitable suffering of life to cultivate peace, love, and joy. The result is a shift in the locus of control from the outer world of people, places, and things, to the inner world of peace, power, and strength—a world of our own definition.

Chapter 7

The Ten Steps

- For a complete review of the ten steps, please read *Healing Power, Revised* (2010), pp. 45–93. Following is a brief summary of the ten steps.

The Ten Steps

1. The Core Drive
2. Duality and Brutal Reality
3. The Compromise
4. Bad Habits
5. Tools Become Barriers
6. The Seeker
7. Soul and Spirit
8. School
9. Spiritual Practice
10. Spiritual Experience

- Step 1: We have an absolute need for unlimited peace, love, joy, and safety. This is called the *core drive*. The core drive is the motivating force behind all of our actions. It does not shut off. It can't. It is built into the genetic code. We have to have it. We want unlimited healing qualities and higher states of consciousness.

- Steps 2–3: We try to achieve the core drive exclusively on the horizontal axis of people, activities, events, and things, but this is impossible. On the physical plane, suffering is inevitable, time is limited, and death wins in the end.

- Steps 4–5: When we persist in our efforts to achieve the core drive on the physical plane, our motor overheats. We get stuck in the mud. We become unnecessarily reactive. The restless mind, highly reactive emotions, excessive material desires, attachments, bad habits, hyperactivity, physical pain, and the ego present an imposing array of problems.

- Step 6: We see the need to get help. We become seekers.

- Steps 7–10: We discover the teachings of the saints and masters of the great faith traditions. They diagnose our problem: we are trying to achieve the core drive *outside*. They give us the good news that it can be realized *inside*. In fact, they tell us, it is already there waiting patiently for our discovery as the true self. They call it the Buddha, image of God, child of God, the soul, love, or higher self. It doesn't matter what you call it. Just practice love, and watch everything improve.

- Steps 1–5 describe our pain.

- Steps 6–10 focus on healing that pain with love.

- Steps 1–10: Love is the great healer. It is more powerful than any painful problem. We know how to make it grow. As it grows, our pain is contained, reduced, or eliminated. We feel better, become better people, and experience higher states of consciousness.

In the next section, you will review the universal healing wheel in detail.

Part 2

The Universal Healing Wheel

The Universal Healing Wheel = PMQ

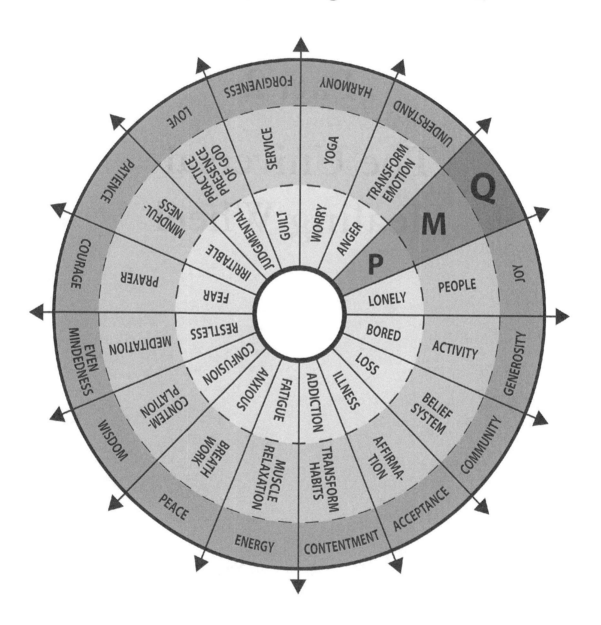

Chapter 8

Setting the Stage to Roll the Wheel
Seven Steps to Mastery

- The medical model has great power, but there is often residual suffering that can only be managed through self-healing. Following are seven conditions necessary to start and maintain a self-healing practice. These steps outline our responsibility in the healing process. If we follow these steps, nothing can stop us. We find our power in the story, keep that power, and make it grow.

Seven Steps to Mastery

1. Hope: Hope opens the door to possibility.

2. Power: We have more power than we are using right now.

3. Responsibility: There is work to do.

4. Roll the Wheel: This is the work.

5. Success: The qualities are growing.

6. Renewal: It's one thing to light your fire. It's another thing to keep it lit. Look for sources of inspiration.

7. Mastery: I am evolving. I am an ever-increasingly skillful pain manager. I feel better. I am a better person. I experience higher states of consciousness. I am ready for the challenges to come.

---

1. Hope

- Healing starts with hope.

- Hope lights the fire of possibility.

- Hope is the great motivator.

- Without hope, we aren't likely to get very far.

- Find hope, keep it, and grow it wherever and whenever you can.

- Here are a few ideas to stimulate hope:
  a. We can increase healing power for body, mind, and soul.
  b. We can learn how to skillfully manage any pain or problem: physical, mental, emotional, interpersonal, or spiritual.

c. We can become better people by cultivating healing qualities such as love, compassion, forgiveness, courage, strength, peace, wisdom, and joy.

d. Our pain is the route to healing through the cultivation of healing qualities.

e. We can find peace and strength within, despite the painful conditions of life.

f. We can exercise and strengthen the mind.

g. We can transform painful emotions into self-knowledge and spiritual power.

h. We can transmute bad habits into peace, strength, and contentment.

i. We can reduce hyperactivity and build stillness into our program.

j. We can use stillness as the doorway to higher states of consciousness.

k. We can reduce the negative side of our ego and replace it with the highest wisdom.

l. We can lock love, compassion, peace, and strength into brain grooves so that these healing qualities become our new mental habits.

m. We can view the body as the carrier of higher states of consciousness as opposed to a source of fear and trouble.

n. There are support networks of like-minded people who have traveled the way of healing. They know the ropes. They know how to sit with their pain and find their power in the story. They can help us do the same.

o. As we move along on the healing path, we become increasingly able to help others with their recovery.

What will you do to the light the fire of hope and keep it going?

2. Power

- We have more power than we are using right now.

- This is true for all of us, no matter our degree of evolution.

- To do the work of self-healing, we need to tap into this latent source of power.

- Deeply embed the following or similar affirmations into the foundation of your consciousness. Never let them go. Make them a permanent fixture in your living room.

    a. I have more power than I am using right now.
    b. I move from hopeless and helpless to power and potential.
    c. I move from *I can't* to *I can*.
    d. I tap into my well of unlimited healing power a little bit more every day.
    e. I got this. I can do this. I will do this.

3. Responsibility

- This is a self-help, self-healing model. There is work to do. No one can do it for you. While there is training, support, and inspiration from others, you have to do the work yourself.

- Are you ready to do some work?

4. Roll the Wheel

- This is the work. Practice PMQ (pain, method, quality). Cultivate healing qualities in response to the pain of life by practicing any one or a combination of any of the fifteen recommended methods.

5. Success

- When you roll the wheel, healing power expands, you become a more skillful pain manager, and you evolve. You feel better, become a better person, and experience higher states of consciousness.

6. Renewal

- It is one thing to light a fire. It's another thing to keep it lit.
- Healing is hard work. Tests and trials are sure to come. There will be good and bad days. Barriers and obstacles will be placed before you. You will sometimes succeed and sometimes fail.
- When energy is low and pain is high, it's easy to lose sight of the goal, back up, and sometimes give up. Everyone goes up and down on the way to higher states, but some people give up and never return.
- We need a way to renew our passion in order to stay the course.
- We need support, inspiration, and traction from a variety of sources.
- No matter how many failures, we need to keep looking for a way to break through.
- This workbook presents a variety of healing principles, methods, qualities, and wisdom pearls meant to inspire.
  a. If you are going to do this work, you will need to strengthen your willpower. Read the section in *Healing Power, Revised* on willpower, pp. 142–50. Here you will learn how to increase your willpower from a spark to a bonfire.
  b. What will you do to light your fire and keep it lit?
  c. How will you reignite your passion?
  d. What is going to sweep you off your feet from moment to moment?
  e. What will keep you going when the going gets rough?
  f. What is going to work for you in the cave of darkness, sometimes referred to as the dark night of the soul? (See *Healing Power, Revised*, pp. 398–400.)

7. Mastery

- If you roll the wheel and persist, the results are profound:

a. High mental and emotional reactivity are replaced by ever-increasing peace, love, joy, safety, and other wonderful healing qualities.

b. Healing qualities become unconditional, spontaneous, and automatic habits. The qualities hold no matter what happens in the world or to our bodies. While we still may suffer, we can hold our ground and move forward. We become more skillful pain managers and better people.

c. We become humble, strong, enthusiastic, and cheerful. We are awake, aware, and ready for anything.

d. We may be called to perform acts of courage and heroism, but most of our work is quiet, anonymous acts of gentle, humble service. We give peace, love, and joy in word, action, and vibration to all we meet.

e. There may be a transformation of consciousness to higher states often referred to as nirvana, the peace that surpasses understanding, ecstasy, Divine Love, the Buddha, or Christ Consciousness. Nothing can touch us. Nothing can ruffle us.

f. Liberated from the bondage of fear and insecurity, we watch the colossal cosmic drama with calm detachment.

Affirmations

- I can do this work.

- I can work with this pain.

- I can manage this pain.

- I am an ever-increasingly skillful pain manager.

- Pain, you can come and go as you please. I will cultivate healing qualities no matter what you, the pain, are doing.

- I respond to pain with healing qualities.

- I use pain as a teacher and stimulant for the cultivation of healing qualities.

- I can't control the inevitable suffering of life. I can put out the fire of my reactivity with the water of healing qualities.

- There may be suffering, but I can hold my ground.

- Nothing can touch me. Nothing can ruffle me.

Points to Remember

- Hope, power, and responsibility set up the conditions for healing. This is the psychology of recovery. Then do the work. Roll the wheel and persist. You will succeed. You will evolve. You will achieve mastery.

In the next seven chapters, we will review in detail the workings of the universal healing wheel or PMQ: pain, method, quality.

In chapter 9, you will find an introduction to the universal healing wheel.

In chapter 10, we will look at pain (P).

In chapter 11, we will study the methods (M).

In chapter 12, we will review the qualities (Q).

In chapter 13, we will study the wheel: the dynamics of how pain, method, and quality work together.

In chapter 14, we will review how the wheel works with traction devices.

In chapter 15, we will review the dynamic relationship between love and pain.

The next chapter introduces the universal healing wheel, the essential healing principle of religion and the essence of mind-body-spirit medicine.

Chapter 9

The Universal Healing Wheel

- Please review chapter 7, The Universal Healing Wheel, in *Healing Power, Revised*, pp. 97–114. Following is a review of this material with some additional principles and exercises.

- Mind-body-spirit medicine: There is ample scientific evidence that people with an active faith system have better outcomes in medicine, surgery, mental health, and addiction. This allows us to bring spirituality and religion into the practice of medicine.

- The next step is to *find and transfer the essential healing principle* from religion to medicine safely and without controversy. This is a difficult task. Religious belief systems present a broad array of complex, confusing, and contradictory principles. This model reduces complicated, controversial religion into a simplified practical spirituality.

- Here is the key principle: the entire story of religion is *the triumph of love over pain*. Love is the supreme healer. It is greater than any painful problem.

- Our job is to respond to our pain with love a little bit more every day. To do this we need:

    1. A definition of pain

    2. A definition of love

    3. A way to implement the principle that love is more powerful than any painful problem

- The universal healing wheel answers that call.

The Universal Healing Wheel = PMQ

PMQ is the essential healing principle of all religion. It is the e = mc2 of spiritual healing. You will find PMQ in every healing model.

- P = Pain

- M = Method

- Q = Quality

- Pain: Let's start with pain. Every health care visit has something to do with pain. We can take some of it away with the medical model, but we are stuck with a great deal of residual suffering. We get hooked to our pain story and can't shake it. We need a way to manage this pain skillfully, but nobody talks about this. We say, "Your pain is your medicine if you know what to do with it. You can turn the tables on your pain and make it work for you. You can become a more skillful pain manager." The saints tell us how to do this.

- The Qualities: The saints recommend adding healing qualities such as love, compassion, understanding, and forgiveness to the pain story to calm it down. After all they would say, "Isn't the whole of religion a story of the triumph of love over pain? Isn't love more powerful than any painful problem? *Love, compassion, kindness and understanding: these are the pain managers and the healers.* But these qualities do not grow on trees. They are in the genetic code, and we need to cultivate them by practicing the recommended methods.

- The Methods: There are fifteen methods extracted from religion, psychiatry, and psychology. These include meditation, mindfulness, breathwork, affirmations, contemplation, the transformation of emotion, and more.

- Rolling the Universal Healing Wheel: In response to your pain, we suggest you pick a method to cultivate a quality. This is called rolling the universal healing wheel. This is universal and works for people of all persuasions.

- Traction Devices: Traction devices are the stuff of religion. We add back the stuff of religion as we think this adds even more power to the healing equation. To stay out of controversy, traction devices are offered as *a cafeteria of options* with the proviso that one person's traction device is the next person's gag reflex.

- How this Works: An atheist or agnostic person with an anxiety disorder might choose meditation to cultivate peace of mind. The PMQ here is anxiety (P), meditation (M), peace (Q). There would be no welcome theological traction devices. A Buddhist with the same problem might want to meditate with the Buddha and focus on compassion. A Christian might add Jesus and the God of love. A Hindu might add Krishna and even-mindedness under all conditions. With the addition of these traction devices, these individuals may find more comfort and solace.

- In summary:
    a) P is any painful problem: physical, mental, emotional, interpersonal, or spiritual.
    b) M is the fifteen methods.
    c) Q is the love = One hundred qualities and higher states of consciousness.
    d) Traction devices are anything from the stuff of religion that gives you traction.

- Study the healing principles outlined in this work long enough to understand how they work. Then roll the wheel and experience the result:
    a) Love contains, reduces, or eliminates pain and guides us through what is left.
    b) Love grows until love is all there is.

- To see how this works, you have to unpack the wisdom through direct personal experience. You have to sit with your pain and ride the pain waves to get to your upgraded, refined love. This workbook shows you how to do this, but you must be the one to do it. Think, reflect, and practice. Use every opportunity and experience—good and bad—to roll the wheel.

- Love is the great healer and great pain manager. It is more powerful than any painful problem. This message is needed now—sorely needed now—as there is so much darkness and pain in the world.

Points to Remember

- This model reduces complicated, controversial religion into a simplified practical spirituality.

- Here are the steps followed in constructing this model:

  1. Deconstruct religion into discrete pieces.

  2. Eliminate dogma, ritual, and other nonessentials.

  3. Extract the essential healing principle = love = healing qualities.

  4. Learn how to make love grow: roll the wheel with or without traction devices.

  5. Love grows until it is unconditional.

- All you need is love and a way to make it grow. The wheel—with or without traction devices— answers that call.

- The universal healing wheel is the essence of and link to all religions. It is the e= mc2 of psychosocial and spiritual healing. It is the unifying theory, what actually works, the Holy Grail. It seems too simple to be true, but this simplicity is its elegance; it has the essential building blocks for healing and the add-ons from the stuff of religion. The wheel with traction devices is the total package.

- Love is the centerpiece of religion. Everything else is a traction device.

- Spirituality = love = healing qualities and higher states of consciousness.

- The wheel with traction devices solves the problem of toxic language and traumatic religious history, as PMQ has no theology and you control the traction devices.

- The wheel with traction devices allows us to capture the power of religion and bring it to health care safely, efficiently, and effectively.

- The number or type of traction devices you use doesn't matter. You can have none, a few, or full-on religion. What *does* matter is love. If a traction device leads to more love, it is good. If not, why use it?

- You will find the universal healing wheel with or without traction devices in a variety of formats throughout this model.

Exercises

1. Health Care Professional, Heal Thyself

- This model offers a host of self-help, self-healing options for health care professionals and their patients.

- When health care professionals are in a self-healing program themselves, they will be better able to help their patients do the same.

- It doesn't matter where you are on the map. We all need more healing power. There is always a next step to take.

- Health care professional, heal yourself first. This is the best way to contribute to the healing of your patient and your organization.

- Those who practice the recommended methods cultivate spiritual qualities such as love, compassion, patience, kindness, humor, forgiveness, and more. When these healing qualities grow, we feel better and become better people.

- Keep going. When the qualities get big enough, they break into higher states of consciousness: the peace that surpasses understanding, pure love, ecstatic joy, intuitive wisdom, and more.

- Practice a variety of healing methods and qualities. See how they work in your life. Practice when you feel well and when you feel bad. Then you can teach your patients how to do the same.

- Don't try to teach unless you have practiced and teach only those who are interested.

2. Health Care Consumer, Heal Thyself

- Medication helps, but you can contribute to the healing process if you are willing to do some work.

- If it's just medication you want, so be it. That is your choice and your right. If you want more, read on.

- While the doctor is working on your problem or when the doctor is done, you can participate in the healing process.

- This model offers fifteen methods, one hundred qualities, and a variety of religious traction devices. These are your choices. You can go as far as you wish using this cafeteria of options for deeper healing.

3. Whether you are a health care professional or patient, when you practice PMQ:

1. Healing power expands.
2. We become a more skillful pain managers.
3. We evolve.
   a. We feel better.
   b. We become better people.
   c. We experience higher states of consciousness.

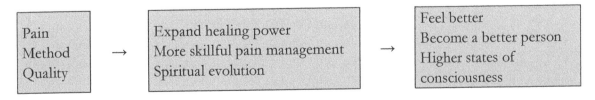

In the next chapter, we will study some important points about pain.

Chapter 10

Pain

- Life is painful.

- *How we manage our pain determines whether we move forward, backward, or stay stuck in this life.*

- When we manage pain unskillfully, we make it worse. We get stuck and go backwards.

- When we manage pain skillfully, we hold our ground and move forward.

- Unskillful pain management is the number one problem on the planet. It can paralyze and eventually destroy our lives and the lives of those around us.

- We need help. We need to learn more about the origin of our suffering so we can manage it more skillfully. Then, instead of dragging us down, our problems become a source of strength and peace.

- *This work is designed to help you become an ever-increasingly skillful pain manager.*

- Skillful pain management will help you safely navigate your way through the many pitfalls that have already come your way and will continue to come your way. Is there anyone who does not need this?

- All of us need to improve our pain management skills, but few pay attention. Our society focuses on the opposite: pleasure seeking, immediate gratification, and pain avoidance. This can work for a time but inevitably leads to more pain.

- *There is nothing more important than learning how to be a skillful pain manager.* Skillful pain management is in the hall of fame of great ideas. It is the missing piece in our lives. It is a big deal.

- Pain is a complex and tricky subject. If we are to become more skillful pain managers, we need to study its ways.

- Facing our pain and learning how to work with it can be frightening. However, when we learn how to do this, we find our power in the story.

- This means we are going to go to our doctor for traditional care, and *we are going to participate in self-healing.*

Following is a review of some principles to help us do this work.

Two Levels of Pain

Pain has two dimensions. It is a good idea to keep these in mind as it helps us see where we do the work. The two levels are:

1. The inevitable suffering of life: we cannot control this.

2. Reactivity: Our reaction to the inevitable suffering of life. This is reversible.

The Inevitable Suffering of Life

- All of us have to face the minor irritations of routine daily living and major life problems such as disease, disability, loss, change, the unknown, and death. This is the inevitable suffering of life. Life is difficult and painful for everyone. There is no way around it.

- The pain can be physical, mental, emotional, interpersonal, or spiritual. It can be any disease, disability, stress, or symptom. While we may be able to reduce some of this pain, there remains a great deal of suffering, no matter what we do.

Reactivity

- Reactivity is what we add to the inevitable suffering of life. Most of us add a lot of reactivity to the pain equation.

- Following is a classic, near universal response pattern that occurs when we are confronted with a stressful problem:

Reactivity

1. Mind: The mind heats up, spins out of control, ruminates, and repeats the pain story. It attaches to the pain story and won't let go.

2. Emotion: Anxiety, depression, anger, fear, guilt, shame, embarrassment, and other painful emotions add up, overlap, pile on, and overwhelm.

3. Desire: Desire, attachments, and bad habits kick in—food, alcohol, drugs, power, sex, shopping, gambling, and more.

4. Body: We experience a medley of uncomfortable physical sensations: tremors, butterflies in our stomachs, tight muscles, sweaty palms, rapid heartbeat, and more.

5. Activity: We become hyperactivity junkies running on the track of life seeking pain relief through people, activities, and things. We distract ourselves from the time we get up in the morning until sleep. This can be good and works to a point, but we don't get to the root cause of our suffering when we use activity to avoid looking at our problems.

6. Ego: The trickster ego adds a layer of confusing maneuvers that get in the way: defensive, paranoid, proud, rigid, judgmental, greedy, selfishness, fixed distorted ideas, power trips, and more.

- Unnecessary high reactivity is a source of untold suffering. But here is the good news. Reactivity is reversible. *We can control these reactions.* We have considerable leverage here. This is where we can do some work. *This is where we can become ever-increasingly skillful pain managers.*

- We can reduce reactivity when we practice the methods and qualities described in this workbook. When we reduce reactivity we have less pain, and we are better at managing the pain we cannot eliminate.

The Universal Healing Wheel Reduces Reactivity

- The key to success in reducing reactivity is matching our problems to a method and a quality. This is rolling the universal healing wheel (UHW or PMQ).

- Review step 8 on pp. 83–86 in *Healing Power, Revised.* Life is school. Pain is the teacher if we open to its lessons. The lessons always have to do with the cultivation of healing qualities.

- Our instinct is to run away from the pain. Skillful pain management is to do the exact opposite, to sit with the pain as the teacher and stimulant for the growth of healing qualities.

- We stop running and sit with the pain, method, and quality in the same space. When we do this, reactivity is contained, reduced, or eliminated. This is where the magic happens. This is transcendence. This is where you rise. This is where you make medicine out of your pain. This is where you find your power in the story. This is when you feel better. And if you don't feel better, at least you stop making things worse.

Points to Remember

- Biological interventions including the medical model and complimentary and alternative medicine are powerful yet limited. Even though medicine, surgery, herbs, vitamins, diet, and exercise are often effective, there is considerable pain left on the table, that inevitable suffering of life and our reaction to it. How you manage this pain will make or break you.

- There is an old commercial for an over-the-counter painkiller with a famous line, "I haven't got time for the pain." The marketers are tapping into our desire to avoid all suffering. But the inevitable suffering of life and our reaction to it is universal. Everyone suffers. We ignore this pain at our peril. When we run and hide, it gets bigger. When it gets too big, it becomes unmanageable. We become desperate, and desperate people do desperate things.

- We need to take a different approach. As long as pain is inevitable, we may as well acknowledge it, use it, and make it work for rather than against us. Our pain is a natural resource. We can exploit and mine its field for gold, diamonds, gems, and jewels. The jewels are the healing qualities described in the next chapter.

Exercises

1. The first step in becoming a more skillful pain manager is to understand the two levels of pain. What is the difference between the inevitable suffering of life and reactivity?

2. It doesn't matter what happens to you as much as how you respond. How does this apply to your life?

3. For a deeper account of the complexities of reactivity, review the first five steps of the ten-step model described in *Healing Power, Revised*, pp. 45–69. Then, focus on step 5: Tools Become Barriers. This step defines and locates the source of our reactivity in six domains: thought, feeling, desire, body, activity, and ego.

4. All of us have to face the minor irritations of routine daily living and major life problems, such as disease, disability, trauma, loss, change, the unknown, and death. This is the inevitable suffering of life. Life is difficult and painful for everyone. There is no way around it.

It is how we respond to the inevitable suffering of life that will determine whether we move forward, backward, or stay stuck in this life.

Following is a list of some common painful problems. We can learn how to manage these problems skillfully by rolling the universal healing wheel or practicing PMQ.

    a. Review the list.
    b. Are there any problems on this list that apply to you?
    c. Do you have any problems that are not on this list?
    d. Make a list of the problems you would like to work on. This will be your P in the PMQ of the universal healing wheel.

Common Painful Problems

1. Restless mind
2. Irritability
3. Quarrelsome attitude
4. Anger
5. Rage
6. Mean
7. Cruel
8. Unkindness
9. Harshness of speech
10. Harshness of thought
11. Impatience
12. Resentment
13. Hatred
14. Vengeful
15. Desire to hurt others
16. Violence
17. Sad
18. Lonely
19. Depressed
20. Anxiety
21. Fear
22. Panic
23. Worry
24. Doubt
25. Insecure
26. Awkward
27. Fear of suffering
28. Fear of disease
29. Fear of the unknown
30. Fear of the abyss
31. Fear of death
32. Financial insecurity
33. Loss of status
34. Loss of possessions
35. Loss of people
36. Loss of self-esteem
37. Feeling abandoned
38. Feeling rejected
39. Feeling left out
40. Feeling ignored
41. Isolated
42. Separate
43. Fear of being alone
44. Hurt
45. Hopeless
46. Helpless
47. Guilt
48. Shame
49. Embarrassment
50. Humiliation
51. Foolish
52. Feeling unworthy
53. Self-hate
54. Desperate
55. Jealousy
56. Craving
57. Covetous
58. Greed
59. Temptation
60. Attachments
61. Needy
62. Bad habits
63. Addictions: alcohol, drugs, sex, food, money, power, shopping, gambling, codependency, and more
64. Hyperactivity: always having to be busy
65. Egotistical
66. Narcissistic
67. Self-important
68. Selfish
69. Pride
70. Arrogance
71. Conceit
72. Any conflict
73. Denial of problems
74. Controlling
75. Rigid
76. Perfectionistic
77. Negative attitude
78. Pessimistic
79. Cynical
80. Bitter
81. Judgmental
82. Racism or prejudice: judging others by their role, body, personality, age, race, religion, nationality, sexual identity, economic class, or disability
83. Indifference
84. Boredom
85. Complacency
86. Mental laziness
87. Physical laziness
88. Procrastination
89. Lack of meaning and purpose
90. Suspiciousness
91. Paranoid
92. Obsessive
93. Compulsive
94. Impulsive
95. Failure
96. Defeated
97. Hypersensitive to criticism
98. Hypersensitive feelings: touchy
99. Lying
100. Cheating
101. Stealing
102. Sex addiction
103. Sex abuse
104. Sexual promiscuity
105. Dishonesty
106. Disappointed
107. Devastated
108. Discouraged
109. Disgusted
110. Misunderstood
111. Overwhelmed
112. Frustrated
113. Inadequate
114. Incompetent
115. Indecisive
116. Inferior
117. Superior
118. Inhibited
119. Trapped
120. Unappreciated
121. Unattractive
122. Ungrateful: taking things for granted
123. Disease consciousness
124. Problem consciousness
125. Any other problem
126. Any other character flaw

The next chapter reviews the methods we can use to manage our pain skillfully.

Chapter 11

Methods

- There are fifteen methods: three on the horizontal axis and twelve on the vertical axis.

- These methods are a compilation of ancient wisdom and modern science. They are evidence-based and have proven to be effective over the ages.

- These self-help methods integrate with traditional, complimentary, and alternative medicine.

- The methods can be used by any person: atheist, agnostic, religious, or spiritual.

- The methods can be used for any problem: physical, mental, emotional, interpersonal, or spiritual.

- The methods help us manage our pain, problem, symptom, disease, or disability.

- The methods help us contain, reduce, or eliminate our pain and guide us through what's left.

- The methods help us cultivate healing qualities which contain, reduce, or eliminate reactivity.

- We can practice the methods anywhere and anytime—at home, at work, or at play.

- We can start anywhere. Pick the method that most appeals to you at this moment.

- Explore them all as time allows.

- No method is better than another.

- No method works for everyone. Pick the ones you want.

- Incorporate and balance the methods according to your current motivation and lifestyle.

The Pain That Doctors Can't Fix

- This work describes fifteen methods we can turn to when doctors and other health care professionals can't solve our problem.

- These methods help us manage the inevitable suffering of life and our reaction to it.

- The methods are organized under the horizontal and vertical axes. Horizontal axis methods include the outer world of people, activities, and belief systems. The vertical axis includes methods we use inside ourselves. These distinctions are made for teaching purposes only. The boundaries between the outer and inner world are arbitrary, and there is overlap.

- You already practice some of these methods. This review will help you become more conscious of what you are doing and help you expand your repertoire.

- These methods are described in detail in *Healing Power, Revised* and are elaborated on in this workbook.

- It doesn't matter if your pain is mild, moderate, severe, or extreme. These methods work no matter the size, shape, or complexity of your problem.

- When we learn how to deal with small problems, we will know how to deal with the big ones. The principles are the same.

- For chronic, severe problems, we will need to practice these methods in a variety of combinations for years.

- With practice, we can learn how to manage our deepest suffering with corresponding healing interventions to match.

- The methods guide us through the roughest patches, including the most brutal reality, dark night of the soul, and cave of darkness.

- The list is not inclusive. You are encouraged to heal by any method that works for you.

- Following is a brief introduction to the fifteen recommended methods. You will find a more detailed review of these methods in chapters 16-32.

The Methods

Horizontal axis: external work

1. People
2. Activities
3. Belief systems

Vertical axis: internal work

4. Affirmations
5. Habit transformation
6. Progressive muscle relaxation
7. Breathwork
8. Contemplation
9. Meditation
10. Prayer
11. Mindfulness
12. Practicing the presence of God
13. Service
14. Yoga
15. Transformation of emotion

Horizontal Axis Methods
External Work

1. People

   - When we are in pain, we instinctively turn to trustworthy loved ones, friends, family, or counselors. We tell our story seeking understanding, validation, comfort, and relief.

   - We have a deep and inherent need to give and receive love, compassion, understanding, patience, kindness, and humor. These qualities are the healers and pain managers.

   - The idea is to have the best possible network of like-minded, warm, wise, and compassionate people: the right people, at the right time, at the right dose.

   - Find a support network of like-minded people.

   - Tell your pain story to a counselor, mentor, sponsor, trusted family member, or friend.

   - Be understood, validated, and supported.

   - Give and receive love.

   - Spiritualize your relationships.

     a. Do you have enough support?
     b. Who is in your life you can really talk to?
     c. Do you spend too much time with people?
     d. Are you codependent?
     e. Is your *people dose* too high or too low?

2. Activities

   - Constructive meaningful activities contribute mightily to pain management and healing.

   - We need a variety of activities such as: school, training, volunteering, work, hobbies, culture, exercise, martial arts, sports, the Internet, TV, radio, music, culture, reading, the arts, and more.

   - We can spend too much or not enough time doing activities.

     a. What is your day like?
     b. Do you have enough to do?
     c. Is your *activity dose* too high or too low?

3. Belief system

   - It doesn't matter whether your belief system is secular, spiritual, fixed, or opened as long is it gives meaning, purpose, and positive thought.

   - We need a strong, healthy belief system rooted in love qualities. This is monumentally important for pain management and healing.

     a. How do you understand the meaning and purpose of life?

  b. Do you have a way to understand the things that happen?

  c. Do you have a spiritual program or philosophy of life?

  d. Do you get support and wisdom from church, synagogue, mosque, twelve-step programs, DBT (dialectical behavior therapy), or other healing ceremonies?

- Many people make the mistake of trying to solve all of their problems on the horizontal axis of people, activities, and belief systems. Some problems can only be resolved by doing some inner work.

- When you have done everything you can in the world of people, activities, and belief systems and you are still in pain, there are twelve additional methods you can use to help you with your painful problem.

- Methods 4–15 describe the work we can do internally. These are the methods of the vertical axis. We can work these methods alone or in a group. Both are good, and they compliment each other. For example, your individual meditation can be enhanced by group meditation and vice versa.

Vertical Axis
Internal Work

4. Affirmation

  - The mind has great power to do harm or good.

  - The science of healing affirmations teaches us how to apply the inherent power of thought for healing and pain management.

  - Thoughts impact disease and healing.

  - Practice affirmations for healing body, mind, and soul.

  - Fill your brain with powerful positive thoughts and wisdom pearls.

  - Keep your mind locked in affirmations rooted in the healing qualities.

  - Let healing qualities be your guide during good and difficult times.

5. Habit Transformation

  - All of us have a mix of good and bad habits.

  - For full recovery and deep healing, we must release the energy captured by bad habits and transfer this power to new good habits.

  - Cultivate the habits of a seeker: fifteen methods.

  - Cultivate the habits of a sage: one hundred healing qualities.

6. Breathwork

   • Breath is always available.

   • We can use it to get centered and calm.

   • Breathwork helps dissolve painful emotions, curb addiction and craving, and convert mental restlessness to peace of mind.

   • Practice any one or a combination of breathing techniques.

7. Progressive Muscle Relaxation

   • Progressive muscle relaxation calms the body and mind through tensing and relaxing the muscles.

   • In addition, when the body and mind are relaxed, it's easier to practice other methods such as contemplation, meditation, and mindfulness.

   • Progressive muscle relaxation helps reduce stress, anxiety, fear, panic, depression, insomnia, and fatigue.

   • You might also do a body scan.

8. Contemplation

   • We do not need a Higher Power or religion to practice contemplation. All we need is some quiet time and our favorite wisdom.

   • The wisdom can come from any source, secular or spiritual.

   • Learn how to crack open the shell of a wisdom pearl to release its hidden secrets and soothing healing powers.

   • Learn how to *fill your brain with wisdom* and how to *sit with a saint*.

   • Convert such great qualities as compassion and any other healing quality or idea from the surface superficiality of mere words to feeling, experience, and action.

9. Meditation

   • Right now, there is a place inside of us that is absolutely still and serene, but our mental restlessness bars us from entering. Meditation is the solution to this problem.

   • When we learn how to meditate, we learn how to slow down the mind, replace negative with positive thought, and eventually get into the room of stillness.

   • The experience of peace in the room of stillness surpasses understanding. Here you will find unfathomable beauty, joy, compassion, light, energy, power, elation, and ecstasy.

   • In meditation: negative → positive → stillness → higher consciousness → infinity.

- Learn how to meditate. Experience deep healing in the room of stillness. This doctor charges no fee.

10. Prayer

- Ask for help from your Higher Power.
- Ask for courage, strength, humility, acceptance, forgiveness, perseverance, self-control, transcendence, wisdom, and more.

11. Mindfulness

- Mindfulness is paying attention in the here and now to one moment at a time.
- Here you will learn how to stay in the present and ride the pain waves just as they are, without adding unnecessary reactivity.
- This technique has four steps:
  a. Stop
  b. Breathe
  c. Present moment
  d. Reframe to the witness, warrior, service, school, entertainment, or ritual
- When we rotate these frames, life becomes one continuous sacred ritual, offering up its knowledge and lessons, entertainment and joy, and opportunities to love and serve.

12. Presence of God

- This is the same as mindfulness for those who have a personal relationship with God.
- Practice the presence of God as peace, courage, strength, perseverance, compassion, love, understanding, or any one of the healing qualities you need at the moment.

13. Service

- In service to humanity, we discover who we really are and what really helps.
- We come to know love as the power that heals the self first and then heals others. As we change ourselves, we change the world.
- The healing power of love is a magnet that draws to itself all good things.
- It is not what you do but how you do it. Add love to every action.
- The way is small acts of gentle humble service without attachment to outcomes.
- When we help others, we help ourselves. Healing power grows. We evolve.

14. Yoga

- Yoga is union of the soul with Spirit through:

    1. Love: Bhakti Yoga
    2. Service: Karma Yoga
    3. Wisdom: Jnana Yoga
    4. Stillness: Raja Yoga

- We can know God or Brahma through love, service, meditation, and wisdom but not until we reduce the restlessness and excesses of the body, mind, emotions, desires, and ego by practicing one or a combination of these four types of yoga.

- The science of yoga teaches us to still the waves of mental restlessness, excessive material desire, and emotional reactivity in both meditation and activity.

- Practice love, service, wisdom, and stillness.

15. Transformation of Emotion

- Emotions are a rich source of information. If we are able to experience sadness or anger without excessive use of alcohol, drugs, food, gambling, sex, or violence, we may discover why we are experiencing these feelings in the first place.

- Painful emotions are a part of the normal, natural, intelligent healing process. When we learn how to process emotion into self-knowledge, we gain strength and peace.

- Emotions tell a story with lessons having to do with the cultivation of healing qualities. When we finish the story, it will stop coming up.

- Learn how to:

    - Let the pain story unfold.
    - Spiritualize the story: infuse the pain story with healing qualities.

Locus of Control

- If you spend most of your time in methods 1–3, your locus of control is primarily outside. Most of us start here.

- When life presents overwhelming problems, it is often necessary to do some inner work. As you begin to practice methods 4–15, healing qualities such as courage, peace, and strength slowly grow. As the qualities grow, your locus of control gradually shifts to your inner self. You become less dependent on the outer world of people, activities, events, and material things when you find inner peace, security, and contentment.

- When we learn how to balance external and internal practices, we become more skillful pain managers. Healing qualities expand. We evolve at maximum speed. At mastery, when your locus of control is deeply rooted inside, you will be even-minded under all conditions. For most of us, even-mindedness under all conditions is an affirmation, not a reality. On the way there, we can have fun with the challenge.

How to Use the Methods
Design Your Own Program

- You will find a detailed description of the methods in *Healing Power, Revised*, pp. 181–357 with supplemental material in this workbook on pp. 135-257.

- Scan the material to see the lay of the land.

- You may already practice some of these methods but want to expand and refine your options.

- Pick a method you would like to add to your toolbox. Start anywhere. It doesn't matter what method you choose. You determine the method based on your life circumstance, motivation, time, energy, and comfort.

- This is like trying on a new pair of hiking boots. If we know we are going on a long and sometimes difficult hike, we would shop for comfortable boots. Similarly, as you review a method, try it on for size, and be sure you are comfortable with it. Then you can use the method to help you manage your painful problems.

- Read and study the chapter on your chosen method in *Healing Power, Revised* and in this workbook.

- Match your method with a problem and a quality.

- Begin your patient daily practice.

Quick Start

- Some people want simple techniques. Others enjoy more complexity. In this work, you will find both. Choose the methods that suit your needs.

- Most of the techniques in this work are built on the template of the following three examples. Note the progression from simple to complex.

    1. The simplest technique

    2. Roll the Wheel

    3. Roll the Wheel with traction devices

The Simplest Technique

- When you are uncomfortable and want to shift gears:

  1. Stop

  2. Breathe

  3. Present moment

  4. Reframe

- The reframe can be a method of your choice. For example:

  1. Stop

  2. Breathe

  3. Present moment

  4. Reframe: choose any one or combination of fifteen methods: affirmations, breathwork, and so forth.

- The reframe can be a quality. For example:

  1. Stop

  2. Breathe

  3. Present moment

  4. Choose any one or a combination of the one hundred qualities: compassion, patience, courage, and forgiveness—to name a few.

  5. Practice your quality for as long as you wish: a day, week, month, or longer.

  6. Some practice one hundred days of love by choosing a different quality every day for one hundred days.

  7. You might review chapter 43 in this workbook. You will find one hundred healing qualities with corresponding affirmations and quotes.

- To expand, try the following format. In this exercise, you connect your pain to a method and quality. This is called rolling the wheel.

Roll the Wheel

When you find yourself immersed in unnecessary reactivity, you can roll the wheel or practice PMQ. Find a problem, choose a method, and cultivate a quality.

1. Stop

2. Breathe

3. Present moment

4. (P) Pain or problem: Realize mindfully that you are in a reaction. Notice what is there. Are you anxious, bored, tired, or angry?

5. (M) Method: Choose any one or combination of fifteen methods: breathwork, affirmations, meditation, and more.

6. (Q) Quality: Cultivate any one or a combination of one hundred qualities, such as peace, compassion, understanding, and forgiveness.

Example:

1. Stop

2. Breathe

3. Present moment

4. (P) Anxiety

5. (M) Meditation

6. (Q) Peace

In the next example, we add traction devices to the wheel.

Roll the Wheel with a Traction Device

When you become aware that you have gone for a ride on the train of thought and you want to get off:

1. Stop.

2. Breathe: Take a slow deep breath.

3. Present moment.

4. (P) Pain: Realize mindfully you are in a reaction. Notice what is there. Are you anxious, bored, tired, or angry?

5. (M) Method: Choose a method.

6. (Q) Quality: Choose a quality.

7. Traction device: This is the stuff of religion or any concept, image, or aspect from any belief system that gives you inspiration. This may be a master such as Jesus, Buddha, Krishna, the God of love, a pearl of wisdom, and so forth.

- Example

  1. Stop

  2. Breathe

  3. Present moment

  4. (P) Anxiety

  5. (M) Meditation

  6. (Q) Peace

  7. Traction device: meditate with the compassionate Buddha

Length of Practice

- There is no universal prescription for length of practice. Just get started and do as much as you can.

- It's like going to the gym. The first step may be hard, but once you get going it gets easier and more enjoyable. Start slow. We climb a mountain one step at a time. Similarly, we build our practice each day by applying a method one step at a time. By taking small steps and building our program gradually, we will have a strong foundation upon which to build higher floors.

- For example, your PMQ might be anxiety, meditation, and peace. You can practice meditation five to ten minutes twice a day and gradually build up your time. If this seems intimidating, try one minute twice a day. Anyone can do that.

- Push the envelope gently. Go back and do it again. More is better. The more you practice, the better you get. Work your way up to forty-five to sixty minutes once or twice a day, if time and circumstance permit.

Adding Methods

- With any pain, fifteen methods, and one hundred qualities, you can individualize your program to suit your needs.

- Your practice may be simple or complex.

- Some will keep it simple and practice one or two methods such as breathwork and affirmations. There are some wonderful affirmations and wisdom pearls in chapter 43, Fill Your Brain With Wisdom, on pp. 288-312

- Others might profit from mindfulness and service.

- Those who want to go deep can practice meditation and transformation of emotion.

- Take your time. You might practice a new method for a few days, weeks, or longer before you decide to add another method. Build it up slowly. We are in this for a lifetime.

- Those who enjoy complexity may practice all fifteen methods.

- Study and practice the methods to see which ones work best. Be creative. Choose problems, methods, and qualities that fit the moment and mood.

The Best Practice Position
Calm Continuous Concentration

- The best practice position combines one-pointed, calm, continuous concentration with intensity, zeal, hunger, and thirst. You can apply this principle to every method described in this work.

- Begin your practice by choosing any PMQ.

- Apply your unwavering focus to your chosen method and quality. Bring all of your attention, intention, and concentration to each moment. Eliminate all distractions. Leave nothing behind.

- Make every moment count and go deeper. Most of the time, we don't go deep enough. Going deeper has to do with motivation, intensity, and passion. Bring some zeal, hunger, and thirst to your practice. Mind, will power, emotions, and energy—everything is channeled in a constructive way towards the cultivation of healing qualities. Don't leave anything on the field.

- However, don't go too far and create tension or strain. All methods are practiced in a relaxed state. You cannot get to higher states if you are tense. There should be intensity without tension. Learn to relax and concentrate at the same time.

The Yo-Yo Effect and Concentration

- As stated, the best practice position combines one-pointed, calm, continuous concentration with intensity. Only a master can hold such a position. The rest of us must deal with the wandering mind.

- When we begin our practice by focusing on an affirmation, the breath, or a mantra, inevitably the mind will lapse into one of its familiar habit patterns. As soon as you notice that your mind has drifted off, gently bring it back to your point of focus. When the mind wanders again—and it will—gently bring it back to its practice position of calm concentration.

- This yo-yo, back-and-forth movement between calm concentration and the wandering mind will go on for years. It is a part of the natural process of meditation, mindfulness, and the other methods described in this work. The yo-yo effect is the route to full power and deep healing.

- Concentration is key. We are learning how to focus the mind, control attention, ignore distraction, and keep the mind where we want it to be. The more we bring the mind back from wandering to a single point of focus, the more we build up our brain groove for concentration.

- The yo-yo effect is frustrating. We want to control the mind but can't. It has a life of its own. We can bypass this frustration and stay calm by accepting the mind exactly where it is at the moment, because it could not be anywhere else. This will help you remain relaxed while you return the mind to its practice position of calm concentration.

- Practicing concentration can be fun or frustrating, depending upon our frame of reference. If we remain gentle, compassionate, and accepting of ourselves, we can play the game of concentration as a sport.

- You progress by taking one step at a time. Little by little, you get there. No matter what comes, press on. Eventually you will perfect the techniques.

- Perseverance is the key. It gets easier, but you must persevere even on difficult days. Give your best effort. Your concentration will expand.

- When the yo-yo slows and finally stops, you can place your needle of attention where you want it to be and keep it there.

A Simple Flick of the Switch or Heavy Lifting

- Sometimes, practicing a method or a quality is easy. It's like the simple flick of a switch. For example, you might practice the one-word affirmation, *compassion*, and bring yourself into alignment with that quality without much effort.

- Sometimes more effort is required. We may be struggling with difficult and painful problems on days when we don't have much energy and we don't feel like practicing anything. Concentration can be difficult—and even more difficult when we don't feel well. Practice on days like this feels like heavy lifting. But we need to do the work both when we feel like it and when we don't.

- A simple flick of the switch or heavy lifting. Be ready for both.

Morning Program

- You may choose to develop a morning ritual consisting of breathwork, progressive muscle relaxation, contemplation, meditation, and prayer.

- If you can't do the full program, do a brief ritual including one or a combination of these methods. Even a few minutes helps set the intent and tone for the day.

- When you finish the morning program, your consciousness is aligned with love and its consort qualities. You can then share these qualities with all whom you meet.

Day Program

- You can maintain the momentum gained in the morning program by practicing mindfulness, the presence of God, service, yoga, and transformation of emotion.

Evening Program

- Every evening, practice the same methods as the morning program: breathwork, progressive muscle relaxation, contemplation, meditation, and prayer.

One Continuous Sacred Ritual

- Morning, day, and evening practice are very beneficial, even if only for a few minutes.

- When you get tired, bored, or overwhelmed with a method, try a different one. Mix and match. Over time you will be able to pair methods to moments with increasing effectiveness.

- Every moment is an opportunity to practice one of the methods. Keep increasing your practice at various points throughout the day. The more we practice, the better we get. Practice the methods as much as you can.

- Advanced students always try to practice one of the methods. This is possible since some methods, such as meditation and contemplation, require solitude, while mindfulness, practicing the presence of God, and service all occur during activity.

- Slowly expand your practice until it is continuous and seamless. When you are always practicing a method, you have reached the pinnacle: one continuous sacred ritual.

Chip, Chip, Chip
Effort is Progress

- Problems can be tiny, small, medium, large, or huge. Some problems are long-term and severe.

- In general, the bigger the problem, the longer it takes to reduce its influence and power. This can be overwhelming. Hope may take a hit. Demoralization results. Some people never begin the healing process because it seems too overwhelming. Others get started but quit early when their pain seems insurmountable.

- To combat this sequence, think of yourself as a sculptor with a chisel, a big block of marble, and a vision of the final product. Go to work. Do a little bit every day. *Chip, chip, chip.* Effort is progress. (See exercise 4, pp. 253-254 in this workbook.)

- Everything gets better slowly with practice, a lot of practice. But the schedule for progress is not up to us. With some problems, we may see improvement right away. Others problems take longer.

- If you have an expectation of how long it takes to feel better and your expectation is not met, you are likely to quit. Then progress is impossible.

- As stated by a student in a class on healing, "If your problem is locked in a big fat obsessive compulsive brain groove and your new method and quality are a tiny little filament, this seems an unfair match. Practice anyway. You have to start somewhere. David beat Goliath." *Chip, chip, chip.* A sculptor does not produce a masterpiece overnight.

- When you do a lot of heavy lifting and see no apparent result, remember this: effort is progress. Keep on keeping on. Results are slow and cumulative. You think nothing is going on, but it is. The qualities are growing, but the growth is too subtle to feel. At some point you will experience peace, love, joy, power, and wisdom. You feel better, become a better person, and experience higher states of consciousness.

Establish the Virtues of the Great Ones

- The supreme goal is responding to painful problems with unconditional patience, peace, poise, compassion, love, understanding, and associated healing qualities. To do this, we need to practice the methods until they become our new mental habits locked in brain grooves so powerful that ultimately this is all we can do. Regular practice of the recommended methods will heal and transform your consciousness. Don't put a cap on your growth. You are unlimited.

- If you do this work, the virtues of the great saints and sages will slowly add on to you: peace and strength, compassion and courage, wisdom, and love expressed in acts of gentle, humble service to all of humanity.

Exercises

1. A Balanced Program

- Of the fifteen pain management options, there are three on the horizontal axis and twelve on the vertical axis. A balanced healing program includes work on both axes. Over time, there is a shift from dependence on the external world of people, activities, places, and things to the internal world of peace, security, and contentment—no matter the condition of the outer world.

- It is up to you to balance the outer and inner methods of the horizontal and vertical axes.

- Which method you choose and how much time you spend on each axis varies according to your stage of life, responsibilities, inclinations, awareness of issues, and degree of suffering.

- For example, if the horizontal axis is working, most people don't take time to retreat for contemplation and meditation. Overwhelming pain is usually the driver that forces people to vertical axis methods.

- Review the fifteen recommended methods for skillful pain management.

- Which ones do you already practice?

- Which ones would you like to add?

2. Prepare for a Rainy Day

- Your current life circumstance determines which methods you choose. For example, bike riding or jogging might be a prominent activity you use for skillful pain management on the horizontal axis. But what methods will you turn to if you break an arm and can't do your favorite sport?

- Most people don't think about this until change is forced upon them by life experience. Why wait for a crisis? Practice some of the vertical axis methods now to prepare for a rainy day.

- Practice when you feel well so you will be more prepared for the difficult painful days that can come at any time.

3. The Inner Gym

- When you realize your mind has gone for a ride on the train of thought and you don't want to be on the train, shift gears by remembering to practice a vertical axis method such as breathwork, affirmations, or mindfulness.

- This is like going to the gym, but in this case you don't have to go anywhere. The gym is inside. Go there and work out as early and often as you remember.

- The benefits are great: a strong, positive, calm, focused, and resilient mind, ready to help you accomplish goals, solve problems, shape meaning, manage pain skillfully, heal, and enjoy the show.

4. The Refrigerator of Life

- The *refrigerator of life* is the world calling you to familiar habits, which keep you from doing vertical axis work. For example, you are sitting in meditation, focusing on your mantra, and experience a good result; the mind becomes more positive and peaceful. You resolve to stay in meditation and go deeper.

- However, an idea or impulse arrives consistent with one of your well-traveled brain grooves, usually in the form of a person or activity in the horizontal axis: find a friend, watch television, check your e-mail, go for a walk, go shopping, eat something, and so forth.

- Watch these impulses and don't respond. If we answer this craving call too quickly, we miss the opportunity to cultivate the new habit of meditation in its new brain groove. It takes time to make a new habit. Resist the craving, and continue your practice for as long as you can.

5. Lifelong Practice

- As with any healthy lifestyle choice—like stopping cigarettes, eating a healthy diet, and physical workouts—practice of the recommended methods is lifelong.

- There is always work to do, whether life is smooth and stable or rocky and chaotic. If we practice the techniques when life is smooth, we can use them more effectively when it gets rough.

- Learning how to do the methods is simple, but it is not always easy. Although practice is enjoyable much of the time, sometimes you will not feel like doing any work. Other days there is considerable discomfort.

- Be ready for anything. Then if life gets rough, you will be less likely to drop the ball and escape to an old, unhealthy pain-killing habit.

- Channel all of your energy and inner faculties in a supreme conscious effort toward expansion of the qualities. This inner workout is like doing mental push-ups. You might call it mental yoga.

- Do as much as you can for the rest of your life. Light the fire and keep it lit. Bring it.

  How deep is your practice? What ignites your passion?

6. A Deep Metaphysical Purpose

- Some of our problems are long-term, chronic, deeply embedded, and seemingly impossible to shake. Like a difficult relative, the problem keeps showing up.

- These disconcerting, anxiety-provoking problems have a deep metaphysical purpose: the cultivation of healing qualities until they become USA: unconditional, spontaneous and automatic habits.

- Long-term severe problems may require more methods and more time than mild superficial problems. Run your problem through any one or a combination of the fifteen methods again and again until it is contained, reduced, or eliminated. It is this repetition that brings forth unconditional understanding, compassion, forgiveness, love, strength, courage, peace, and more.

- You will find more suggestions on how to manage long-standing problems in chapter 32, a Balanced Healing Program, on p. 244 in this workbook.

Points to Remember

- Pain has two levels: the inevitable suffering of life and our reaction to it. We cannot control the inevitable suffering of life, but we can control how we respond. This is where we have leverage. This is where we do the work. The work is reducing reactivity.

- Healing qualities are water for the fire of reactivity. Love, compassion, understanding, forgiveness, patience, kindness, humor, courage, and strength are the antidotes to impatience, frustration, anger, jealousy, judgment, selfishness, restlessness, and the like.

- In this work, you will find a versatile toolbox of fifteen methods. The list of methods is not intended to be all-inclusive. You are encouraged to heal by any method that works for you.

- The methods help us heal and manage our pain skillfully. With practice, you can wire the methods in the neurocircuits of your brain and make them your new good habits. Once these habits are in place, you can call upon them to help you manage your pain and problems.

- When practicing the methods, we learn how to turn it down a notch so we can enter a difficult situation with a wise mind, which is even-mindedness.

- You can practice any one or a combination of methods for any length of time. Study and practice the methods to see which ones work best. Start with one or two, and build from there at your own speed. Take your time. Build it up slowly. We are in this for a lifetime.

- Start wherever you wish. You are encouraged to choose the methods that work best for you in any combination. Some people may only practice affirmations and breathwork. Others focus on meditation and mindfulness.

- You progress by taking one step at a time. Little by little, you get there. No matter what comes, press on. Eventually you will perfect the techniques. Perseverance is the key. It gets easier, but you must persevere even on difficult days. Give it your best effort. Your concentration will expand. Eventually you will learn to stay with a method at will throughout the day.

- Focus on the cultivation of healing qualities in the moments of your life. The expansion of healing qualities is the result of every little effort in each moment. Results are subtle, but they accumulate minute by minute, thought by thought, and breath by breath.

- Use every circumstance and every moment as an opportunity to practice. Eventually you will experience the wonderful expansion of peace, love, joy, power, and wisdom.

- Healing qualities are the route to higher states of consciousness. Keep going and you will experience the peace that surpasses understanding, pure unconditional love, and ecstatic joy.

- In ordinary consciousness, we ride the inevitable pain waves of life and add unnecessary reactivity. In higher states of consciousness, we still feel the pain but we do not add unnecessary reactivity. It still hurts, but we get the best possible ride when we respond with love and its associated qualities.

- At mastery, we can ride the inevitable pain waves of life perfectly without reactivity. We remain even-minded under all conditions. No provocation can disrupt a master's love: a tall order, a wonderful goal.

- The only criterion for progress is doing your best. Practice PMQ and you will move forward. At some point you will feel it.

- Don't worry about perfection. Just do your best and leave the rest. There is only one report card. If you do your best, you get an A.

- You may start your practice on your own and later find the need for a teacher.

In the next chapter, we will study how the qualities help us manage our pain and evolve.

Chapter 12

Qualities

- Place all of the religions in a blender and swirl them into liquid religion. Take out your magical filter and command it to remove everything from the liquid that is not absolutely essential. Now pour the liquid through the filter into a small perfume bottle. The filter does its job of removing ritual, dogma, and other nonessentials. The perfume bottle now holds a product called the *elegant essence of religion*. If you were to drink this one night before sleep and wake up in the morning transformed into a Christ, Krishna, Buddha, favorite master, saint, sage, or the highest person you can imagine, what would be in the bottle?

- If you did the same exercise with every other healing model you can think of—including the psychotherapies, twelve-step programs, DBT (dialectical behavioral therapy), and other mindfulness-based cognitive therapies—what would be in the bottle?

- On the next page, you will see a list of one hundred qualities. These qualities would be in the bottle.

- These qualities make up *the essential healing principle* of all psychological, social, religious, and spiritual belief systems.

- The Bible, Koran, Bhagavad Gita, and all sacred texts and stories speak to these qualities.

- Christ, Buddha, Krishna, Rumi, The Baal Shem Tov, saints, sages, gurus, Zen masters, and yogis teach these qualities.

- The qualities are at the core of every spiritual story. They represent the basics, the alphabet, and the periodic table of spiritual elements.

- Likewise, all psychosocial healing models ultimately point to these qualities as the goal of inner healing work.

- These are the qualities we are going to study.

- *These are the qualities we will use to heal, manage our pain, and evolve.*

- Following your review of the list, there will be a more detailed discussion about how the qualities help us to do this work.

The one hundred healing qualities are:

HEALING QUALITIES

1. Acceptance	35. Honesty	69. Pure awareness
2. Appreciation	36. Hope	70. Pure consciousness
3. Balance	37. Humility	71. Purity
4. Beauty	38. Humor	72. Receptivity
5. Belief	39. Immortality	73. Reverence
6. Changelessness	40. Infinity	74. Rhythm
7. Cheerfulness	41. Integrity	75. Safety
8. Clarity	42. Interconnectedness	76. Security
9. Community	43. Introspection	77. Self-control
10. Compassion	44. Intuition	78. Service
11. Confidence	45. Joy	79. Silence
12. Contentment	46. Justice	80. Simplicity
13. Courage	47. Kindness	81. Sincerity
14. Creativity	48. Knowledge	82. Spaciousness
15. Desirelessness	49. Laughter	83. Stillness
16. Devotion	50. Light	84. Strength
17. Endurance	51. Listening	85. Success
18. Energy	52. Loyalty	86. Surrender
19. Enthusiasm	53. Mercy	87. Sweetness
20. Equality	54. Mindfulness	88. Tenderness
21. Eternity	55. Mystery	89. Thoughtfulness
22. Even-mindedness	56. Non-attachment	90. Tolerance
23. Faith	57. Non-injury	91. Trust
24. Fearlessness	58. Oneness	92. Truthfulness
25. Forbearance	59. Openness	93. Unconditional Love
26. Forgiveness	60. Order	94. Understanding
27. Freedom	61. Patience	95. Unity
28. Friendship	62. Peace	96. Usefulness
29. Fun	63. Perfection	97. Warmth
30. Generosity	64. Perseverance	98. Will
31. Gentleness	65. Play	99. Wisdom
32. Gratitude	66. Positive thinking	100. Witness
33. Harmony	67. Power	101. Other
34. Healing	68. Practicality	

Important Points About the Qualities

- You have an army of one hundred healing qualities.

- They are in the genetic code, the inherited wisdom of the body.

- They are not just words but actual healing powers.

- We can deploy them in response to any painful problem.

- They are more powerful than the painful problem.

- We know how to make them grow.

- Grow one, and the others grow with it. They are interconnected.

- The goal is to make them unconditional, spontaneous, automatic habits.

- As they become unconditional, spontaneous, automatic habits, the locus of control shifts from outside to inside.

- Expansion of healing qualities leads to higher states of consciousness.

- Life presents unlimited opportunities to evolve the qualities.

- Every moment of every scene is an opportunity to grow a quality.

- We can bring the qualities to every aspect of life: thought, feeling, choices, actions, listening, talking, working, eating, relaxing, relationships, conflicts—everything; you name it.

- There is no limit on the growth of a quality. There is always a next step.

- We always need more of all of the qualities, but from moment to moment some stand out as more important than the others. Work there.

- Reactivity is that part of our pain that is reversible. *Healing qualities contain, reduce, or eliminate reactivity and guide us through what is left.* This is skillful pain management.

- Armed with healing qualities, we are ultimately bigger than our pain.

- Good mental health is when the qualities are in charge.

- Good spiritual health is when the qualities are in charge.

- The most important question: are the qualities growing?

In the next section, we will study these important healing principles in more detail.

1. Healing Power

- The qualities are not just words but *actual healing powers*. Cultivation of the qualities leads to expanded healing power. When the qualities are in charge, we heal.

- Everything is on the table. As the qualities grow, everything inside and outside is renegotiated, rearranged, rebalanced, and polished. Negativity melts. We heal. We rise.

- The cultivation of these wonderful qualities is essential for complete recovery. We need them for deepest healing.

2. Pain Management

- Healing qualities are the *pain managers*. We can deploy the qualities in response to any pain or problem. The qualities are more powerful than any painful problem.

- Healing powers such as love, compassion, understanding, forgiveness, courage, perseverance, gratitude, acceptance, and humility will contain, reduce, or eliminate any barrier we face.

- Responding to painful problems with healing qualities is skillful pain management.

3. Spiritual Evolution

- We know how to make the qualities grow. This workbook teaches fifteen methods that will help you grow the qualities in response to any painful problem.

- As the qualities grow, we evolve spiritually:
  a. We feel better.
  b. We become better people.
  c. We may experience higher states of consciousness.

4. Love

- For our purposes, each time you read the word *love*, you can consider that as one or a combination of these qualities.

- If you don't favor the word love, you are encouraged to use any label that gives you inspiration: truth, power, wisdom, higher self, true self, soul, Buddha, Atman, image of God, spiritual qualities, spiritual alphabet, healing alphabet, spiritual properties, healing qualities, life savers, attributes of love, or any label that gives you inspiration.

- It doesn't matter what we call it.

- What does matter is the recognition that at the very core of our being exists a host of healing qualities that can help us manage any painful problem.

5. The True Self

- The roles we play in life, our educational level, economic status, race, ethnicity, and age obscure our true nature. Our bodies, personalities, or roles do not ultimately describe us.

Similarly, we are not our problems, flaws, or illnesses. These superficial identifications veil our inner identity or true self, the soul where we find all of the healing qualities.

- The qualities are our true identity, the higher self, our Buddha nature, the image of God within. It is who we really are. At the very core of our being, we are warm, loving human beings filled with strength, courage, wisdom, and joy.

- When we lose touch with this higher self, we are in trouble.

6. Interconnected

- The list of healing qualities is long and may appear overwhelming. It need not be. All the qualities are interconnected, and love is their root.

- If we improve our ability to love, the rest of the qualities simultaneously grow. Similarly, if we cultivate any one of the qualities, our love grows.

- We can pick one or a few qualities to work on at any given time. It doesn't matter which ones we choose. Grow one, and the others grow with it. They are interconnected.

7. Universal with Variation

- The qualities are universal. Every person has all of the qualities.

- The qualities are in every religion. They don't belong to one religion. No religion owns them. They apply to all faiths or no faith.

- The cells in the body do not ask your religion. They don't care about theology or lack of theology. They don't care if you are atheist, agnostic, religious, or spiritual. They do care if you are in peace-love-joy.

- All of us have the qualities, but each manifests the qualities in a unique way. We are the same being in different disguises.

8. Love Is More Powerful Than Any Painful Problem

- Love is the great healer and the great pain manager.

- Love qualities contain, reduce, or eliminate our pain and guide us through what is left.

- Love is a part of the solution to any painful problem.

- Our problem may be complex, but the solution is simple: love and its consort qualities. We need love, compassion, patience, and kindness no matter the nature of our problems however complex they might be.

- When we add love qualities to our story, it may not eliminate all of our pain, but it is the line of least resistance.

- Following the way of love is the least painful way to go through life. All other routes are more painful. Love is the best possible ride.

- Look for love over pain as a means of expressing creativity and evolution.

9. **Water on the Fire of Reactivity**

    - Reactivity is that part of our pain that is reversible.

    - *Healing qualities are water on the fire of reactivity.* (See illustration below)

    - Patience, kindness, love, compassion, and forgiveness heal anger, judgment, resentment, jealousy, anxiety, fear, cruelty, and more.

The Triumph of Love Over Pain

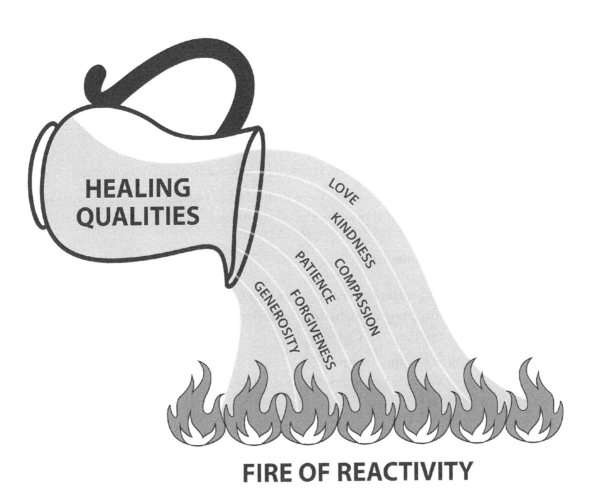

10. **Precision Guidance**

    - Religious, spiritual, and psychological healing models can be complex, confusing, and contradictory.

    - The qualities, on the other hand, are *concrete, specific, clear, simple, focused, crystallized, and precise.*

- Let the qualities be your guide. These are universal truths we can live by. They are easy to follow.

11. Unconditional, Spontaneous, Automatic Habits

- When we practice the methods recommended in this work, the qualities grow and become strong inner-being muscles. At mastery, the qualities are USA: unconditional, spontaneous, automatic habits.

- This is a tall order. The qualities are relentless taskmasters. It takes years to cultivate peace, love, compassion, and understanding, no matter the condition of the world or your body.

12. Locus of Control Shifts from Outside to Inside

- As the qualities become USA—unconditional, spontaneous, and automatic habits—the locus of control shifts from outside to inside.

- As you build your external world of people and activities, you can also build an inner world of peace, power, and strength.

- As the healing qualities slowly grow, you will be less reactive and more relaxed.

- The ultimate goal is to shift your locus of control from outside to inside in order to be less reactive and to remain at peace under all conditions.

13. Higher States of Consciousness

- Expansion of healing qualities eventually leads to higher states of consciousness. When the qualities become strong enough, they can no longer contain themselves. They inflate by nature.

- Ever-expanding love and compassion eventually break into superconsciousness: unfathomable peace, pure unconditional love, and ecstatic joy. This pure consciousness expands to infinity.

Exercises

1. Your Power in the Story

- No one can give you the qualities or take them away. You already have them, and you make them grow or shrink by the choices you make. This is your power in the story.

- An old Cherokee Indian was speaking to his grandson. "A fight is going on inside me," he said to the boy. "It is a terrible fight between two wolves. One is evil—he is anger, envy, sorrow, regret, greed, arrogance, self-pity, guilt, resentment, inferiority, lies, false pride, superiority, and ego. The other is good—he is joy, peace, love, hope, serenity, humility, kindness, benevolence, empathy, generosity, truth, compassion, and faith. This same fight is going on inside you, and inside every other person, too."

The grandson thought about it for a long minute, and then asked his grandfather, "Which wolf will win?"

The old Cherokee simply replied, "The one you feed."

- This wonderful Native American parable speaks to the evil and good wolf in each of us. The evil wolf creates pain. The good wolf heals.

    a. Are you mindful of the battle between the two wolves in you?
    b. Which wolf have you been feeding?
    c. What changes would you like to make?
    d. To find your power in the story, choose the good wolf—love—a composite of one hundred healing qualities.
    e. Often, our only place of power in the story is love. When we get this, we are really moving along.

2. An Army of One Hundred Healing Qualities

- We are born with an army of one hundred healing qualities. They are standard equipment, built into the body from the start. They are in the genetic code as the inherited wisdom of the body.

- The jewels of this life lie at the very core of your being. You have within you right now the habits of a sage. You are not just good; you are very good.

    a. Did you know you are born with an army of healing qualities?
    b. How does that make you feel?
    c. Review the list of one hundred healing qualities. The list is not dogmatic. Take what you need and leave the rest.
    d. Notice quality 101: *Other*. You are encouraged to add any quality you personally find inspiring. Can you think of some qualities you would like to add?
    e. You are also encouraged to delete any quality you wish. Which quality or qualities would you delete?
    f. What does your list look like?
    g. Your army of one hundred healing qualities awaits marching orders. Have you called them up? If not, what are the barriers?

3. The Most Direct, Quick, Simple, and Efficient Way to Access Healing Power

- To access healing power, all we have to do is place our needle of attention on a quality.

- Let's use compassion as an example.

- Compassion is already embedded in the genetic code, neural structures, and consciousness, waiting to be tapped, free of cost.

- When we think, feel, and visualize compassion with affirmations, mindfulness, and meditation, we *activate it and make it grow.*

- When we do this, our healing power expands, we become more skillful pain managers, and we evolve.

- Evolution means we feel better, become better people, and experience higher states of consciousness.

- *Compassion itself is the healer, pain manager, and spiritual transformer.*

- Let it radiate out from the center of your being to every cell in your body, surrounding space and other people.

- Cultivating the qualities is the most direct, quick, simple, and efficient way to access healing power. There are no circuitous routes. This is direct healing for you and others.

4. The Higher Self

- The roles we play in life, our educational level, economic status, race, ethnicity, and age obscure our true nature. Our bodies, personalities, or roles do not ultimately describe us. Similarly, we are not our problems, flaws, or illnesses. These superficial identifications veil our inner identity or true self, the soul, where we find all of the healing qualities.

- The qualities are our true identity, the higher self, our Buddha nature, the image of God within. It is who we really are. At the very core of our being, we are warm, loving human beings filled with strength, courage, wisdom, and joy. When we lose touch with this higher self, we are in trouble.

    a. Do you allow your problem or illness to define you? If so, how does that make you feel?
    b. Read the list of one hundred healing qualities. As you read, realize this is your true or higher self. How does this make you feel?
    c. You are a warm, kind, loving, compassionate, strong human being. You are not just good. You are very good. How does this make you feel?
    d. Affirm. Contemplate. Meditate. Go deep. Realize your Buddha nature. You *are* the qualities.

5. Love Is More Powerful Than Any Painful Problem

- Review the list of painful problems on p. 58 and the list of healing qualities on p. 79.

- Now, remember this: healing qualities are more powerful than any painful problem.

- Healing powers such as love, compassion, understanding, forgiveness, and humility will contain, reduce, or eliminate our pain and guide us through what is left.

- When we add love qualities to our story, it may not eliminate all of our pain but it is the line of least resistance. Following the way of love is the least painful way to go through life. All other routes are more painful.

- There is a jewel with many facets at the center of our being. The jewel is love. The facets are the healing qualities. No matter what happens, always stay in touch with love and its consort qualities.

    a. Can you think of a time when the lack of love on your part caused problems?
    b. Can you think of an example in your life where love healed your pain?
    c. Can you think of a time in your life when love helped you manage a pain that wouldn't go away?

- A member spoke about how the qualities impact his PTSD cycle. "My PTSD cycles are shorter when I throw the healing qualities into it. It shortens the episode," he said.

    a. Can you think of a problem and a healing quality you used to help you manage the problem?
    b. Can you think of a time in your life when a healing quality helped you heal at a deeper level than usual?
    c. The entire story of psychosocial and spiritual healing is the triumph of love over pain.
    d. Look for love over pain as a means of expressing creativity and evolution.

6. **Water on the Fire of Reactivity** (See illustration p. 83)

- We already have all of the qualities but not enough. When we overreact, it is a result of a shortage in the qualities.

- Reactivity is that part of our pain that is reversible. Healing qualities are water on the fire of that reactivity.

- Patience, kindness, love, compassion, and forgiveness heal anger, judgment, resentment, jealousy, anxiety, fear, cruelty, and more.

    a. Review those scenes you wish you could rewrite and replay in a different way. Usually this involves a lack of self-control resulting in a string of negative consequences. Words slip out, you raise your voice, you yell, throw things, hit the wall, or worse.
    b. In these scenes, notice the relationship between reactivity and healing qualities. The more patience, kindness, compassion, and understanding, the less anger, judgment, resentment, fear, and cruelty. When healing qualities are big enough, reactivity can't get in.
    c. Can you think of some examples in your life when a healing quality helped you reduce your emotional reactivity?

7. **Skillful Pain Management = Love**

- The qualities are pain managers. We can deploy them in response to any pain or problem.

    a. When we respond to painful problems with healing qualities, we manage our pain skillfully.
    b. Can you think of an example in your life when you managed your pain unskillfully?

87

   c. Now consult the list of healing qualities. Which qualities would have helped you manage that pain more skillfully?

   d. Can you think of an example in your life when you managed your pain skillfully by responding with healing qualities?

   e. Love and skillful pain management are one and the same. Do you see the connection?

> Love = Skillful Pain Management

8. Interconnected

- The list of healing qualities is long and may appear formidable. It need not be. All of the qualities are connected, and love is the root.

- If we improve our ability to love, the rest of the qualities simultaneously grow. Similarly, if we cultivate any one of the qualities, our love grows.

- We can pick one or a few qualities to work on at any given time. It doesn't matter which ones we choose.

- If we cultivate compassion, we automatically become more patient and understanding.

- If we practice kindness, we automatically become more forgiving and loving.

- When we practice courage and perseverance, we automatically become stronger and more peaceful.

- Gratitude leads to reverence.

- Patience, kindness, sweetness, and gentleness move together.

- When we grow even one quality, the rest follow.

- It does not matter which ones we choose. Each quality is connected to the others, and they all lead to love.

- Which qualities would you like to grow first, knowing the rest will grow with it?

9. Protection, Guidance, and Wisdom

- Religious, spiritual, and psychosocial healing models can be complex, confusing, and contradictory. The qualities, on the other hand, are concrete, specific, clear, simple, focused, crystallized, and precise.

- We can use the qualities for protection, guidance, and wisdom when we conduct family meetings, business meetings, and conflict resolution. We can use the qualities in our marriage and in all of our relationships.

- We need and crave the qualities. No matter what happens, always stay in touch with the qualities. They are the teacher, the guru, and the master. Let the qualities be your guide in thought, feeling, and action. They are easy to follow.

  a. How might you be able to use qualities such as compassion, kindness, and understanding to guide your thoughts, feelings, choices, and actions?
  b. Pick a quality in the morning, and let that quality guide you throughout the day.
  c. Affirmation: *Compassion, love, and understanding guide me every moment throughout the day.*

10. Simple But Difficult

- Cultivating healing qualities in response to the painful problems of life may sound simple, but it is difficult. The qualities do grow if we practice the recommended methods, but growth is slow and sometimes it hurts. There is work to do. It involves discipline. It takes time.

  a. Is this a time in your life when you are willing to do some work?
  b. What barriers stand in your way?
  c. Are you willing to do some work today?
  d. Are you willing to do some work every day for the rest of your life?
  e. Are you willing to work, one moment at a time, for the rest of your life?

11. Diversity

- All of us have the qualities. Each of us manifests the qualities in our own way. We are the same being in different disguises.

  a. Can you think of some ways you manifest healing qualities in your life?
  b. Can you think of some ways others manifest healing qualities in their lives?
  c. Enjoy the diverse way others express the qualities. This can be a source of inspiration to you.

12. Creativity

- The list of one hundred qualities seems long, but it is good to have a variety of options. There is no limit to the number of ways we can use the qualities to heal, create, and evolve.

- A member said this about the qualities: "There are so many options and so much room for play. I use the qualities in different ways. To me, compassion is an idea, and kindness is a behavior. It is easier for me to be compassionate mentally, but being kind is another order of depth as it means I have to be kind, not just in my head but in my behavior. I am talking about my head, how I treat people in my head. Kindness helps me behave mentally and in the real world as well."

- Life presents unlimited opportunities to evolve the qualities. Every moment of every scene is an opportunity to cultivate a healing quality.

   a.   We always need more understanding, forgiveness, strength, and forbearance.

   b.   We always need warmth, thoughtfulness, and sensitivity to the needs of others.

   c.   There is always a need for justice and equality.

   d.   We crave happiness, friendship, humor, laughter, and fun.

   e.   We have an unbending need for peace, love, joy, and wisdom.

- We always need more of all the qualities, but from moment to moment some stand out as more important than the others. Some of us need to focus on courage, strength, and perseverance, while others work on patience, kindness, and compassion.

- We may need a different set of qualities from one day to the next or different qualities for different parts of the day.

- Review the list of qualities. Which one or combination of qualities do you need most right now?

- The quality you choose may vary depending on your readiness, mood, the problem you are working with, or how much energy you have. For example, practicing forgiveness is difficult. One has to be ready. It requires energy and perseverance. On a day when you are already overwhelmed and tired, this might not be the best quality to choose. With a list of one hundred qualities, you are likely able to find at least one that appeals and fits your current need. Notice how the qualities you need the most can change from scene to scene.

- You can practice a quality for a minute, hour, day, week, month, or year.

- We can bring the qualities to every aspect of life: thought, attitude, feeling, choices, actions, listening, talking, working, eating, relaxing, relationships, conflicts—everything; you name it.

- With one hundred qualities, there are so many options and so much room for play. Be creative.

- You might try practicing one hundred days of love. Choose a different quality every day for one hundred days.

- Can you think of some unique ways you can use the qualities in your life?

- What works for you?

13. Locus of Control

- As you build your external world of people and activities, you can also build an inner world of peace, power, and strength. As the healing qualities slowly grow, you will be less reactive and more relaxed.

- The ultimate goal is to shift your locus of control from outside to inside, to be less reactive, and to remain strong and peaceful under all conditions. We may not be safe outside, but we are always safe inside with the qualities.

- Discuss how shifting the locus of control from outside to inside applies in your life.

14. Superconsciousness

- Healing qualities help us in every aspect of life. When we bring out the qualities in response to life's difficulties, our consciousness will rise to a higher state. Our life is smoother and easier. We feel better and become better people.

- When the qualities become strong enough, they can no longer contain themselves. They inflate by nature. The expansion of healing qualities leads to higher states of consciousness: the peace that surpasses understanding, pure love, ecstatic joy, cosmic sound, cosmic light, unfathomable stillness, and more.

- For more on superconscious experience, read chapter 14, The Universal Healing Wheel with Traction Devices, on p. 116 in this workbook.

  a. Have you ever had a superconscious experience?
  b. What was it like?
  c. How long did it last?

15. Self-Esteem and Soul-Esteem

- Self-esteem is based on success and failure in the outer world. We feel good about ourselves when we succeed, and feel bad when we fail.

- Soul-esteem is a reflection of the true self, the Buddha, or image of God within. The qualities are in charge inside, independent of success or failure in the outer world. We have love, compassion, understanding, forgiveness, strength, and humor inside no matter what happens outside.

  a. Notice how self-esteem is associated with an external locus of control. Your image is determined by what others think of you.
  b. Notice how soul-esteem is associated with an internal locus of control. Your image is determined by what you think of yourself.
  c. Notice how self-esteem and soul-esteem play out in the movie of your life.
  d. As we evolve and soul-esteem grows, the locus of control shifts from outside to inside.
  e. Affirm, "What others think of me is none of my business."

16. Goodness

- Everyone brings something deeply good to the table right now.

  a. Which qualities are you good at?
  b. Which would you like to grow?
  c. Look for the healing qualities in others. Focus on those qualities rather than any negative characteristics.

17. Kindness

- The Dalai Lama says, "This is my simple religion. There is no need for temples, no need for complicated philosophy. Our own brain, our own heart is our temple; the philosophy is kindness."

    a. Do you see? The one thing every religion, spiritual program, twelve-step program, and any other healing model have in common is the cultivation of healing qualities.

    b. When you have a painful problem, consult the list of one hundred spiritual qualities. Determine which qualities you need to help you manage your problem. Now, focus on your chosen quality. Give it all of your attention.

    c. You can use the qualities as one-word affirmations throughout the day.

    d. Practice one or a combination of the healing qualities throughout the day, and evaluate how you did at night. Did you respond to the day's events with those qualities or in a negative fashion?

    e. Identify areas for improvement, and start anew the next day.

18. The Most Important Question

- "Are the qualities growing?" This is the most important question.

- To see if you are growing, review the qualities you are working on and ask:

    a. Am I becoming more patient, kind, understanding, and peaceful?

    b. Am I growing in acceptance, compassion, forgiveness, and gentleness?

    c. Is there more love in my life, both giving and receiving?

    d. Is there more strength, courage, and perseverance?

    e. Is there more gratitude and humility?

    f. Is there more balance, rhythm, and harmony in my life?

    g. Am I more awake, aware, and alive?

    h. The answers to these questions make up your spiritual report card.

    i. Choose any one or combination of qualities and see how you are doing.

19. Contagious

- One member noted how kindness and safety were the two qualities he felt when he first started going to AA meetings. Then he became those qualities and was able to give them to others. His conclusion: the qualities are contagious.

    a. Drop kindness, safety, or any other healing quality into the center of your consciousness. Feel the healing vibrations throughout your system, and then send those vibrations to others and surrounding space.

    b. Start your day with a healing quality, and focus on that quality all day long. Invoke a powerful memory of this quality working in your life. Think, picture, and feel the quality healing yourself and others. Keep it for a week, month, or longer.

20. Clusters

- You can bundle the qualities and use them for your walking meditation, affirmation, or mantra. This is a great exercise. It feels really good.

- Here are some examples you can use on different days depending on your mood, energy level, and need at the time. Give yourself these one-word commands:

  a. Acceptance, courage, endurance
  b. Compassion, love, understanding, forgiveness
  c. Balance, rhythm, harmony
  d. Patient, kind, sweet, tender, gentle
  e. Stillness, silence, spaciousness, serenity
  f. Courage, strength, perseverance
  g. Soft, yield, open, silence
  h. Humility, devotion, surrender, trust
  i. Love, truth, beauty, goodness
  j. Peace, love, joy, power, wisdom
  k. Faith, trust, belief, positive thought
  l. Surrender, obey, accept, attune, receive
  m. Love, service, courage, faith
  n. Simplicity, oneness, humility
  o. Create your own quality cluster

21. Rivet Them In

- The qualities can be our organizing principle, core beliefs, backbone, or the hub of the wheel.

- The goal is to manifest the qualities in full bloom at all times, but this is impossible. Our imperfections get in the way. But we can make them grow a little bit each day by making them our lifelong affirmations. There is always another step to take.

  a. Get the qualities in your mind first, then in your heart, then in your bones.
  b. Fix your mind to the qualities and the qualities to your mind, and don't let go. Rivet them in. Don't let anything knock you off that pedestal.
  c. Focus on one or a combination of qualities, not just for a few minutes but throughout the day, 24/7 for the rest of your life.
  d. Give the qualities to yourself and others at all times. This is true mindfulness. This is wisdom in action.

22. The Three-Story House

- We live in a three-story house.

- The first floor of the house is where we live out our story. It becomes turbulent or chaotic at times.

- The second floor of the house is filled with unlimited healing qualities. We can go there for solace and comfort. No matter the problems we face, the second floor offers peace, safety, harmony, and strength.

- When we bring second floor qualities down to the first floor, everything gets better.

- When the qualities become strong enough, they expand through the roof of the second floor to the third floor of the house. Here there are no walls or ceiling. This is the Big Space, the land of the Higher Power and higher states of consciousness, sometimes referred to as superconsciousness. Here you will experience unfathomable peace, pure unconditional love, and ecstatic joy.

- When your consciousness is high, nothing can touch you. Get to the second floor of the house and eventually the third floor. That is all you need. That is the key and the solution to life's problems. The way and the goal is expansion of healing qualities. This is wisdom.

- For an expanded version of The House, see chapter 44 on p. 315 in this workbook.

23. Low Tide

- When you are at low tide or when you drift, re-energize each moment by practicing the following method:
    a. Stop
    b. Breathe
    c. Present moment
    d. Pick a quality

Points to Remember

- Love qualities are the healers, the pain managers, and the spiritual transformers.

- The qualities are concrete, specific, clear, simple, focused, crystallized, and precise.

- The qualities are the quickest and most direct path to expanded healing power.

- We use the regular alphabet to learn language. Spiritual qualities are the alphabet of life.

- Love is a unified force field with infinite possibilities. We are the same being in different disguises. Each of us manifests the qualities in a different way.

- No matter what barriers might stop us, we can respond with healing qualities. These are our tools, the habits of a sage, the jewels of this life. When your back is against the wall and you are in pain, you can call up your army of one hundred healing qualities.

- Love qualities are the goal, the product, and the true measure of our success. When you are in alignment with the qualities, everything falls into place. Don't leave home without them.

- The answer to our painful problems is simple. Grow some qualities. How? Practice PMQ, also referred to as rolling the universal healing wheel. When we practice breathwork, affirmations, mindfulness, and meditation, healing qualities grow, painful problems are contained, reduced, or eliminated, and we evolve. We feel better, become better persons, and may experience higher states of consciousness. PMQ is the essential healing principle, the e = mc2 of all psychosocial and spiritual healing models.

- Love qualities are the gold standard, the ideal, the best. They guide us. They set the boundaries and pathway. We are either in or out of bounds, on or off the path. When our thoughts, feelings, and actions are not in alignment with love, we have work to do. The work is to practice any one or a combination of methods to expand love until it is unconditional.

- We are afraid of suffering, disease, disability, the unknown, and death. This fear makes the inevitable suffering of life worse and slows down the healing process. *The essence of mind-body medicine is reducing this reactivity and replacing it with healing qualities such as compassion, love, understanding, strength, courage, and peace.* Bring out healing qualities in response to life's difficulties. Your life will be smoother, easier, and you will feel better.

- Healing qualities adding up to love are more powerful than any painful problem. Clearly establish the cultivation of healing qualities as your goal, and keep this goal ever shining before you. Make the qualities the central organizing principle of your life. You may get overwhelmed, but you won't get lost. The qualities are your radiant light. Let them burn brightly and illuminate your way.

- The techniques described in this book will show you how to place your needle of attention on healing qualities referred to as love. You will learn how to think, feel, visualize, and ultimately become these qualities. The qualities will then help you broker and buffer any painful problem.

- Skillful pain management, reduced reactivity, increased healing qualities, and love are all the same thing. The simple way to say this is: love is the great healer.

- When we apply the qualities to our serious problems over the years, we will see how they broaden, deepen, and have a totally different meaning: faith, surrender, courage, and so forth. There is no limit to their creative healing powers. The most important question: are the qualities growing?

Memorable Quotes from Groups and Classes

- Each quality is a light switch from negative to positive.

- The qualities will make you *prrrrrr* like a kitten, maybe not right away but eventually.

- You can hold on to your snark or throw the qualities into the mix and move out of it.

- Healing qualities are safe. They open the door without toxicity.

- The qualities feed each other.

- I pick a quality the first thing in the morning, one I am not familiar with.

- Whether we have a problem or not, we need the qualities.

- I practice when the weather is good, so I can call on them when the wind blows.

- The qualities are your toolbox.

- When I match my problem with a quality, it doesn't damage me or others.

- Gratitude is a muscle. The more I practice, the stronger it gets.

- Let the qualities be your guide. What would the qualities do? How would love, courage, patience, kindness, and perseverance guide me now?

- The qualities are a corrective guiding force. When I'm off, they get me back on course.

- Continuously affirm and practice the qualities you wish to manifest. When old habits persist, keep practicing anyway.

- Start where you are. You have the qualities. Gently build from there.

- The qualities are not just an affirmation, prayer, or checking in a couple of times a day. No, the qualities are our new habits locked into neurocircuits, so we can respond automatically and spontaneously. We get there by rolling the universal healing wheel, described in the next chapter.

- Now that you have completed your review of pain, method, and quality, we can study how these three work together. In the next chapter, you will learn how to roll the universal healing wheel.

Chapter 13

Rolling the Universal Healing Wheel

Skillful Pain Management

- We have studied pain, method, and quality in chapters 10--12.

- In this chapter, we will put it all together. We will study how pain, method, and quality work together.

- In this work, PMQ—or problem, method, quality—is called the universal healing wheel

- (P): The problem can be any problem of body, mind, or soul. Remember, this is about the residual suffering that can't be relieved by your doctor or other health care professionals. This pain-ball is in your court and can only be managed by you through self-help, self-healing methods.

- (M): To address these problems, the workbook describes fifteen self-healing methods.

- (Q): The result is the cultivation of one hundred spiritual qualities adding up to love.

- To evolve, all you have to do is find a problem, practice a method, and cultivate a quality.

- When we practice PMQ:

    1. Healing power expands.
    2. We become more skillful pain managers.
    3. We evolve.
        a. We feel better.
        b. We become people.
        c. We experience higher states of consciousness.
- Following are a variety of exercises illustrating the dynamics of the universal healing wheel.

1. Roll the Wheel

- The first step is to realize mindfully that we are in a reaction (P) and don't want to be there.

- Then we need to pick a method (M) and quality (Q) to reduce that reactivity.

- Here is a simple technique to help you do this.

When you realize you have gone for a ride on the train of thought and want to get off the train:

1. Stop
2. Breathe
3. Present moment
4. (P) Pain: Any painful problem
5. (M) Method: Choose a method
6. (Q) Quality: Choose a quality

(P): Problem:

- Find a problem you would like to work on. (see list on p. 58)

- This can be any problem: physical, mental, emotional, interpersonal, or spiritual.

- It can be any size: tiny, small, medium, large, or huge.

(Q): Quality:

- Go to the list of one hundred healing qualities (p. 79)

- Pick one or a combination of qualities you need right now to help you with your problem.

(M): Method:

- Pick one or a combination of methods that will help you grow that quality. (See p. 60)
    a. Now, gently bring the quality and method to the pain. Everything is done gently.
    b. Focus on the method and quality, not the pain.
    c. Practice your method and quality for a day, a week, or longer.
    d. Read about that quality.
    e. Think about it.
    f. Discuss it.
    g. Contemplate it.
    h. Affirm it.
    i. Breathe it.
    j. Feel it.
    k. Visualize it.
    l. Concentrate on it.
    m. Permeate your being with it.
    n. Invoke powerful memories about it.
    o. Create from it.

    p. Make it your faithful guide and companion.

    q. Write your experience.

    r. Share in a group or with a friend.

- Example: Perhaps you want to reduce your tendency to judge others harshly by practicing compassion. When you have gone for a ride on the judgmental train of thought and want to get off the train:

  1. Stop
  2. Breathe
  3. Present moment
  4. (P): Realize you are in a judgmental frame of mind.
  5. (M): Affirm: My heart is always open and willing to forgive.
  6. (Q): Compassion

- There are many options. You might choose patience for irritability, courage for fear, forgiveness for resentment, acceptance for physical pain, community for loneliness, and so forth.

- For some examples, see the Universal Healing Wheel, p. 100

- You might also review the list of painful problems on p. 58 and manifestations of the trickster ego on pp. 345-346.

- The universal healing wheel works for any problem: tiny, small, medium, large, or huge. The dynamics are the same.

- Choose any problem and match it to a method and quality. Practice the method, and cultivate the quality in response to the pain. The quality is more powerful than the painful problem. As it slowly grows, it will contain, reduce, or eliminate your pain.

- We must still deal with the inevitable suffering of life. But now there is less reactivity and more strength and peace. This is skillful pain management by rolling the universal healing wheel.

The Universal Healing Wheel

Problem	Method	Quality
Any problem of body, mind, or spirit	15 methods	100 qualities
Lonely	People: meet a friend	Joy
Bored	Activity: volunteer	Generosity
Loss	Belief system: go to church or AA meeting	Community
Physical illness	Affirmation	Acceptance
Addiction	Habit transformation	Contentment
Fatigue	Progressive muscle relaxation	Energy
Anxious	Breathwork	Peace
Confusion	Contemplation	Wisdom
Restless	Meditation	Even-mindedness
Fear	Prayer	Courage
Irritable	Mindfulness	Patience
Judgmental	Practicing the Presence of God	Unconditional Love
Guilt	Service	Forgiveness
Worry	Yoga	Harmony
Anger	Transformation of emotion	Understanding

2. Pain, Method, and Quality in the Same Space

- Once you define your pain, method, and quality, the goal is to focus on the method and quality—not the pain. Often, however, our concentration muscle is not strong enough to do this. We try to focus on the method and quality but the force of the pain is compelling and commands our attention.

- We can manage this common scenario by gently holding the pain, method, and quality in the same space.

- Place your needle of attention on the method and quality. When the mind lapses into one of its negative habit patterns, bring it back to your method and quality.

- For example, your PMQ might be (P) anxiety, (M) breathwork with affirmation, and (Q) peace.

- (P) anxiety

- (M) breathwork and affirmations

- (Q) peace

- When you feel anxious, breathe slowly and deeply while you affirm: "Breathing gently, calming down. Breathing gently, problem melts."

- When the mind lapses back into anxiety or fear thoughts, all you have to do is shift your attention from the anxiety back to slow deep breathing and your affirmation and hold it there until it wanders again. And it will.

- The back and forth movement between the old negative habit pattern of anxiety and the new point of focus on your breath and affirmation is called the yo-yo effect.

- The yo-yo effect applies to all of the exercises in this workbook and is a natural part of the healing process.

- As your concentration improves with practice, you will be able to focus more and more on the breath and affirmation until you can stay there at will.

- This is hard and counterintuitive. Holding the pain, method, and quality in the same space hurts. There is friction, conflict, and discomfort. There may be more pain before there is less pain. It feels like going to a mental dentist, jumping off a cliff, or a wrestling match. In this example, the wrestling match is between anxiety and the affirmation, "Breathing gently, calming down. Breathing gently, problem melts."

- We don't want this fight, but there is no healthy alternative. We must sit with the pain, quality, and method in the same space for however long it takes.

- Being aware of the pain, method, and the quality at the same time is the key. This is where the magic happens. Peace wrestles with anxiety and eventually pins it to the mat. But to get to the pin, you have to sit with the wrestling match.

3. Four Stages of Growth

When We Roll the Wheel, Change Occurs in Four Stages

- Stage 1: *No change is noticeable*: We do the work and nothing happens. The qualities are growing, but the increase is subtle and imperceptible. Many people quit here, as they are looking for immediate gratification and are not prepared for work, struggle, and discipline. Don't put a schedule on this stage. If we do—and our expectations are not met—we may become discouraged and give up our quest.

- Stage 2: *We feel better and become better people*: There is a tangible experience of ever-increasing peace, love, strength, courage, compassion, and the other love-qualities.

- Stage 3: *Superconscious experience* Love qualities inflate by nature. At some point, they cannot contain themselves. They break into superconscious states that defy description. Words are only signposts. We have to go there. When we reach an expanded superconscious state, we know it, experience it, and feel it. These experiences last for a few minutes or hours to several days. But there is inevitably a return to ordinary consciousness. Back to school. Back to work.

- Stage 4: *Mastery*: A sustained state of superconsciousness reserved for masters. This is a very advanced stage and requires decades if not lifetimes of discipline. For a more detailed description of this stage, see *Healing Power, Revised* p. 88 and pp. 134–35. Alternatively, you can study the lives of Jesus, Buddha, Krishna, Rumi, or any God-realized master.

---

4. What Do We Do If We Roll the Wheel and Our Pain Doesn't Go Away?

- This is a very important question. Most of us want a quick fix. If we don't get it, we quit.

- It is not possible to predict how long we have to roll the wheel or practice PMQ before we experience pain relief. Some may feel better right away. Others will have to practice for a while before they feel better.

- Review the four stages of growth in exercise 3 above. Stage 1 has no defined timetable. We don't know how long it will last. However, if we persist with our practice when there are no apparent results, we will progress to stages 2, 3, and 4.

- To illustrate how this works, let's use the PMQ: anxiety, breathwork/affirmation, peace as in exercise 2 above.

- At first, we experience anxiety while practicing the breath and affirmation. There is no peace. We repeat the affirmation "Breathing gently, calming down. Breathing gently, problem melts." In the beginning, this affirmation is stuck at the level of thought. It is not realized. The thought stays in our head. There is no change in consciousness. The anxiety persists untempered by the affirmation. In PMQ language: we have the P (anxiety) and the M (affirmation/breathwork), but there is no Q (peace).

- This is the critical zone. In the beginning, the new brain groove is not big or strong enough to hold against its bigger opponent brain groove carrying the anxiety habit pattern. This is a difficult phase of the work. It hurts. We are in pain. The pain may be severe.

- However, if we persist in our practice, we build up the brain groove carrying the new good habit: affirmation, breathwork, and peace. *Persevere. Keep on keeping on. Practice your method and quality whether or not your pain goes away.*

- In response to your pain, focus on your method and quality as much as you can. When the pain captures your attention, gently return your focus to your method and quality.

- Notice the back and forth yo-yo effect between the pain and your method and quality. In the beginning, the pain has its way with you. With practice, however, your ability to maintain your focus on the method and quality will improve. *The growth of concentration is key.* Eventually you can concentrate on your method and quality, no matter what the pain is doing.

- Back to our example of anxiety, breathwork/affirmation, peace. Anxiety is intense. It draws all of our attention. Keep breathing and affirming into the anxiety. The back and forth battle between anxiety and breathwork/affirmation and peace is slowly being won by peace because of our *work, effort, and practice.*

- When we do this work and don't try to escape, we will succeed. The new brain groove carrying our affirmation and breathwork slowly grows. Peace fights off anxiety and finally takes over.

- Riding the pain wave without acting out is the most important principle of skillful pain management. In this case, the pain wave is anxiety. You ride the wave with your breathwork and affirmation. Peace wins in the end.

- The goal is to shift your pain story to a healing story by practicing the methods and qualities recommended in this work. But we may not be able to shake our pain story easily when it is loaded with prior negative actions, personality flaws, symptoms, attachments, bad habits, and addiction. We want the healing story to dominate our consciousness, but there are times when we have to hang out with and travel through the pain.

- There will be many layers and many rounds. You don't just do an affirmation and get the cure. The healing quality must go to progressively deeper layers to soothe, ease, and quiet the pain down. And it will. The quality will sink into the deepest part of your consciousness and become part of a foundation that cannot be broken. It will become a new and eventually unconditional habit, housed in a brain groove that will not quit.

- It doesn't matter what pain or quality you pick. The dynamics are the same. You may be countering resentment with compassion, anger with understanding, or craving with contentment. Hold your pain and quality in simultaneous awareness. The pain and quality

103

wrestle, dance, cook, simmer, marinate, merge, overlap, and play. Eventually the quality will soothe, ease, and replace your pain or guide you through what is left.

- When the pain is reduced or gone, keep up your practice. It is a good idea to practice when you feel well, as you are building a reserve. You are putting qualities in the bank so you can call them out for tests and trials that are sure to come. Practice with intensity and duration. You are creating new neurocircuits that contain the methods and qualities. To do this, you need to practice when you feel well *and* when you are in pain.

- In summary, when pain persists, keep practicing your method and quality. The magic happens when the P, M, and Q occupy the same space. In this heat, the healing quality slowly grows and takes over. This is transcendence. This is where you rise. This is where you find your power in the story. This is when you feel better. If you don't feel better, at least you won't make it worse.

- Love is the great healer. Roll the wheel. Love grows. All you have to do is apply your will, thought, and concentration to your method and quality and persevere. Love will come in to save the day.

- Remember this: armed with the healing qualities, you are ultimately bigger than your pain. But you must practice this to prove it to yourself.

5. Embrace the Gap: Getting Comfortable with the Uncomfortable

- To become ever-increasingly skillful pain managers, we must become familiar with the great variety of ways pain manifests.

- Pain hits our inner being and body with a medley of uncomfortable thoughts, feelings, cravings, and sensations. It can be frightening and overwhelming.

- This is why mindfulness, meditation, and the other recommended techniques are so important, as they help us get in touch with our pain so we can navigate our way through it skillfully. We learn how to get comfortable with the uncomfortable.

- We drop our resistance to the pain, name it, face it, and we move with it and through it to go forward.

- To do this, we must tune into the varieties of stress and how they manifest in our thoughts, feelings, sensations, desires, fantasies, impulses, choices, and actions.

- Feel the pressure of the problem. As it takes shape and form, use it to propel yourself in the direction of the healing methods and qualities.

- If we persevere, we will see the quality is more powerful than the painful problem.

- Love, understanding, compassion, forgiveness, patience, kindness, courage, and strength will contain, reduce, and eliminate reactivity and guide us skillfully through any pain that persists.

- Practice PMQ as much as you wish. More is better.

6. **Find Your Power in the Story**

- When overwhelmed, we feel frail or inadequate. Nevertheless, we always have more power than we are using right now; this is true no matter where we are on the path of healing and enlightenment.

- We can tap into our latent healing power by rolling the universal healing wheel = practicing PMQ.

- To find your power in the story: (1) define your painful problem, (2) choose a method, and (3) choose a quality.

- You have one hundred healing qualities. The qualities are your power in the story no matter what form or direction your story takes.

- Find healing qualities most useful to you in the moment, and cultivate these with your method or methods of choice.

- The universal healing wheel is packed with wisdom. Practice PMQ and you will see how it works. You will learn how to sit with your pain, ride the pain waves, and find your power in the story.

7. **Ride the Pain Wave** (See illustration p. 106)

- Our instinct is to run away from the pain.

- Skillful pain management is to do the exact opposite, to sit with the pain as the teacher and stimulant for the growth of healing qualities.

- Instead of running, let the pain in, face it, name it, and work with and through it. How?

- Imagine yourself on a board, surfing the pain wave.

- The goal is to stay on the board no matter what shape or form the wave takes.

- Sometimes the wave gets bigger before it dissipates. There may be more pain before it gets better. This can be frightening.

- To stay on the board no matter the size or shape of the wave, match your problem to a method and quality.

- Focus on the method and quality as the wave changes size and shape.

- Eventually, the quality comes in to manage the pain skillfully.

- I am anxious (P), I practice meditation (M), and I cultivate peace (Q). Peace eventually comes in to contain, reduce, and eliminate anxiety.

- We fall off the board countless times on the way to mastery. This is a natural part of the process. Be gentle with yourself when you make mistakes. Make kindness and generosity toward yourself your new mental habits.

Ride the Pain Wave

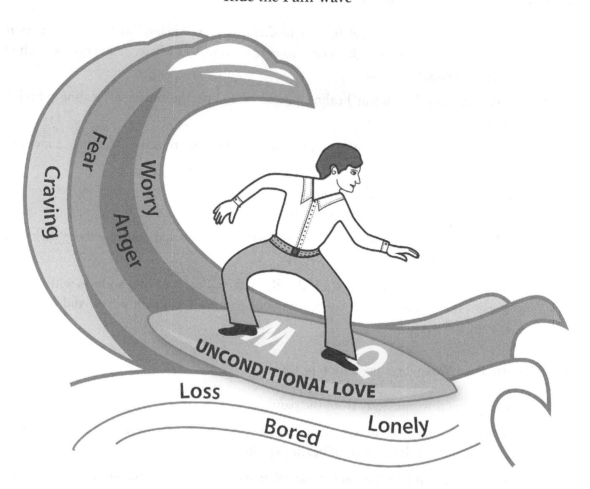

8. **A Mindfulness Exercise: Two Doors** (See illustration p. 107.)

- Life is painful no matter what route we take, but how we manage our pain will make or break us.

- The difference between a cocaine addict and a saint is how pain is managed. A cocaine addict is an unskillful pain manager. A saint is a skillful pain manager.

- Pain killing devices such as excessive use of drugs, alcohol, money, the Internet, power, sex, gambling, food, and shopping work in the short run to reduce suffering, but they create greater pain and destruction in the long-term. We get locked in powerful negative brain grooves carrying bad habits and addiction. Our pain story takes hold and we can't get out.

- Skillful pain management techniques such as meditation and mindfulness sometimes bring more pain in the beginning but lead to strength, power, peace, and courage in the long run.

- Here is a good mindfulness exercise. Everyone has two doors:

a.   Door #1: unskillful pain management. Make a list of your unskillful pain management practices. (See. P. 58.)

b.   Door #2: skillful pain management: Review the list of fifteen skillful pain management practices on p. 60. Which of these do you already have, and what would you like to add to your current program?

c.   Review the list of one hundred healing qualities on p. 79. We always have all of them but always need more. Which of these qualities do you need to cultivate now?

d.   Mindfulness exercise. When you find yourself reacting and want to shift gears:

- Stop

- Breathe

- Present moment

- Notice which door you are choosing from moment to moment.

- Ask yourself, is this door # 1 (unskillful pain management)? Or is it door # 2 (skillful pain management)?

Two Doors

Door No. 1
Unskilled Pain Management

Door No. 2
Skilled Pain Management

9. Trust the Process

- Healing qualities are more powerful than painful problems. We have to prove this to ourselves through direct personal experience. There is no other way to gain trust in the process.

- We have to let the pain in, match it with a method and quality, experience the growth of the quality, and then observe how it slowly contains, reduces, and eliminates the problem and guides us through what is left.

- We can start by riding small pain waves and then building up to bigger ones. Practicing on and having success with smaller waves gives us the confidence to handle bigger waves.

- Breathe into your pain instead of pushing it away. Give the pain its due respect by inviting it in as a guest teacher.

- Use your pain as a teacher and stimulant for the growth of healing qualities.

- Embracing our pain this way can be frightening. But after several successful experiences with this, we come to trust our ability to ride the pain waves without drowning.

- After many cycles, you will learn to trust the process. When new problems show up, you will not doubt yourself or the healing process. You will know your job is to roll the wheel and persist. The healing quality does the rest. It comes in to save the day but not on our schedule.

- We would like healing and pain reduction to occur more quickly, but it doesn't work that way. We have to wait and be patient. True lasting value only comes with patient daily practice.

10. Deep Suffering and Deep Healing: How Far Are You Prepared to Go?

- The universal healing wheel works for any problem: tiny, small, medium, large, or huge. The dynamics are the same.

- Take any problem and match it to a method and quality. Practice the method and cultivate the quality in response to the pain. The quality slowly grows and will help you contain, reduce, or eliminate your pain.

- Don't miss your smaller problems. They are training for bigger problems.

- Bigger problems present the biggest opportunity. They require more time, effort, work, and struggle. But the reward is great: even more peace, love, joy, power, and wisdom.

- The deepest suffering requires the deepest healing. How deep are you prepared to go?

11. Start Slowly and Build to One Continuous Sacred Ritual

- PMQ is a simple formula but difficult to do. It requires patient daily practice, moment to moment, for the duration.

- Everyday you can use the circumstances of your life as the springboard for the work. Don't change anything. Just go about your business and roll the wheel.

- Start slowly and build your practice until you are always practicing a method and a quality.

- It's good to practice when times are good, so that you'll be able to maintain your practice when times are difficult. If you don't do this and really bad things happen, you can be so overwhelmed that you won't be able to do the work.

- A pain wave will come that is bigger than you. Build some reserve in the bank. The goal is to have the qualities in place so strongly that they can field the pain and manage it for you when it comes.

- There will be times, however, when the pain is greater than your ability to manage it skillfully. For example, you may become more patient with practice, but a big stressor might overwhelm your patience. You become irritable and inadvertently share this negative feeling with others. When this occurs, intensify your practice until patience replaces irritability.

- The greater the pain, the bigger the quality needs to be. This is a lot of work, and it doesn't go in a straight line. When you master a certain level of difficulty, the bar is raised for the next problem, pain, or test. There are ups and downs. We are skillful and then unskillful pain managers. We go forward and backward on our way forward. Pain is the driver. It forces us to upgrade our program to one continuous sacred ritual.

  a. Notice how your progress is not in a straight line. This is normal. We all go forward and backward on our way forward.
  b. Practice your methods and qualities until they are a part of *one continuous sacred ritual.*
  c. Practice your methods and qualities until they become *unconditional, spontaneous, automatic habits.*

12. How to Manage a Backslide

- You may have made some progress and then gone backwards. Join the crowd. All of us go up and down on the way up. Healing does not happen in a straight line.

- Sometimes we make bad decisions. Old habits return. Character defects replay. We lose control of emotions. We get lazy or discouraged. We stop going to church, synagogue, AA, or other healing meetings. We stop practicing methods and qualities. The pain story gets bigger. Self-esteem takes a hit. We are more locked up. What to do?

- When you go backward, you can say to yourself, *I know how I got here, and I know what to do. I still have the qualities. The qualities are always inside waiting to be tapped, free of cost.*

- To get back on track, start another cycle of hope, power, and responsibility. Then roll the wheel. You will experience success, renewal, and mastery. (See chapter 8, Setting the Stage to Roll The Wheel: Seven Steps to Mastery.) Here is a brief review of that seven-step cycle.

  1. Hope: Hope opens the door to possibility.

2. Power: We have more power than we are using right now. See the story about two frogs in trouble in *Healing Power, Revised*, pp. 143–44.

3. Responsibility: There is work to do.

4. Roll the wheel: This is the work.

5. Success: The qualities are growing.

6. Renewal: It's one thing to light your fire. It's another thing to keep it lit. Look for sources of inspiration.

7. Mastery: I am evolving. I am an ever-increasingly skillful pain manager. I feel better. I am a better person. I am ready for the challenges to come.

13. Physical Healing and Spiritual Healing

- When you roll the wheel, your painful problems may get better, worse, stay the same, or disappear. However, no matter the pattern or direction of your pain, the qualities are growing. Spiritual healing—or the growth of healing qualities—occurs no matter what the body is doing.

- Always roll the wheel, and don't worry if problems get worse, better, or stay the same.

- Just do your best moment to moment, day to day, year to year, decade to decade, and lifetime to lifetime; you will see the slow but definite increase in love, compassion, understanding, strength, courage, and wisdom.

- You may or may not get a physical healing, but you can always heal spiritually by growing the qualities in response to your pain.

14. Pain and Healing: A Marriage of Wisdom

- There are two phases of healing: the pain story and the healing story.

The Pain Story = Let the Story Unfold

- This is the first step of the healing process. This is the P in PMQ.
- We learn how to face our pain.
- We let the pain story unfold.
- We accept the painful conditions of our current reality that cannot be changed.
- We ride pain waves without resisting, running, or hiding.
- We learn how pain is the teacher. It carries our personal story, meaning, and lessons.
- We face our pain thoroughly and completely, as our most triumphant assets (the qualities) reside in the depths of our suffering.

- Ask the pain:

  1. What do you want?

  2. What do I need to learn?

  3. What are the lessons?

- For more information on how to let the story unfold, review:

  1. Chapter 23, Transformation of Emotion, *Healing Power, Revised*, pp. 345–57 and p. 236 in this workbook.

  2. Chapter 10, The Serenity Prayer, *Healing Power, Revised*, with particular reference to the section on surrender or acceptance on pp. 151–54 and p. 336-339 in this workbook.

  - It is necessary to go through the pain story, but we get stuck here. This is not a good idea and can be dangerous to our health.

  - We need to shift gears and focus on the healing story, the second phase of healing— also called *spiritualizing the story.*

The Healing Story

- The second phase of healing is called the healing story or spiritualizing the story. This is the Q in PMQ.

- To shift gears from the pain story (P) to the healing story (Q), infuse the pain story with healing qualities such as strength, courage, endurance, compassion, understanding, peace, harmony, and a host of other qualities.

- Healing qualities are more powerful than any painful problem. The healing story trumps the pain story and takes over the dominant position in consciousness. It determines our true identity as peace, love, joy, power, and wisdom manifested as serene and compassionate service to humanity.

- This sounds good and is the right thing to do, but we can't just make this happen without practicing the methods.

- When pain is unbearable, we try to kill it with unhealthy actions such as overeating, sex, substance abuse, excessive shopping, and so forth. We don't bring in the healing qualities. Pain and healing remain separate or they get a divorce.

- The alternative is to match the pain with one or a combination of methods and qualities. The methods are the matchmakers in the marriage of wisdom between pain and healing. When we get this right—when we marry our pain to a quality with a method—the product is ever-increasing love. When we get it wrong—when painful problems and healing get separated or divorced—we are in trouble.

- There is great power and wisdom in the pain, method, and quality healing dance. Follow it. Watch it. Get the rhythm of it. Master it. Teach it.

15. Saints Are Skillful Pain Managers

- Look at the lives of the saints.

- Many had tremendous pain, but they were highly skillful pain managers. They learned how to endure in the cold, hard light of day.

- St. Francis, St. Theresa of Avila, and Sri Gyanamata had great pain, but their love was greater. By practicing techniques similar to those recommended in this work, they learned how to be in pain and maintain their love and higher states of consciousness at the same time.

- We are also bigger than our pain, but to know this we must integrate the following principles in our lives.

  - We have the qualities.

  - We are the qualities.

  - We can make the qualities grow.

  - The qualities are more powerful than any painful problem.

  - The size of our problem determines the size of the quality we need to manage it. Big problems are good, as they offer a big opportunity to grow the qualities. *The bigger the pain or problem, the bigger the quality must be.*

  - We need to manage our pain well or it recurs until we get it. When we master a certain level, the bar is raised. Pain and tests escalate. When we pass a test, class, and grade, we get another class, test, and grade. We must respond with ever-increasing qualities to pass a test and transcend to the next level.

  - Those who continue their practice become ever-increasingly skillful pain managers. A profound sense of peace and strength come to those who maintain their practice. We have to prove this to ourselves through direct personal experience. There is no other way to gain trust in the process.

  - There can be no love without pain on this plane of existence. Let the pressure of your pain push you deeper into love until your love is greater than your pain. Let love be your relentless taskmaster until love is all there is.

16. A Palette of Colors

- PMQ is like a palette of colors. The pain, methods, and qualities are your colors.

- With any pain, fifteen methods, and one hundred qualities, there are so many options and so much room for play.

- There are virtually unlimited possible combinations to fill a variety of moods and moments. Paint your own picture.

- You decide which method and quality you want to use for your problem.

- The method and quality can vary over time. For some problems, affirmations and breathwork will suffice. Other problems require deeper work, such as transformation of emotion and meditation.

- Matching problem, methods, and qualities is an art that can be developed over time through patient trial and error.

- As you practice and try different methods, you will see which ones work for which kinds of problems, thus becoming increasingly skillful at the matching process.

- Enter anywhere. By attuning your intuition, you will be able to identify which healing qualities and methods are best suited for you in any given moment.

- This highly individualized approach is the advantage of this model. You are the one who knows what will work best for you.

- We can roll the wheel 24/7, any place, any time, anywhere—at home, work, or play in a variety of combinations to fill a variety of moods and moments.

- One continuous sacred ritual: I roll the wheel every moment of every day at work, home, and play.

A Summary of PMQ Dynamics

- Healing qualities are the spiritual solution to any pain, problem, conflict, symptom, disease, or disability.

- You already have an army of one hundred spiritual qualities. You can call up any one or a combination of these qualities to help you win the battle of life.

- Healing qualities are part of the wisdom of the body. We need them for deepest healing. They are the jewels of this life. They are the healers. They buffer the pain of life.

- Our muscles are weak or strong depending on how much exercise we get. Healing qualities are the same. Without exercise they remain dormant and flabby. With exercise, they become strong and powerful.

- Roll the wheel. Exercise your qualities. Make them big and bigger still. Armed with healing qualities, we are ultimately bigger than our pain.

- The qualities are circulating around in our system with everything else—all the junk and all the negatives. When overwhelmed with pain, we can't know this. We won't feel them. All we feel is pain. But the qualities are there. Don't panic. Go to work. Pick a method and dig them out.

- Remember, pain has two levels: the inevitable suffering of life and our reaction to it.

- We are afraid of the inevitable suffering of life: disease, disability, the unknown, and death. This fear or stress makes the inevitable suffering of life worse and slows down the healing process.

- While we may not be able to eliminate the inevitable suffering of life, we can always reduce reactivity. We can calm everything down. We can turn down the idle point and bring the whole machine to homeostatic balance. We do this by reducing reactivity and replacing it with healing qualities such as compassion, love, understanding, strength, and peace. Healing qualities put out the fire of reactivity.

- It doesn't matter what method we use, where we start, or how much we practice. Start anywhere and build from there. If we persist in our practice, we will see the qualities slowly grow and contain, reduce, and eliminate unnecessary reactivity.

- Bring out the healing qualities in response to life's difficulties and you will see how much better you will feel. The qualities will help you in every aspect of your life. Your life will be smoother and easier.

Points to Remember

- PMQ is the essential healing principle common to all religions and other psychosocial healing models.

- PMQ is the e = mc2 of psychosocial spiritual healing.

- PMQ is the backbone of any and all of the processes described in this book.

- PMQ = Buddhism = the link to all religions.

- PMQ is cognitive behavioral therapy (CBT), in which you shift from a negative painful problem to a positive healing quality.

- Jesus, Buddha, Krishna, and other God-realized masters are supernova cognitive behavioral therapists.

- PMQ cannot be reduced any further. It is necessary and sufficient.

- PMQ addresses the root cause of much of our suffering.

- PMQ is the inner physician-healer-counselor.

- PMQ is universal. Everyone has this.

- PMQ solves the problem of traumatic religious history and toxic language as there is no theology or deity. It is not invasive, threatening, or noxious.

- PMQ is enough for some people. That is all you need.

- Some need traction devices. Tractions devices are equivalent to the stuff of religion, described in detail in the next chapter.

- Any question of religion can be answered with PMQ. Then add traction devices or not.

- The wheel is and is not a stand-alone tool. We can plug it into our belief system or operate it independently. We can use the wheel to just get through the day and not make any connection to religion, spirituality, or enlightenment. Or we can connect it. It plugs into any belief system.

- PMQ is the essence of mind-body-spirit medicine. We can build the methods and qualities into the brain as a tool.

- With PMQ, we work with, through, and past any painful problem, so it doesn't define us. We are not our problems. We are the qualities.

- We must have PMQ for full recovery and deep healing. When we roll the wheel, we evolve. We become love itself.

- To practice PMQ, all you need is will, thought, concentration, and the breath.

- In the next chapter, we will learn how to roll the wheel with traction devices.

Chapter 14

The Universal Healing Wheel
With Traction Devices

- In the last chapter, we discussed how to roll the universal healing wheel.

- In this chapter, we will discuss traction devices for the wheel.

- The universal healing wheel is the essential healing principle of any psychosocial or spiritual model. The wheel is universal. It works for persons of any persuasion: atheist, agnostic, religious, or spiritual. For many, PMQ is enough. Others need traction devices for the wheel.

- A traction device is any concept, image, or aspect of a great wisdom tradition that gives inspiration. A few examples are: ritual, story, metaphor, parables, Higher Power, mystery, the unknown, God of Love, Father, Mother, Friend, Beloved, Omniscience, Omnipotence, Omnipresence, Christ, Krishna, Buddha, Image of God, karma, reincarnation, grace, nature, the collective unconscious, archetypes, the subconscious, reason, traditional worship, sermons, music, art, committee work, and many more.

- Traction devices help us get traction so we do not get stuck when the going gets rough. Healing is work, and traction devices help us do the work. They help us stay in the game when we feel like quitting. Traction devices add more power to the healing equation. They help us manage our pain and heal.

- Traction devices include the stuff of religion and the nature of God. There is great controversy here. Arguments rage within and between religions, and between atheists, agnostics, religious, and spiritual people. The trails of history and current events are populated with tragic stories about confrontations concerning "the one true way."

- We can do better. We can learn how to talk about these profoundly important principles without getting into trouble. If we do this, we profit greatly. Healing power expands. We become more skillful pain managers. We feel better, become better people, and experience higher states of consciousness.

- In this chapter, we will study:

1. Higher Power options

2. Rolling the wheel with a traction device

3. Complexity, speed, and depth

4. The difference between religion and spirituality

5. How to have an enjoyable and safe discussion about traction devices without destructive debate

6. Superconsciousness

7. The scientific method in metaphysics

8. Starting a practice without answers to the big questions

Exercises

1. Higher Power Options

- There is an invisible unseen mountain sparkling with healing quality gems and jeweled higher states of consciousness.

- When you decide to make your climb, you will need some equipment.

- No one but you knows what equipment you'll need.

- You must try it on for size, see how it fits and feels, start your climb, and modify accordingly.

- You must be comfortable with the equipment, and it must work for you, as the climb is rigorous.

- Try a variety of traction devices on for size. See if they fit. See if they are comfortable.

- Following are some examples of traction devices. Which one of these might work for you?

    a. The God of your understanding

    b. Omniscient, omnipotent, omnipresent: a personal relationship with an omniscient, omnipotent, omnipresent God to whom you may appeal and get a response through grace. In Christianity, Judaism, Islam, Hinduism, and certain aspects of Buddhism, God is present everywhere as an all-knowing, all-powerful, conscious universal being.

    c. God is love: a personal relationship with the God of Love manifesting as Father, Mother, Friend, Confidant, Beloved, Teacher, Protector, Guide, Creator, Healer, Counselor, Giver, or Physician.

    d. The masters: a personal relationship with a saint, sage, prophet, or God-realized master as the embodiment of the great spiritual qualities: Christ, Buddha, Krishna, Rumi, Baal Shem Tov, and more.

    e. The Changeless One: This is the one life that flows through, pervades, and unites everything—the eternal source of all that is and the place to which we all return. It is the infinite and immortal formless form within which all form exists. There is no body, only pure consciousness and awareness. It cannot be cut, burned, or hurt in any way.

    f. Infinite Intelligence: Omniscience is the intelligent power that creates, operates, and sustains the cosmos, from the tiniest particle to the grandest stellar system. Omniscience is omnipresent. It occupies every millimeter of space. Omniscient power organizes and expresses itself on Earth—not to mention in faraway galaxies and solar systems—in a seemingly endless parade of spectacular forms that often exceed the imagination. This power operates every particle, molecule, cell, tissue, organ, and system within our body so that we can hear, see, feel, think, and love. We can use this supreme intelligence to help us solve our problems by cultivating the soul quality of intuition. (See chapter 27, Humility, *Healing Power, Revised*, pp. 394–96 and chapter 32, Intuition, *Healing Power, Revised*, pp. 451–58.

g. Infinite Love: We live in an infinite ocean of love. This unified field of peaceful, joyful, loving energy cannot be broken. We are in it, and it is in us. It permeates every cell of our bodies, every atom, and all space. When we immerse ourselves in this ocean, we experience unity with all of life. In the stillness of the ocean, we contact the pure, formless consciousness that is at once the source of everything and the link that connects all. This consciousness fills all space. It cannot be born, confined, limited, divided, or destroyed. When we experience this power, we know that we are immortal, indivisible, and connected to all.

h. Infinite healing power: A vast unified field of Omniscient Love filled with infinite spiritual qualities and healing powers. This omniscient loving power underlies and unites all. It is inside, outside, everywhere, extending forever in any direction, uniting all things and people. This is God as the Great Physician with infinite healing power. We can enter this unified field of healing energy via meditation, contemplation, visualization, and prayer.

i. God is everything, and everything is connected.

j. God is in everything and beyond: immanent and transcendent, form and formless.

k. The Creator: the source of all. One creates many.

l. The Teacher: life is school. God is the teacher in every event, person, and experience.

m. Consciousness: Many people do not feel comfortable relating to their Higher Power in a personal way. They believe any attempt to think of God in human terms is limiting, if not confusing. These individuals may pursue an elevation in consciousness but do not believe in a God to whom they can appeal. For example, some who practice Buddhism may focus on expanded awareness, energy, and consciousness.

n. Superconsciousness: the peace that surpasses understanding, ecstatic joy, pure love, unfathomable silence, intuitive wisdom, bliss, nirvana, God, and more.

o. The infinite mysterious unknown: no words can describe this state. It is beyond the meager adjectives of human conception.

p. Higher meaning and purpose: for example, compassionate service to humanity. The tools for growth are reason, morality, and actions performed for the greater good.

q. Higher or true self: seek healing qualities such as love, compassion, understanding, forgiveness, courage, strength, and endurance as part of the higher self.

r. Nature

s. Energy

    t. Mother Earth

    u. Great Spirit

    v. Grandfather

    w. Grandmother

    x. Cosmic consciousness

    y. Christ consciousness

    z. Divine love

    aa. The one and the many

    bb. The Giver and the gift

    cc. The one in everything

    dd. The source: Everything comes from and returns to the source.

    ee. The Big Space

    ff. A host of other names. This is not a comprehensive list. There are many other images, concepts, and ideas. What would you add?

- Define the aspects or images of a Higher Power that are comfortable, approachable, and accessible.

- Make it personal. Visualize a favorite saint, master, bird, flower, mountain, ocean, or whatever ignites your passion.

- Install that image in your consciousness, and use it as a source of continuous guidance and inspiration.

- Because the mind is limited, we may find it difficult to think of God in absolute terms. This is why spiritual books offer a variety of aspects we can relate to such as Father, Mother, Friend, Beloved, the masters such as Christ, Buddha, Krishna, and more. An aspect is like a window, an object of reverential focus that opens to infinity.

- We can reach higher states of consciousness through worship of the beloved aspect. If you think of Christ or Krishna, love is there and God is there. Will you pick a master such as Jesus, Buddha, the Baal Shem Tov, Rumi, or Krishna as an embodiment of spiritual qualities?

- Are there any other prophets, saints, or sages who give you inspiration and guidance?

- Will you find guidance and protection from omniscience?

- Will you seek healing power from the Great Physician?

- Will you expand your understanding, compassion, patience, kindness, and forgiveness through immersion in the Ocean of Love?

- Will you observe nature and see in her the rhythm, harmony, beauty, intelligence, and power that can carry you through anything?

- Will it be the mystery, the unknown, or the absolute beyond conception?

- Will it be reason, morality, and the higher self?

- Is God your teacher, present in every moment, event, person, and experience?

- Will you choose love and service to humanity and surrender to the mystery—accepting God as unknowable?

- Do you have any other images, concepts, or ideas that work for you?

- Try an option on for size. If it fits and is comfortable, wear it for a while. See if it helps you with your pain and problems.

- Look at life through the lens of your option. Stay opened. Give it some time. See if the data comes in for Jesus, Buddha, the God of Love, infinite intelligence, and so forth.

- There is great variability in the number of traction devices we need. You can have as many as you like. You can choose none, a few, or the totality of a religion.

- You can hold onto your traction device tightly, loosely, or not at all. Just love. Love is more important than the vehicle.

- Choose Higher Power options that are personal, intimate, compelling, and relevant to your tasks and problems. If none of the options work, just go with the qualities.

- Your concept can help you in your relationships with people, in conducting the business of life, with minor irritations, or in major crisis.

- Sometimes we experience overwhelming pain. Sometimes we feel that we might shatter and never put the pieces back together again. Sometimes we do shatter. In any case—whether our problems are minor or extreme—our Higher Power can be a source of strength, courage, and wisdom.

- What is going to help you get through the worst pain, evil, or problem that arises?

- What is going to help you withstand any test or trial?

- In the next exercise, you can apply your traction device to the PMQ of your choice.

2. Rolling the Wheel with a Traction Device

Rolling the Wheel with a Traction Device

- When you realize you have gone for a ride on the train of thought, and want to get off the train:

  a. Stop

  b. Breathe

  c. Present moment

  d. Pain

  e. Method

  f. Quality

  g. Traction device

- Choose the PMQ you would like to work on at this time. This can by any problem, method, or quality.

- Now choose the traction devices that will give you inspiration and guidance. For some examples, review exercise 1 above.

- An atheist with an anxiety disorder might choose meditation to cultivate peace of mind. The PMQ here is anxiety (P), meditation (M), and peace (Q). There would be no welcome theological traction devices.

- A Buddhist with the same problem might want to meditate with the Buddha and focus on compassion. The PMQ would be the same: anxiety (P), meditation (M), and peace (Q). With the addition of the compassionate Buddha as the traction device, the meditation would have more power.

- A Christian might visualize Jesus and the God of Love during his or her meditation. A Hindu might add Krishna and even mindedness under all conditions. With the addition of these traction devices, these individuals may find more comfort and solace.

- Choose any PMQ.

- Then choose a traction device for the wheel that works for you.

- Then roll the wheel with your traction device.

- If you get bored with a traction device, try another to keep it interesting.

- Traction devices with no appeal now may become more interesting later.

- Observe how traction devices help you move through rugged terrain.

- See how traction devices give inspiration and keep you from getting stuck.

- Who gives you traction? Jesus, Buddha, Krishna, other masters, saints, sages, Freud? Perhaps a combination of these?

- It doesn't matter what you use to get traction as long as it improves your ability to love.

3. Complexity, Speed, and Depth

- You can build your own program with the wheel and traction devices.

- You can keep it as simple or complex as you wish.

- If you want to keep it simple, you can stay with a single PMQ. Pick your problem, favorite method, and favorite quality, and work right there for as long as you wish.

- For more complexity, you can choose any one or a combination of traction devices from the entire palette of religious colors.

- Furthermore, you can change the problem, method, quality, and traction device in the moment, according to your needs and how you feel.

- With these working parts, you can go at your own speed and as deep as you wish.

- When the time is right, you can respond to your deepest suffering with the deepest healing.

- You control complexity, speed, and depth.

- How much complexity do you need or want?

- How fast do you want to go?

- How deep do you want to go?

4. The Difference Between Religion and Spirituality

- There are a great variety of ways to define religion and spirituality. Following is how these terms are defined in this work.

- Religion includes story, metaphor, parable, concepts, images, aspects, sacred texts, wisdom pearls, rituals, traditional worship, attending services, listening to sermons, prayer, social gatherings, committee work, music, architecture, and more.

- Spirituality is comprised of the *healing qualities and higher states of consciousness* that permeate the religious traction devices listed above.

- Healing qualities and higher states of consciousness are attributes of love.

- Spirituality = healing qualities and higher states of consciousness = love.

- Love is the essential healing principle of all religion.

- The goal of religion is ever-expanding love.

- Love is the centerpiece of religion. Everything else is a traction device.

- Are you a Christian, Jew, Buddhist, ethical humanist, Sufi mystic, atheist, or agnostic? This is the wrong question.

- Are you in love or "something else"? That is the question. (*Something else* refers to any negative that takes away from love. See the list of painful problems on p. 58 and ego tricks on p 345-346.

- It's about the qualities, not the vehicle. Your cells don't care about your religion. They *do* care about the qualities.

- When we practice the methods recommended in this work, we evolve spiritually.

- Spiritual evolution means you feel better, become a better person, and experience higher states of consciousness.

- When you practice PMQ, you feel better. If you look through the microscope to find out why you feel better, it is because the qualities are growing. There is more peace, love, joy, patience, kindness, compassion, courage, strength, perseverance, forgiveness, understanding, humor, and the other qualities listed in the spiritual alphabet. Healing qualities feel good. Love feels good. Get more and you feel better. Keep going. Eventually you will have a superconscious experience, which feels even better. There is no end to this progression.

- If religious or spiritual work does not lead us to ever-expanding love, why are we even talking about it?

- Don't worry or argue about religious traction devices. The work is about love and how to make it grow.

- Affirm, "Love is my religion. The universe is the book."

- There is no end to this love. How far will you travel?

5. How to Have a Safe and Enjoyable Discussion about Traction Devices without Controversy and Destructive Debate

- Review the group guidelines on pp. 19-20. If we follow these suggestions, we can turn a potentially volatile argument into an enjoyable and highly productive discussion. Following is a summary of some key points.

- The wheel is universal. It applies to atheists, agnostics, religious, and spiritual persons. Everyone needs PMQ for deepest healing and full recovery.

- Traction devices, on the other hand, are personal and individualized.

- Choose your traction devices from a cafeteria of options.

- Take what you need and leave the rest.

- One person's traction device is the next person's gag reflex.

- Nuke offensive language, and substitute your own.

- Stay in your own lane.

- Reform yourself and not others.

- Do not proselytize (try to convert others to your point of view).

- Discuss without debate.

6. Superconsciousness

- In ordinary human consciousness, we experience the world within a limited range of vibrational frequencies.

- In superconsciousness, there is an unmistakable transformation sometimes described as the peace that surpasses understanding, pure love, ecstatic joy, unfathomable stillness, intuitive wisdom, a feeling of oneness with everything, and other wonderful expressions of spirit. These experiences may last from a few minutes or hours to several days, but there is inevitably a return to ordinary consciousness—unless one is a spiritual master.

- Superconscious states can only be understood through experience, not words. Words are directional signals. That is all.

- Superconsciousness is the result of a change in your vibration to a higher state resulting from your PMQ practice. You have to go there. You have to do the work. The work is PMQ.

- When you practice PMQ, healing qualities expand. You will feel better, become a better person, and eventually experience a new place in your consciousness—a higher vibration of love, peace, and joy.

> Roll The Wheel → Reduce Reactivity → Expand Healing Qualities → Superconsciousness

- Roll the wheel with or without traction devices. Grind it out in your daily routine. Practice loving-kindness affirmations, mindfulness, breathwork, service, and meditation. Expand your practice until it becomes one continuous sacred ritual. At some point—and this can be in either meditation or activity—the door opens. Your consciousness expands. You have a superconscious experience.

- Some people refer to superconsciousness as the Buddha, Christ, Image of God, the Big Space, bliss, or nirvana. It doesn't matter what you call it. Retrofit the label of your choice to describe your experience.

- What does matter is this: One taste of superconscious love is addicting. Hooked for eternity, we yearn for more forever. We are willing to do whatever it takes to get more until we become pure love itself.

- There are an unlimited number of rooms in your house filled with a variety of higher states of love you have yet to discover. Go there. Find those rooms. Absorb the love there, and give it to all whom you meet.

7. The Scientific Method in Metaphysics

- In the domain of Higher Power and higher states of consciousness, there is a great deal of controversy and confusion. There is an enormous literature from a variety of cultures covering thousands of years of history. It is a big map. We need to review some of this, but the ultimate proof is in our personal practice and experience.

- We need to read, study, and discuss some key points and important ideas, but at some point we have to stop talking and go to work.

- Review the scientific method in metaphysics in *Healing Power, Revised*, pp. 40–41.

- We need to float a hypothesis and conduct an experiment. We need to practice PMQ in order to have a direct personal experience of how healing qualities help us feel better, become better people, and eventually lead to higher states of consciousness. Otherwise, the model remains at the level of an intellectual conversation or an unrealized affirmation.

- We get caught up in words. Stop the words, get quiet, and roll the wheel with or without traction devices. Don't talk about it. Just do it. Then you will see the difference between words and experience.

- When you have had some experience with the wheel and traction devices, come back together and talk about it some more.

Unpack the Wisdom of the Ages in Your Consciousness

- If we follow this sequence, we can unpack the wisdom of the ages and realize it through direct personal experience in our very own consciousness.

- Read → Contemplate → Discuss → Practice → Experience → Repeat → Mastery.

---

8. **Starting a Practice without Answers to the Big Questions**

The Big Questions

a. Who am I?

b. Why am I here?

c. What is the purpose of life?

d. Why is reality so brutal?

e. Is there anything to hold onto as I go through the brutal realities of life?

f. How do I get through all of this?

g. Is there a God?

h. If there is a God, what is its nature?

i. Is God love?

j. If God is love, why is there so much suffering and evil in this world?

k. Does the body harbor the God of the universe?

l. How can I find peace, love, and joy in the face of suffering?

m. Is our search for permanent love and safety futile on this earth where limitation and insecurity seem to have the upper hand?

n. If the physical plane cannot satisfy our deepest yearning, is there another dimension to life, perhaps higher or subtler, that can help?

o. Is there something in this life and after death that we can trust?

p. Is there anything that doesn't change that gives stillness and peace?

q. Do karma and reincarnation exist?

r. What is death?

s. Is there life after death?

- These are difficult questions to answer. The spiritual mathematics in these shadows presents a big challenge, and knowledge of the absolute is elusive.

- Are you plagued by some of these questions?

- Have you run into a dead-end street?

- Is it difficult for you to start your practice without definitive answers?
- Some suggestions:

  a. Define the difference between religion and spirituality. Love is the goal.
  b. Read, contemplate, discuss, practice, and experience. Then repeat this sequence.
  c. Follow the scientific method in metaphysics.
  d. Roll the wheel with or without traction devices.
  e. Stop thinking and talking and just practice the methods.
  f. Don't worry about the big questions or the nature of the Higher Power. You supply the answers or float the questions in the mystery and just go to work on PMQ.
  g. Roll the wheel with or without traction devices, and observe for expansion of healing qualities and superconscious experience. See if you feel better, become a better person, and enter the Big Space.
  h. The Big Space is a good term because there is no implied theology or deity. When you have a superconscious experience, you can call it anything you want.
  i. Words are signposts only. You have to go there. When you reach an expanded superconscious state, you will know it, feel it, and share it vibrationally.

9. Given the proposed definition of religion and spirituality here, can you be religious and not spiritual?
10. Can you be spiritual and not religious?
11. What is your definition of religion and spirituality?

Points to Remember

- Superconsciousness is beyond and above the body and mind. It is like a powerful smooth jet stream. Mantra and breath will get you there.

- Some people say there is no Higher Power or superconsciousness. But how can one know if one doesn't do the work?

- If you have never had a superconscious experience, keep practicing. Roll the wheel. When you do have one, you will know.

- Spirituality = love = healing qualities and higher states of consciousness.

- Love is the centerpiece of religion. Everything else is a traction device.

- The number or type of traction devices you use doesn't matter. You can have none, a few, or full-on religion. What does matter is love. If a traction device leads to more love, it is good. If not, why use it?

- Your concept of a Higher Power may change as you evolve. Maintain your practice and stay open. Be scientific. Float a hypothesis and avoid premature conclusions. Watch. Observe. Collect experiential data. The sum total of your current knowledge remains infinitesimal in the face of the infinite. This intellectual humility will carry you a long way.

- Don't argue about the nature of the Big Space. Stop thinking and talking. Just go there. Then we talk.

- The wheel with traction devices allows us to capture the power of religion and bring it to health care safely, efficiently, and effectively.

- The wheel with traction devices solves the problem of toxic language and traumatic religious history, as PMQ has no theology, and you control the traction devices.

- The wheel with traction devices allows us to mobilize our assets and preferences in the moment. You control complexity, speed, and depth of practice.

- PMQ is the essence of and link to all religions. It is the unifying theory, what actually works, the Holy Grail—too simple to be true it seems, but this simplicity is its elegance; it has the essential building blocks for healing and the add-ons from the stuff of religion that makes it the total package.

- It doesn't matter what religion we practice. Nor does it matter if we practice a religion at all. What does matter is the level of our development of our souls' qualities, or love. If the fruit of a religion or other healing model is love, it is good; if not, there is a problem. Just practice PMQ. You will evolve.

- In the next chapter, you will review the guiding principles upon which the wheel is built. You will study the relationship between love and pain in greater detail.

Chapter 15

The Foundation

- We all need individualized support and conversation, but there are some universal truths that apply to all. This chapter reviews key universal principles upon which this work is built. A good understanding of these truths will help you start and maintain a self-healing spiritual practice.

- You will find these guiding principles repeated and elaborated on in example and exercises throughout this work. We need the repetition. It takes time to understand spiritual wisdom.

- Often in the beginning, we cannot grasp the meaning of a universal truth or a deep wisdom pearl. The pearl may sound good and attract our interest, but it stays in our head as an idea. We barely get a glimpse of its true significance.

- The sacred wisdom of the ages requires ongoing study, contemplation, and practice. The meaning of a true pearl of wisdom is often well beyond our reach and may take years or decades of contemplation and practice to realize its full significance. Deeper realization occurs only with patient daily practice.

- Review the following principles. Read first, and then contemplate them one at a time. Go slow. Go deep. These are very important concepts. They are the foundation of this work.

- Don't worry if you don't understand the first time around. Most don't. I didn't. It takes time to understand. Just keep studying and begin your practice.

- Once you get even a glimpse of the power behind these words, you will be well on your way to learning how to heal your deepest suffering, *to make medicine out of your pain.*

The Triumph of Love over Pain

- Life is painful.

- How you manage your pain determines whether you move forward, backward, or stay stuck in this life.

- The goal is to become an evermore skillful pain manager.

- Pain has two levels: the inevitable suffering of life and our reaction to it. We have no control over the inevitable suffering of life, but we can control our reactivity.

- Skillful pain management is responding to reactivity with healing qualities.

- Healing qualities are water on the fire of reactivity. Patience, kindness, love, compassion, and forgiveness heal anger, judgment, resentment, jealousy, anxiety, fear, cruelty, and more. (See illustration p. 83)

- Healing qualities add up to love.

- Love is more powerful than any painful problem.

- This work is about the triumph of love over pain.

- When we respond to pain with love, we are skillful pain managers.

- Skillful pain management = love.

- Becoming a more skillful pain manager is the same thing as becoming a more loving person.

- Love is the great healer.

- Love is the great pain manager.

- When we respond to the inevitable suffering of life with love, we get the best possible deal. We find our power in the story.

- Love is the true secret, the pearl of great price, the greatest gift, and the ultimate healer. It is greater than any painful problem. But saying this is not enough. We need a mechanism, a way to transform the idea that love is greater than pain to a reality. The mechanism for doing the work is the universal healing wheel or PMQ.

- When we roll the wheel, we hold our pain, method, and quality in the same space. This is where the magical combustion happens. (See illustration p.132). In this crucible, in this heat:

  a. Love contains, reduces, or eliminates the pain and guides us through what is left.
  b. Love slowly grows until love is all there is.
  c. We feel better, become better people, and experience higher states of consciousness.
  d. At mastery, we are love itself.

- Love is the centerpiece of religion. Everything else is a traction device.

- The wheel with traction devices solves the problem of toxic language and traumatic religious history, as PMQ has no theology and you control the traction devices.

- The number or type of traction devices you use doesn't matter. You can have none, a few, or full-on religion. What does matter is love. If a traction device leads to more love, it is good. If not, why use it?

- The wheel with traction devices allows us to capture the power of religion and bring it to health care safely, efficiently, and effectively.

Points to Remember about Pain

- Pain is any painful problem: physical, mental, emotional, interpersonal, or spiritual.

- Pain has two dimensions: the inevitable suffering of life and our reaction to it. We cannot control the inevitable suffering of life, but we can control our reactions.

- Reactivity is what we add on to the inevitable suffering of life. There is a lot. We are going to look at this closely. We will dissect reactivity and demonstrate how it works, how we add on, and what to do about it. We will learn how to contain, reduce, or eliminate it. This knowledge is indispensable. We all need it. Now is the best time to get it because we will need it sooner or later.

- We are going to review how the ego causes a high degree of unnecessary reactivity when it spins out of control. This is to be distinguished from the heightened emotions and sensitivities resulting from major mental illness: schizophrenia, bipolar disorder, PTSD, anxiety and depressive disorders, traumatic brain injury, and more. In these instances, there is a biological and/or genetic contribution to heightened reactivity that may or may not respond to the techniques recommended here.

Points to Remember about Love

- The number one goal is love.

- Love is the great healer. It is more powerful than any painful problem. It is a fundamental solution to all of our problems. It is who we really are.

- In this work, love is defined as any one or a combination of any of one hundred healing qualities. These qualities are the essential healing principle of every psycho-social-spiritual belief system.

- Love = one hundred healing qualities and higher states of consciousness = spirituality.

- Love and its consort qualities are the healers. Healing qualities are water on the fire of reactivity. They broker and buffer the pain of this life. Such healing powers as compassion, understanding, forgiveness, and humility are more powerful than any painful problem. They will contain, reduce, and eventually eliminate our reactivity.

- Consult the list of healing qualities. (See p. 79 in this workbook.) These qualities are the attributes of love, and they reflect the character of the higher self, true self, or soul. We have these qualities. They are in the genetic code. We know how to make them grow.

- We can have a variety of goals related to the outer world of people, activities, work, training, recreation, volunteer, sports, culture, and so forth. While we work on these outer goals, the inner goal is always cultivation of love qualities. Once that inner goal is established, we can continuously affirm, feel, and visualize the qualities we seek to cultivate.

- We can use the qualities from moment to moment to manage our pain for the rest of our lives. Affirm compassion over cruelty, self-control over a bad habit, forgiveness over resentment, patience over irritability, understanding over judgment, or any PMQ of your choice.

- All you need is love and a way to make it grow. The universal healing wheel is the way. When we roll the universal healing wheel, love slowly grows until love is all there is. As our love becomes an unconditional, spontaneous, and automatic habit, our locus of control shifts from outside to inside.

- Love is expansive by nature. At some point, it cannot contain itself. It breaks into a higher state of consciousness commonly known as the divine love, ecstasy, nirvana, or bliss. Kind and compassionate service to all of humanity is the natural product of this exalted state of consciousness.

- Repetition is the key to success. Throughout this work, you will discover a variety of practices that will help you grow love and keep this illumined goal before your eyes.

- It is in the daily victory of love over pain from moment to moment, thought to thought, and breath to breath that we find our liberation.

Exercises

1. **The Crucible** (See illustration p. 132)

    - Love is the great healer and great pain manager. It is more powerful than any painful problem. To put this healing principle into practice, we have to learn how to hold love and pain in the same space. In other words, we need to learn how to be in love when we are in pain.

    - This is not easy. When pain comes, we instinctively turn to escapist pain killing devices that are not consistent with love, such as: substance and sex abuse; excessive eating, shopping, the Internet, TV, or other addictions; power and control over others; verbal and physical abuse; greed and selfishness.

    - The magic happens when we don't escape. We stay with the pain and bring our love to the pain with a method. This is rolling the wheel or practicing PMQ. When we roll the wheel, we hold the pain, method, and quality in the same space. It is in this heat, in this crucible, that the magic happens.

    - When we hold love and pain in the same space with a method, love grows. As it grows, it contains, reduces, or eliminates the pain and guides us through what is left. This is transcendence. This is where you rise. This is where you find your power in the story. This is when you feel better. If you don't feel better, at least you won't make it worse.

    - It doesn't matter what the pain does. We keep coming back with love. When we get this pain-love dance right, the reward is great. We evolve spiritually. We feel better, become better people, and experience higher states of consciousness: ecstatic joy, intuitive wisdom, bliss, nirvana, God. We bring that refined and purified gentle, compassionate love to all whom we meet. This is skillful pain management by responding to pain with love.

The Crucible

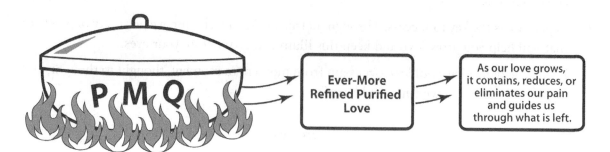

2. **Love and Medical Practice**

- Love is the great healer and the great pain manager. It can help our medical practice if we figure out a way to integrate it without controversy. To do this, we need a definition of love and a vehicle for its implementation.

- Love is defined as one hundred healing qualities and higher states of consciousness.

- The universal healing wheel or PMQ is the vehicle for cultivating love in response to pain.

- The simplest method is this. When you see that you have gone for a ride on the train of thought and want to get off the train:

  a. Stop
  b. Breathe
  c. Present moment
  d. Pain
  e. Method
  f. Quality
  g. Traction device (optional)

- This method extracts and transfers the essential healing principle from religion to medical practice safely, efficiently, and effectively.

- When we practice this method, healing power expands, we manage our pain more skillfully, and we evolve.

- You will find variations of this method throughout this work.

In the next section, you will find a comprehensive review of the fifteen methods.

Part 3
Methods

Chapter 16

Horizontal and Vertical Axis Methods

- This work describes fifteen methods that help us manage the inevitable suffering of life and our reaction to it. These are the methods we can turn to when doctors and other health care professionals cannot solve the problem.

> ### The Methods
>
> Horizontal Axis
>
> 1. People
> 2. Activities
> 3. Belief systems
>
> Vertical Axis
>
> 4. Affirmations
> 5. Habit transformation
> 6. Progressive muscle relaxation
> 7. Breathwork
> 8. Contemplation
> 9. Meditation
> 10. Prayer
> 11. Mindfulness
> 12. Practicing the Presence of God
> 13. Service
> 14. Yoga
> 15. Transformation of emotion

- **External Work: Horizontal Axis.** Methods 1–3 describe our work in the external world of people, activities, and belief systems.

  1. People: When we are in pain, we spend time with family and friends for solace and comfort.

2. Activities: We engage in constructive meaningful activities, such as work, school, training, volunteering, recreation, sports, exercise, martial arts, culture, hobbies, nature, and events.

3. Belief system: We go to church, synagogue, or temple for traditional worship or to a group like Alcoholics Anonymous for support and wisdom.

- All of this helps and may be enough for some people. Others need to do some additional work on the vertical axis.

- **Internal Work: Vertical Axis**. Methods 4–15: When we have done everything we can in the world of people, activities, and belief systems and are still in pain, there are twelve additional methods we can use to help us with our problem.

- In the next three chapters, we will review a few key principles on how people, activities, and belief systems help us manage our pain and heal on the horizontal axis.

Chapter 17

People

- Unconditional love is the pearl of the great price, the greatest gift, and the ultimate healer. We are here on this earth-school to perfect our love, to make it unconditional, and to learn how to love when we do not. Our power in the story is always love. When we find love, we find our power.

- Love is a composite of one hundred healing qualities. We know how to make these qualities grow in two dimensions:

  1. Horizontal axis: human love

  2. Vertical axis: Divine Love

- Human and Divine Love work together in a continuum for the cultivation of unconditional love. Below are a few key points to illustrate how this works.

Horizontal Axis
Human Love

- We have a deep inherent need to give and receive love. We cultivate love on the horizontal axis through meaningful relationships in a variety of roles. There are unlimited opportunities to practice love—as a father, mother, son, daughter, brother, sister, husband, wife, romantic partner, aunt, uncle, cousin, grandchild, grandparent, friend, colleague, coworker, neighbor, stranger, even enemies.

- When we are in pain, we instinctively turn to trustworthy loved ones, friends, family, or counselors. We tell our pain story seeking understanding, validation, comfort, and relief. This works. Social support helps us heal and manage our pain.

- The idea is to have the best possible network of like-minded, warm, wise, and compassionate people. However, many people make the mistake of trying to solve all of their problems in the human domain. Some problems can only be resolved by doing some inner work through the cultivation of Divine Love.

Vertical Axis
Divine Love

- The vertical axis corresponds to Divine Love, sometimes referred to as Cosmic Love, Big Love, Christ Consciousness, Krishna Consciousness, The Love of God, and more.

- Divine Love is pure and unconditional. It is omniscient, omnipotent, and omnipresent. It embraces all people, creatures, and creation. It is always inside, waiting to be tapped, free of cost. We can use it as a universal balm for any pain or problem.

Human and Divine Love Work Together

- We can use our current relationships as a starting place. We give and receive love in the variety of roles described above: father, mother, friend, lover, and so forth. In the daily grind of these relationships, problems inevitably emerge. We can use these problems as opportunities to expand and purify our love. To do this, we can do some interpersonal work to improve communication and solve problems. (See the exercises in the next section.)

- However, the transformation of human to Divine Love is ultimately about self-reform and self-mastery. It is not about others' behavior. It is about our response.

- Instead of looking to others, we bring love from within ourselves. We give love, no matter what others do. This higher love gives complete satisfaction while setting up the condition for others to change when they can.

- When we look for love on the outside we are vulnerable. We may or may not get it. But we already have the love we need inside. When we learn how to love within ourselves, we are in a position of strength.

- We can cultivate Divine Love by practicing mindfulness, meditation, affirmations, prayer, the presence of God, and other vertical axis methods. When we practice these methods, we learn how to love unconditionally from the inside out. With this expanded and purified love, we will be able to manage our interpersonal relationships with more skill.

- For a more in-depth discussion of human and Divine Love, read chapter 25 on Love in *Healing Power, Revised* (pp. 363-82) and the chapter in this workbook on Love on p. 261.

- Following are some exercises designed to help us improve our human and Divine Love.

Exercises

1. The Right People

- Healing requires good people. We can't recover alone. We can do some of this alone but we need like-minded people doing the work at a higher level. We can draw from their presence. They are in a higher place. They help us get to a higher place.

  a. Are you with the right people?
  b. Do you have enough support?
  c. Do you need to meet some new people?

2. The Right Dose

- People are like medication.

- If we get the right medication at the right dose and at the right time, we heal.

- If we don't get enough medication, there is no healing.

- If we get too much medicine, there are side effects. There may even be danger to health or life.

- And of course, the wrong medication will be useless or negative.

    a. Are you at the *correct people dose*?
    b. Do you need to spend more time with people?
    c. Do you need to spend less time with people?
    d. Are you codependent?
    e. Notice how the correct people dose changes. Sometimes we need more and sometimes less.

3. The Pain Story

- When we are in pain, we instinctively turn to the right people: those loved ones, friends, family, counselors, or mentors who have earned our trust.

- We tell our pain story seeking understanding, validation, comfort, and relief. This works. This is a big part of healing.

    a. Who gets you?
    b. Who is in your life you can really talk to?
    c. Do you need a counselor, therapist, mentor, or teacher?

4. Hot Potatoes

- How you manage your pain will determine whether you move forward, backward, or stay stuck in this life.

- Unskillful pain management is a source of untold difficulty. We give a huge amount of pain to each other unnecessarily.

- To illustrate, let's say each of us is born with one hundred hot potatoes.

- A hot potato is an unresolved painful problem that surfaces when we are stressed.

- Our job is to cool off the hot potato so we don't give it to others, but it is too hot to handle. We don't know what to do with it, so we flip it to the next person's lap—adding to their burden. They don't like it, so they flip it back and give you a few of theirs. Alternatively, they absorb it and get sick.

- If we keep giving each other hot potatoes, everyone's burden increases. Examples include irritability, rudeness, yelling, passive aggressive behaviors, addiction, control and power trips, greed, physical and sexual abuse, and more. Most of us do this at some level. It happens even if we are totally dedicated to not doing it.

    a.   Give some examples of others giving you their hot potatoes.

    b.   Give some examples of how you give your hot potatoes to others.

- The alternative is to manage our pain skillfully, to protect others by cooling off our own hot potatoes and not passing them along.

- Do you need some help in cooling off your hot potatoes? Try rolling the universal healing wheel. The wheel has fifteen methods and one hundred qualities designed to help you become a more skillful pain manager, to help you cool off your hot potatoes before you pass them on to others.

5. Interpersonal Problem-Solving Discussions

- All relationships have conflict at some point. To get back in harmony, we need to have interpersonal problem-solving discussions. The goal is to give and receive constructive feedback and minimize reactivity. However, receiving critical feedback can be very painful. We react. We argue and fight. We get too big. We manage the pain unskillfully. Instead of helping the relationship, things get worse. Following are some suggestions to help reduce reactivity.

> **Interpersonal Problem-Solving Discussions**
>
>   a.   The Golden Rule
>
>   b.   Right speech
>
>   c.   Focus
>
>   d.   Listen
>
>   e.   Give feedback
>
>   f.   Receive feedback
>
>   g.   Time out
>
>   h.   Go to your room
>
>   i.   Persist
>
>   j.   Mastery

a. The Golden Rule

- When people feel supported and encouraged, they are much more likely to respond.

- Be aware and sensitive to other people's needs.

- Treat others as you wish to be treated.

b. **Right Speech**

- Harsh or brutal criticism is like hitting someone over the head with a club. It does not work.

- When giving critical feedback, give a warning to reduce surprise and shock.

- Your words should be true, necessary, kind, firm, and gentle.

c. **Focus**

- Do not bring up multiple problems at the same time. This causes people to be overwhelmed and shut down.

- Discuss one problem at a time.

d. **Listen**

- Listen carefully.

- Do not interrupt unless one person is dominating.

- Cultivate an attitude of open reception and reflection.

- Try to get the other person's experience.

- Look for solutions acceptable to both people.

e. **Give Feedback**

- Giving and receiving constructive critical feedback on each other's problem behaviors are the most important and sensitive steps in the process.

- Define each other's triggers and avoid them when possible.

- When you discuss the other person's problem behavior, own it. There should be no third party comments. Describe the effect the problem behavior has on you.

- Make suggestions about the changes you would like to see.

- Do not interpret what you think are the causes of the behavior. This is usually felt as invasive.

f. **Receive Feedback**

- When you receive painful feedback, you may feel hurt.

- If you are hurt and your emotions are rising, use your breath to create space and buy time. Practice this:

  1. Stop

  2. Breathe

141

3. Present moment

4. Affirm a healing quality or one of the following affirmations:
    a. Sometimes there is more pain to have less pain.
    b. I can hear the truth without attacking the messenger.
    c. I can hear the truth without making defensive comments.
    d. I have this problem, but it does not define me. I am the *qualities*.
    e. I am patient.
    f. I am kind.
    g. I am loving.
    h. I am understanding.
    i. I am thoughtful.
    j. I am calm.
    k. I am wise.
    l. I am responsible for myself.
    m. I have to do this.
    n. I can do this.
    o. I got this.
    p. In the gap-abyss, a pearl of wisdom forms.

g. **Time Out**

- If your hurt or anger leads to debate, fighting, or retaliation, take a time out.

- This is very important. If we learn how to do this, we can avoid destructive fighting.

- Leave the room immediately so you do not do any damage with abusive language, which can lead to more anger and possible physical violence.

h. **Go to Your Room**

- It is easier to find fault with others than it is with yourself. However, a searching and fearless inventory of your issues goes a long way in the healing process.

- Take the painful feedback you have received from your family, friend, teacher, supervisor, or mentor.

- Go to your room. Introspect. Take responsibility for your problems.

- As you discover your own problems, be sure to remain kind and gentle with yourself.

- Practice vertical axis methods: meditation, breathwork, affirmations, contemplation, and prayer. This will take some pressure off the horizontal axis.

i. **Persist**

- Return to your problem-solving discussion when both parties are calm and receptive.

- Do not wait too long, as this might lead to smoldering resentment.

- Communicate until there is a strategy agreeable to both people.

j. Mastery

- Practice the new strategy or plan.

- Meet again as needed on old and new problems.

- Observe the growth of healing qualities: mutual respect, empathy, compassion, humility, love, understanding, strength, peace, forgiveness, and wisdom.

6. Spiritualize Your Relationships

- Don't divide your life into a spiritual life and the rest of your life. Everything is spiritual.

- Spiritualize everything, including your relationships.

- You can spiritualize your relationships by infusing them with healing qualities: love, compassion, understanding, forgiveness, patience, kindness, and so forth.

- Love everyone all of the time, no matter what. When you fall short—and you will—be gentle and compassionate with yourself and continue your practice of PMQ. This will expand your little love until Big Love is all there is.

7. Human and Divine Love

- We have an absolute need for unconditional love. When we look to people for pure love, we fail; human love is imperfect. We all have egos, flaws, attachments, and bad habits. These barriers impede our ability to manifest perfect love.

- When our need for unconditional love remains unmet, we get anxious, angry, and depressed. In frustration, we desperately seek love in all the wrong places. We end up with codependency, multiple partners, addiction, and other such bad habits. Many of us become hyperactivity junkies, immersing ourselves in activities from morning to night, trying to avoid the work that must be done inside.

- When we learn how to cultivate love on both axes in a balanced way, our love purifies and expands at maximum speed. Learn how to maximize the healing power from relationships on the horizontal axis by finding the right people at the right dose, and balance that with the healing power of Divine Love on the vertical axis.

- Read chapter 25 on Love, in *Healing Power, Revised*, pp. 363–82. Here you will find a description of how to purify and expand your love on the horizontal and vertical axes.

- Also review chapter 33 on Love in this workbook on p. 261.

8. Love Is a Field of Infinite Possibilities

- We have a deep and inherent need to give and receive love. We express that love in a variety of ways: compassion, understanding, validation, forgiveness, courage, humor, strength, grounding, comfort, inspiration, laughter, connection, reality testing, mirroring the qualities, and more.

   a. Review the thirty ways to practice love in *Healing Power, Revised*, pp. 374–77.
   b. Think of the variety of ways you already help others.
   c. Can you think of some other ways to give and receive love? Be creative. Love is a field of infinite possibilities.
   d. Start an epidemic. Send your little love wave out into the Big Love Field. It keeps going. As in homeopathy, a tiny cause can have a big effect.

9. Gratitude and Humility

- In ordinary consciousness, we take things for granted and miss the blessings that are already there. Don't miss the blessings and the help you are getting.

   a. Love comes in a variety of forms. Be mindful of the many ways you get help from others.
   b. Cultivate gratitude and humility. This power couple will help you attune to the countless blessings already there.

10. Karma

- Love is more powerful than any painful problem; or if you prefer, love burns karma: mine, yours, and ours.

- What others do to you is important. How you respond is even more important. No matter what others do, respond with love and associated qualities.

- When you respond to others with love, you will contain, reduce, and eventually dissolve your karma while setting up the condition for others to successfully manage theirs.

Points to Remember

- We can find the right people at the right dose.

- We can share our pain story and be understood, validated, and supported.

- We can learn how to cool off our hot potatoes (painful problems) without flipping them into our neighbors' laps.

- We can improve our ability to have interpersonal problem-solving discussions involving critical feedback without destructive reactivity.

- We can spiritualize our relationships.

- We can improve our ability to love on the horizontal axis.

- We can learn how to cultivate Divine Love on the vertical axis.

- We can learn how human and Divine Love work together for maximum purification and speed of evolution.

- At mastery, there is no distinction between human and Divine Love. Love is one, and love is all there is.

- The next chapter provides a brief summary of how we can use the right activities at the right dose for maximal healing and pain management.

Chapter 18

Activities

- **Right Action:** Constructive meaningful activities contribute mightily to pain management and healing. We need a variety of options in the activity domain, both alone and with other people: school, training, volunteer, work, hobbies, culture, exercise, sports, the Internet, TV, radio, music, culture, reading, the arts, nature, and more. All of these activities help us manage our pain and heal.

- **Right Dose:** When we find the right activities at the right dose, we have more healing power, and our ability to manage suffering improves. But even if we have a perfect activity program filled with the right action at the right dose, we are going to have residual pain. Most of us get into trouble with bad habits because we try to eliminate this inevitable suffering of life with unhealthy pain killers: substance, sex, and food abuse, gambling, materialism, power trips, and hyperactivity.

- **Perpetual Motion:** In our culture, we are encouraged to surround ourselves continuously with stimulating activities. Between work, relationships, recreation, sports, culture, television, and the Internet, we have plenty to keep us busy. In fact, most of us have become activity junkies, staying in motion the entire day. We walk, talk, work, shop, cook, clean, care for children and parents, exercise, study, read, play, go to church, mosque, or synagogue, play sports, and so forth. Most of us are in a state of perpetual motion from the time we get up in the morning until we go to bed at night.

- **Outer Life:** In the course of living, we find that the joys and pleasure of the outer world are limited and ephemeral. The world of events, objects, and people is always changing. Everything has a beginning, middle, and end. Joy alternates with sadness, peace with anger, health with sickness, success with failure, and pleasure with pain. We cannot avoid the ups and downs of life. Worldly pleasures do not last, and suffering is inevitable.

- **Inner Life:** Although we cannot be completely satisfied with our lives on the physical plane, the wisdom traditions point to our inner being as a source of lasting peace. Discovering the inner path to contentment is difficult, however, as the external world is powerful and attractive, continuously seducing us into the illusion that happiness is within our grasp and that the price is right.

- **Stillness:** Activity becomes a barrier to spiritual growth when it is compulsive, addictive, or used as a substitute for searching within for the superconscious peace, love, and joy bred of stillness. We can bring stillness into our lives when we practice vertical axis methods: contemplation, introspection, and meditation.

Exercises

1. **Right Action:** When we are in pain, we can turn to school, training, volunteer, work, hobbies, culture, exercise, sports, the Internet, TV, radio, music, culture, reading, the arts, nature, and more. Constructive meaningful activities contribute mightily to pain management and healing.
   a. What is your day like?
   b. Do you have enough activities that involve other people?
   c. Do you have enough activities that you can do alone?
   d. What activities would you like to add?
   e. Are there any barriers that keep you from expanding your activity program? If so, what steps do you need to take to move through these barriers?

2. **Activity Dose:** You can spend too much or not enough time in activities.
   a. Are you at the *correct* activity dose?
   b. Are you a hyperactivity junkie?
   c. Are you spending too much time on the horizontal axis with people and activities and not enough time on the vertical axis in retreat for contemplation and meditation?
   d. Have you learned how to balance activity with stillness?

In the next chapter, we will review how belief systems help us manage our pain and heal.

Chapter 19

Belief System

- Across cultures and time, people have gone to temple, church, synagogue, mosque, or engaged in related healing ceremonies for solace and comfort. Now there is evidence that religion stimulates healing power. The connection between spirituality and healing has been made.

- In this chapter, we explore the mind-body-spirit connection. Mind-body-spirit medicine is now an established part of modern medical practice. It is scientifically grounded and evidence-based: people with an active faith system have better outcomes in medicine, surgery, mental health, and addiction.

- Belief systems are monumentally important in the healing process. How does this work? What is the mind-body-spirit connection?

Key Principles of Mind-Body-Spirit Medicine

- There is no separation between mind and body.

- The mind is connected to every cell in the body through electromagnetic and chemical waves.

- What goes on in the mind affects the cells in the body and how they do their work.

- In some yet-to-be-determined way, thoughts impact disease and healing.

- Negative thoughts and feelings contribute to the disease process.

- Positive thoughts and feelings promote healing.

- Healing power expands when people exercise their spiritual beliefs.

- Healing power expands when we find our connection to something greater than ourselves, something that pulls us—secular or spiritual—be it a Higher Power, service to humanity, family, work, children, or volunteer work.

- There is an essential healing principle secreted in the religions. If we can define it, extract it, and transfer it to medical practice, it will help us manage disease, stress, and pain. This model defines and operationalizes that principle as the universal healing wheel with or without traction devices.

- In the following exercises, we take a deeper look at belief systems and how they help us manage our pain and heal.

Exercises

1. What is a Belief System?

- Belief systems are a composite of thoughts, values, rituals, and actions.
- Belief systems are religious, spiritual, political, national, cultural, racial, familial, psychological, and personal.
- Belief systems are fixed or opened, secular or spiritual.
- The essential function of a belief system is to create a story.
- The story may be literal, allegorical, or both.
- The story is usually comprehensive and compelling. It tries to make sense out of life by explaining everything that happens to us and around us.

2. Why Are Belief Systems Important in Health Care?

- Belief systems help us manage our pain and heal. This is the business of health care.

3. How Do We Talk about Belief Systems?

- We have respect and tolerance for the great variety of ways to understand and practice spirituality.
- We provide a common language that enables us to talk to each other about religion and spirituality without getting into trouble.
- We promote universal healing principles that can work for as many people as possible: atheist, agnostic, religious, and spiritual persons.
- We support people to stay in their program of origin, secular or spiritual, expand their practice, or build their own program.
- We work on ourselves, not others. We are not here to change others. We are here to change ourselves.
- We do not proselytize.
- We engage in discussion without debate.
- For additional points on this subject, see pp. 19-20 in this workbook.

4. What Do We Get from Belief Systems?

- Belief systems have many functions. Some of these activate at the time of illness and suffering.
    a. Meaning and purpose
    b. Story and metaphor
    c. Knowledge and wisdom

    d. Positive thought, positive feeling, positive vibrations

    e. Comfort and solace

    f. Pain relief and healing

    g. Guidance and protection

    h. Inspiration and strength

    i. Identity

    j. Self-control

    k. Self-esteem

    l. Truth

    m. Expansion of healing qualities: love, compassion, understanding, forgiveness, and more

    n. Community and service

    o. Grounding

    p. Connection to every day life

    q. Connection to all events: tiny, small, medium, large, and huge

    r. Connection to the moment: any moment, every moment

    s. Connection to all levels of detail from microscopic to macrocosmic: infinitesimal, tiny, small, medium, large, and infinite

    t. Pulls us out of ourselves and brings us to higher ground

    u. Deals with the big questions of life

    v. Manage brutal reality, the cave of darkness, or the dark night of the soul

5. Brutal Reality and the Cave of Darkness

- Review step 2: Duality and Brutal Reality, pp. 52–53 and The Cave of Darkness, p. 398–400 in *Healing Power, Revised*.

- Brutal reality is death, pain and suffering, and the unknown. No one escapes. It asserts itself in the life of anyone at any time in a seemingly endless variety of ways: illness, disability, trauma, loss of loved ones, crime, domestic violence, sex abuse, war, earthquakes, economic depression, tyranny, racism, ethnic cleansing, hunger, unemployment, poverty, homelessness, and more.

- In the cave of darkness, we face severe pain without immediate answers to our questions. The cave is dark. All evidence of spiritual life is gone. The world seems to be against us. There is no solace from our usual sources of family, friends, work, the arts, or recreation. Sometimes even going to church, synagogue, or temple brings no relief. We feel alone separate, powerless, and frightened.

- Belief systems are geared to protect us, even when brutal reality strikes, even when terrified at the abyss, and even in the cave of darkness. If our sacred knowledge holds here, it will hold anywhere. However, when pain is overwhelming, our belief system comes under its most rigorous challenge. Some lose all but a thread of their system and hold onto that. Some people lose their entire system. Others have enough spiritual infrastructure and deep healing wisdom to match whatever shows up, so they can move through and out of crisis with new wisdom and strength.

- It is a good idea to get your belief system in shape for life in general and for pain management and healing in particular. We need something to help us get through our trials, to help us face the abyss, to help us get through any condition, however long or severe— something more powerful than the worst case scenario life can bring.

- Following are some exercises to help us do that work.

6. The Interface of Medicine with the Big Questions of Life

- The big questions about the meaning of life and suffering come up anytime, especially when suffering or ill. They are always there, but they get bigger when we are sick. The medical model, despite all of its power, does not address these questions. Doctors and health care professionals ignore the big questions. They are the elephant in the room. They are left on the table without any conversation or direction from the biological healer.

- If we don't journey these questions, our pain can be overwhelming and cause disintegration. Review the following and contemplate where you stand. Take your time. These questions do not yield answers so easily.

The Big Questions

a. Who am I?

b. Why am I here?

c. What is the meaning of life?

d. Why is there so much suffering?

e. How do I understand suffering?

f. Is there a way to heal my deepest suffering?

g. How can I find peace, love, and joy in the face of suffering?

h. What is death?

i. Is there life after death?

j. How do I get through all of this?

k. Is our search for permanent love and safety futile on this earth, where limitation and insecurity seem to have the upper hand?

l. If the physical plane cannot satisfy our deepest yearning, is there another dimension to life, perhaps higher or subtler, that can help?

m. Is there anything to hold onto?

n. Is there something in this life and after death that we can trust?

o. Is there a God, and, if so, what is its nature?

p. If God is love, why is there so much evil and suffering?

q. Is there anything that doesn't change that gives stillness and peace?

r. What can be done about my character defects?

- We ignore these questions at our peril. If we don't journey the questions—if we don't deal with the inevitable suffering of life, with the mystery of suffering and evil, with the unknown and death, and with our reaction to all of this—we inevitably run the risk of making things worse.

- We repress the pain in the subconscious and body, douse it with unhealthy pain killing devices like substance use, or share it in unhealthy ways with others through cynicism, irritability, hostility, anger, and verbal or physical abuse. In the worst-case scenario, a failure to journey the big questions successfully can lead to disintegration and grave danger to self and others.

- What to do? This is potentially dangerous territory. Whether we are atheist, agnostic, religious, or spiritual, we protect our belief systems with fierce tenacity. How do we address the big questions in health care without getting into trouble

- The saints, sages, masters, teachers, and gurus from the great wisdom traditions offer answers to these questions. I have transferred their ideas and float them as a cafeteria of options. *This work does not push a particular point of view. You make the choices. The choices are embedded within the universal healing wheel or PMQ, with or without traction devices*

- PMQ is the essential healing principle within the religions. P is any painful problem. M is fifteen methods. Q is one hundred qualities. With these options, you design your own healing program. You choose the level of work you want to do at this time. You pick the pain, method, quality, and traction device, and go as deep as you wish.

- You may choose to work on a minor problem with breathwork and affirmations for a few minutes twice a day. Others may want to go deep, leave no stone unturned, and confront brutal reality: death, pain and suffering, and the unknown. If you can manage that, you can manage anything.

- In short, this model puts the pain ball back in your court and gives you a racket to hit it. That is to say, it offers a boatload of practical tools to help you manage your pain and heal. The rest is up to you.

7. Meaning, Purpose, and Positive Thought

- Whether our belief system is fixed or opened, secular or spiritual, we need:
    a. Meaning, purpose, and positive thought
    b. Something compelling, not an abstraction
    c. Something that connects us to the moments and details of everyday life
    d. Something that gives meaning to small and big events
    e. Something that impacts and informs
    f. Something that grounds us and guides us
    g. Something that inspires us
    h. Something that gives us love and healing qualities
    i. Something that supports community and service
    j. Something from beyond that pulls us out of ourselves to higher ground

Healing Power: The Workbook

    k. Something to help us manage brutal reality and the cave of darkness

        1. What will this be for you?

        2. How do you understand the meaning and purpose of life?

        3. Do you have a way to understand the things that happen?

        4. Do you have a spiritual program or a philosophy of life?

        5. Do you go to church, synagogue, mosque, a twelve-step program, DBT (dialectical behavior therapy), or other healing ceremonies?

        6. Do you have a Higher Power, service to humanity, family, work, children, volunteer, nature, other?

8. Religion and Spirituality

- We can recover and heal whether we are atheist, agnostic, religious, or spiritual. For those who include religion and spirituality in their program, following are some points for discussion.

- There are a great variety of ways to define religion and spirituality. Here is how these terms are defined in this work.

- Religion includes story, metaphor, parable, concepts, images, aspects, sacred texts, wisdom pearls, rituals, traditional worship, attending services, listening to sermons, prayer, social gatherings, committee work, music, architecture, and more.

- Spirituality encompasses the *healing qualities and higher states of consciousness* that permeate the religious elements listed above.

    a. Are you atheist, agnostic, religious, or spiritual?

    b. What is your definition of religion and spirituality?

    c. Some need a fixed system with a lot of structure and clarity. Others want an opened system with more ambiguity, mystery, and personal choice.

    d. Where do you fit in the spectrum?

    e. How much structure do you need?

    f. Do you need your system to be signed, sealed, and delivered? Or do you prefer freelance?

    g. Choose your own adventure book.

9. The Universal Healing Wheel

- PMQ is the essential healing principle of any psychosocial or spiritual belief system.

- We can use PMQ to help us manage any painful problem: tiny, small, medium, large, or huge.

- It doesn't matter what your beliefs are. You can be agnostic, atheist, religious or spiritual. The inevitable suffering of life, our reaction to it, and the qualities as antidote to the reactivity cut across each of these categories. These are universal principles.

153

- We pose the big questions but do not provide answers. We float a cafeteria of options. You pick.

- You don't have to change your belief system to practice PMQ.

- There are fifteen methods and one hundred qualities. Most of us are doing some of these methods and qualities already.

- How might you expand your practice?

10. Traction Devices for the Wheel

- The universal healing wheel is the essential healing principle of any psychosocial or spiritual model. The wheel is universal. It works for persons of any persuasion: atheist, agnostic, religious, or spiritual. For many, PMQ is enough. Others need traction devices for the wheel.

- A traction device is any concept, image, or aspect of a great wisdom tradition that gives inspiration. Here are a few examples: ritual, story, metaphor, parables; wisdom pearls, affirmations, prayers, Higher Power, mystery, the unknown, God of love, Father, Mother, Friend, Beloved, omniscience, omnipotence, omnipresence, Christ, Krishna, Buddha, Image of God, karma, reincarnation, grace, nature, the collective unconscious, archetypes, the subconscious, reason, traditional worship, sermons, music, art, committee work, and much more.

- What works for you?

11. Higher Power?

- We need something beyond the self to pull us up and out of the mud when we get stuck. Here are some options:

> ### Higher Power Options
> a. Higher meaning and purpose
> b. Higher self
> c. The God of your understanding
> d. Higher states of consciousness

- Do you have a Higher Power?

- What is the nature of your Higher Power? (See chapter 14, exercise 1 on pp. 117-120.)

12. Love is the Report Card

- Your belief system may be religious, spiritual, atheist, or agnostic. It doesn't matter as long as love is the product.

- Nor does it matter how much structure you need. Some need a fixed belief system with a lot of structure, as in the orthodox wing of a religion. Others need an opened belief system with choices and flexibility. Love is the report card, not the vehicle. An ethical humanist may have more love in his or her heart than an orthodox religious person and vice versa.

  a. Mindfully ask yourself the most important question: Am I in love or something negative?

  b. When you find yourself in any kind of negativity, practice PMQ. Define the negativity as your pain, and respond with a method and quality of your choice.

  c. When you roll the wheel, your expanded love transforms your consciousness to the next highest level possible at that moment.

Notable Quotes from Groups and Classes
About Belief Systems

- Some go to church, synagogue, or mosque for formal worship. Others have God in their heart. Others want to have nothing to do with this.

- With positive thought and prayer, it always gets better.

- We seek not to know all the answers but to understand the questions.

- Breakfast feeds you. Medication adjusts you. Meditation lifts you.

- Believe in yourself.

- Job gets it all back and more in the end.

- I am a humanist. I do not have a concept of God. I do believe there is a Spirit that can help me get stronger by going through the pain. We all have pain. We are all frail. I need to be alone with the healing power within me. I can get through this.

- I am in the arms of God, protected.

- Things are not okay. We need to address it. We need to look after one another. We are all one. We need loving guidance.

- I suffered a great loss. It was too much. I shattered into a thousand pieces. There was relief and elevation eventually, with prayer.

- Desperation is a gift. It forces me to ask for help. Help comes. I understand more about Spirit.

- It's all about finding out how the elevator works.

- Recovery means changing our story by replacing fixed negative core beliefs with positive thought and wisdom.

- What goes on in the mind counts a lot in health care outcomes. I choose positive thoughts grounded in healing qualities such as patience, kindness, love, and understanding. This helps me get through troubled times.

- Here is how we work with belief systems. We spiritualize the old story and in so doing create a new story, new beliefs, new identity. The link: change looking for love in all the wrong places to looking for love in the right way.

- Start your day with pearls of healing wisdom, and use this to combat fear, insecurity, worry, and doubt throughout the day.

- Bring the wisdom of the ages to the street and health care, and translate that through the universal healing wheel as love.

Notable Quotes from Groups and Classes
About the Ultimate Meaning of the Universe

- This is personal. It's up to you to decide.

- Shift negative to positive.

- Christianity.

- It all happens for a reason.

- It's about mindfulness. Today is why. What can I do today? It's not about past and future. Be of use here and now. Seize the moment.

- The goal is self-knowledge. Who am I? This is the key. When you figure this out, you can deal with the daily grind.

- There is no reason. Religion is created to reduce fear.

- Do we create religion to help manage fear of the unknown and death, or is there an absolute truth and reality that awaits our discovery?

- The goal is knowledge. Seek your personal brand of knowledge about how to make it through, and then share that wisdom with others to help them get through.

- Jesus spoke about the God of Love. Buddha taught compassion and joy. Billions are attracted to these and similar messages in other religions. We don't push a particular brand here. We support individual choice. The healing qualities, however, are universal and good for healing and recovery.

- It does not matter what religion we practice. Nor does it matter if we practice a religion at all. What does matter is the level of our development of healing qualities, or love. If the fruit of a religion or other healing model is love, it is good; if not, there is a problem. Just practice PMQ. You will evolve.

- In chapters 20-31, you will find a detailed review of vertical axis methods.

Chapter 20

Affirmations

- Please review chapter 12, Affirmations, in *Healing Power, Revised*, pp. 183–205. In this chapter you will find some suggestions for creating powerful and effective affirmations and a technique for practicing affirmations during activity and meditation. Following are some additional principles and exercises.

- The mind in ordinary consciousness hops like a bunny by free association. Some call it busy brain or monkey mind. The mind is not only hyperactive. It is all too often filled with a host of junk thoughts: negative, violent, wrong, frightened, insecure, worry, doubt, hysterical, reactive, ruminative, and more. In a recovery and healing meeting, one member said, "There is a bad neighborhood up there. The six inches between my ears is the scariest place I know. Don't go in there alone!" A busy, hyperactive, monkey mind with junk thoughts! What to do?

- Since we are always affirming something, why don't we fill our brains with wisdom rather than let junk thoughts play?

- We can notice our train of thought and shift gears to an affirmation or wisdom pearl when the mind goes negative.

- An affirmation is a beautiful idea or a positive thought that we would like to be true—and can be true—but is currently out of reach.

- A wisdom pearl is not just a positive thought but also a super-positive deep thought with the potential power to help us heal, not just in the moment but over the course of a lifetime. Wisdom pearls have the potential to help us in every domain of life, but it takes time to understand them. A deep wisdom pearl can grow throughout our lives and even then not be fully understood.

- The idea behind practicing affirmations is very simple. We fill our brains with positive thoughts and wisdom pearls. We make our self-talk say better things. We take a positive thought and make it our own. We make it real. We become it. This takes practice, lots of practice. In the beginning, we set intention and direction. Slowly, we realize the affirmation. We become that wisdom.

- This whole book is an affirmation. It is way ahead of most of us. Take a little piece at a time and work on it. Following are some exercises to help us do this work.

157

Exercises

1. A Calm, Positive, Focused, Strong, Resilient Mind

- We do our best when the mind is calm, positive, focused, strong, and resilient. It is awake, alert, and ready for problem solving, creative intelligence, shaping meaning, goal accomplishment, pain management, and the creation of health, success, harmony, and joy. This is the definition of good mental health and the goal of recovery and healing work. Along with the other methods prescribed in this work, affirmations help us accomplish this lofty goal. There is no end to this work. We can always make our minds stronger and more positive.

- Try the following or similar affirmations:

  a. I prepare my mind daily.
  b. I train my mind daily.
  c. I develop my mind daily.
  d. I strengthen my mind daily.
  e. I can always make my mind stronger.
  f. I make my mind stronger with positive thought.
  g. I need to fear less, train more, and rely on positive thought and wisdom.

2. Replace Fixed Negative Core Beliefs with Healing Qualities

- Review pp. 185–87 in *Healing Power, Revised*. Here you will find a discussion about automatic negative thoughts, which emanate from fixed, deeply embedded, negative core beliefs.

- Negative, false subconscious thought patterns can build up over the years. We need to reprogram our thinking by shifting from a negative brain groove carrying a negative thought pattern to a positive one.

- Our goal is to root out the negative core belief and replace it with thinking patterns related to the healing qualities: peace, love, joy, power, wisdom, strength, courage, patience, kindness, compassion, and understanding. We are the healing qualities. This is the true self. To realize the true self, we have to get rid of every last trace of conscious and subconscious negativity.

- Do you struggle with fixed negative core beliefs? They might be beliefs like: *I am invisible; I don't matter; I am wrong; I am bad; I am not good enough; I am weak;* or *I can't change.*

- Find your most negative thought and write a polar opposite affirmation to counter that thought. Replace *I can't* with *I can.* Challenge *I am an awkward, homely loser* with *I am compassionate, loving, kind, and warm.*

- What affirmations will you create to counter your negative fixed core belief?

- Remember, this is a slow process. It does not work overnight. It takes time and effort to build up the new brain groove so it can compete with the old one that has had the power for years, if not decades.

- The mind is like a jukebox. Brain grooves are the records. Practice affirmations related to healing qualities. Eventually you will cut the new song habits of your true self, songs of peace, love, strength, courage, perseverance, forgiveness, understanding, and humor.

3. Two Great Powers: Thought and Will

- Thought and will are two great powers. We don't realize their full potential because we don't exercise them enough. Many spend enough time working out physically but not enough on the inner workout.

- We need to build up our mental endurance. We can do this by exercising our will and thought. We can use will and thought when the world or body gives us trouble. Find an affirmation that you need. Then apply all of your muscle to that thought.

- For example, if you are in pain, send loving-kindness thoughts to the body part in pain, to all the cells of your body, to all people, and to all creation. This practice expands love. If you maintain your practice, your love becomes unconditional. At mastery, no trouble of the world or body can ruffle you.

- Thought and will are two great gifts. Don't forget to exercise them. Apply your thought power and willpower to all of the methods and qualities described in this work. There is no limit to their potential. But you must do the work. You must persevere. Even when backed in a corner, you can always do something with will and thought.

4. Quality of the Week

- (P): Choose a problem you would like to work on.

- (Q): Consult the list of healing qualities. Choose one or a combination of qualities that will help you manage that problem skillfully. For example, if you are working on fear, choose courage and peace.

- (M): Choose your method. You might decide to practice affirmations, mindfulness, or presence of God.

  a. Affirmations: Practice affirmations of courage and peace throughout the day.
  b. Meditation: Bring in as much stillness as you can.
  c. Mindfulness: Cultivate the witness—affirm stillness, silence, spaciousness, and serenity.
  d. Practice presence of God as the peace that permeates all—inside, outside, above, below, left, and right.
  e. Practice your method and quality for a week.

159

5. Note Cards

- Keep a 4 x 6 card with affirmations in your pocket. When you have a free moment, read one of your favorite affirmations.

- Drop that affirmation down to the center of your being and let it radiate out to all of your cells, surrounding space, and to other people.

- As you do this, you are healing yourself and spreading your good healing vibrations to other people.

6. Thought Glasses

- Thoughts are like glasses. We see the world through them.

- If your thought glasses are smudged and you can't see clearly, try cleaning them with positive thoughts.

- Choose a healing quality such as love, gratitude, or humor. Look at the world through the lens of that quality.

- You will see what a difference a thought makes.

7. Replace Junk Thoughts with Healing Qualities

- Mark Twain said, "My life has been filled with misfortunes, most of which never happened." Junk thoughts: we all have them. Some are more common than others. *I am a loser. I don't deserve to get well. I can't do this.* What is in your hall of fame of junk thoughts?

- Change your thinking. Keep your thoughts consistent with the qualities. When negative or junk thoughts arise, switch to positive thoughts synchronized to the qualities. Stay with the qualities when the going gets rough.

- Review the list of one hundred healing qualities. These one-word affirmations have unlimited potential healing power. They give off electromagnetic healing waves that hit every cell of your body, surrounding space, and other people.

- When your mind wanders:

  1. Stop

  2. Breathe

  3. Get in the present moment

  4. Affirm peace, courage, compassion, or any of the listed qualities.

  5. Practice these like physical pushups; the more you do, the stronger you get.

8. Affirmations and Meditation

- Practice affirmations and meditation. This potent combination leads to the following sequence:

Negative thought → Positive thought → Stillness → Higher Consciousness → Infinity.

- With affirmations, you replace negative with positive thoughts. Meditation breeds stillness and expansion to higher consciousness.

- Affirmations have more power when planted in stillness. When you plant your affirmation thought seed in a quiet field, it has a better chance to take.

  a. Stop thinking and talking.
  b. Sit, be quiet, and feel.
  c. Meditate and bring in as much stillness as you can.
  d. Choose a wisdom pearl.
  e. Let everything else go and focus only on the pearl.
  f. Drop it down to the center of your consciousness. Let it simmer and cook there.
  g. Don't let any negativity from the outside or inside take it away.
  h. The thought-seed planted in stillness vibrates and eventually spreads to every cell in your body. It becomes a part of you and affects surrounding space.
  i. As you proceed in meditation, you will experience the unlimited peace, love, and joy we all crave.

9. Right Speech

- Words are bullets that cause great destruction or healing powers for you and others.

- Review the list of healing qualities. Align your thoughts and speech with the qualities.

- Avoid gossip, criticism, judgment, debate, and harsh words.

- Your words have the vibratory power to spread truth, healing, and love. Speak truth guided by sweetness of speech.

10. Loving-Kindness Affirmations

- Loving-kindness affirmations help us move from our selfish ego to our serving soul. This training in service to others reduces anxiety.

- This is a long-term practice. It can be done in both meditation and activity. It is a great walking meditation.

a. Start with yourself. Wish others the same. Think of those who are good to you and those who are not good to you. Include family, friends, strangers, and even enemies.

b. Keep your mind locked in your affirmation.

- May I be healthy and content. May you be healthy and content. May we all be healthy and content.

- May I be relaxed and safe. May you be relaxed and safe. May we all be relaxed and safe.

- May I be happy and strong. May you be happy and strong. May we all be happy and strong.

- May I be free from suffering. May you be free from suffering. May we all be free from suffering.

- May I feel peace, love, joy, power, and wisdom. May you feel peace, love, joy, power, and wisdom. May we all feel peace, love, joy, power, and wisdom.

- As I heal, may I give this healing to those I love and those I don't.

- Create your own affirmation.

11. Mind Over Matter

- Remember the inevitable suffering of life and our reaction to it. We cannot control the former but we can always reduce reactivity. Many suffer from chronic physical illness that does not respond completely to medical interventions. There can be considerable residual disability and pain, made worse by our reaction to it. To put out the fire of reactivity, practice affirmations and breathwork.

- Don't underestimate the power of affirmations and breathwork. These techniques work.

- Even when the body hurts, the mind can remain calm, positive, and strong. It can be even-minded under all conditions. What a good idea!

- When the body hurts, practice this mental yoga:

1. Stop

2. Breathe

3. Get in the present moment

4. Choose a healing quality such as courage, strength, patience, endurance, perseverance, or even-mindedness. Affirm your quality and breathe gently, slowly, and deeply.

5. When the mind wanders, bring it back to the breath and quality.

12. Your New PRN (as-needed medication)

- Klonopin is used for anxiety or agitation. It is very effective but can be addicting. Try affirmations instead. Make these your new PRN medication.

  a. Identify your negative problem and assume the polar opposite positive. For example, if you are anxious, practice peace.

  b. If your affirmation of peace doesn't feel true, affirm it anyway.

  c. Concentrate on peace. Picture it, feel it, and visualize it.

  d. When your mind wanders, stop, breathe, get in the present moment, and affirm peace.

  e. Don't give up. Apply all of your concentration and attention to the breath and peace. At some point, the work pays off. Peace is restored.

13. Wisdom Pearls

- A wisdom pearl has multiple layers of meaning. We can only realize such wisdom with patient daily practice. We have to sit with it, work with it, contemplate it, practice it, and intend it over weeks, months, years, and even lifetimes. Here are some examples:

  a. Love is the great healer.

  b. Even-minded under all conditions.

  c. Make medicine out of your pain.

  d. Pain is the teacher and stimulant for the cultivation of healing qualities.

  e. Healing qualities are more powerful than any painful problem.

  f. Fearlessness

  g. The perfect peace of the soul.

  h. Acceptance

- One super pearl is enough. We don't need hundreds or thousands. Take one super pearl tablet in the morning. This is your potent medication for the day. Swallow the pill. Let it dissolve in the blood stream. It will permeate and purify your entire system a little bit each day. Wisdom is a great cleanser. Be patient. Remain calm. Slowly the wisdom pearl becomes real.

- Following is an example of how this works. Most of us have moments throughout the day when we get frustrated or angry about things we cannot change. We consult our doctor and ask for help. She reminds us of the serenity prayer: *God, grant me the serenity to accept the things I cannot change.* She says this medicine will help us stay even-minded, even when things don't go our way. She says the pill will work for hours at a time, but there may be a need for an extra dose. She gives us an unlimited supply of pills and says we can take as many as we need. There are no side effects. She reminds us that acceptance is more powerful than the painful problem, but we must put this principle into practice. She writes the following script.

163

1. Take one super-powerful acceptance pill first thing in the morning.

2. Let it dissolve in your bloodstream and permeate every cell in your body.

3. Let it determine every thought, feeling, decision, and action you take.

4. If a problem comes up that you cannot change and you get frustrated or angry,
   a. Stop
   b. Breathe
   c. Get in the present moment
   d. Affirm, feel, and visualize acceptance until peace is restored

14. Two Schools of Thought: Cognitive Behavioral Therapy (CBT) and Mindfulness

- With affirmations and CBT, we replace negative thoughts with positive thoughts.

- In mindfulness, we don't engage in a battle of negative versus positive thought. We accept the mind just as it is, noting that thoughts are just thoughts, not a reflection of reality. This takes the steam out of the overheated mind's engine.

- While some may debate the merits of these schools, why not combine the two for maximum healing power?

- When we have a negative thought, we can work against it with a positive thought or we can leave it there and change our relationship to it with the mindfulness practice called *the witness*. When we practice the witness, we don't try to change our thoughts. We change our relationship to thoughts by cultivating a space for them just as they are. Then we can watch the mind-movie as entertainment rather than get entangled in the drama.

- When we do CBT and mindfulness together, the sequence is:

  Negative thought → Positive thought → Stillness

- The positive thought is an affirmation. This is CBT.

- Stillness is a product of the the witness. When we cultivate the witness, we don't try to change our thoughts. We create space for them by affirming stillness, silence, spaciousness, and serenity.

- When you discover a negative thought pattern:
  a. Stop
  b. Breathe
  c. Get in the present moment
  d. Choose an affirmation to counter your negative thought.
  e. Affirm the stillness, silence, spaciousness, and serenity of the witness.

15. Horizontal and Vertical Axis Affirmations

- Review the list of fifteen methods on p. 60 of this workbook.

- We can have affirmations for both the horizontal and vertical axis.

- Horizontal axis affirmations focus on our relationship to the world: health, success, and prosperity.

- Vertical axis affirmations relate mostly to getting our inner house in order.

- We need affirmations for the outer world and our inner life. Both are necessary. Both require work and discipline.

16. Stay in Reality

- Positive thought is good, but avoid magical thinking. Don't use affirmations to go out of reality.

- Be sure to see your doctor when you have a medical problem.

Chapter 21

Habits

- Please review chapter 13, Habit Transformation, pp. 207–19 in *Healing Power, Revised*. In this chapter, you will find a discussion on how habits are formed through brain grooves, attention, and repetition, and a ten-step method for transforming bad to good habits. Following are some additional points and practices.

- A member of our community shared the following wisdom in a recovery and healing meeting: "Addiction is like a gorilla in a cage. The gorilla always wins if you let him out. Sometimes if he gets out, we may not be able to get him back in." Even when we know this truth, we find it difficult to follow. What keeps us from taking on our bad habits? Why do we fail so often when we do take them on?

- Picture a battle between two brain grooves: the old and the new. Our bad habit resides in a big, fat, obsessive-compulsive brain groove. It has had its way with us for years. It has great power.

- In the beginning, the new brain groove carrying a new good habit is a tiny filament. It takes time and practice to build it up so it is strong enough to compete with and eventually dominate the old, bad habit brain groove.

- When we first start to do the work, it is an unfair match. The big, bad habit brain groove has more power than the tiny filament new habit brain groove. As a result, we may lose some of the battles, return to our bad habit, get demoralized, and quit trying. This can be dangerous and, in some cases, lethal.

- What will help? How do we get motivated to take on our bad habits? How do we stay safe in this early phase of healing? Following are some suggestions.

Exercises

1. Following is a Review of the Fifteen Methods Described in this Workbook

We can use these methods to combat addiction. As you review the methods, remember this. The brain is malleable. When we practice the methods, we are literally rewiring the brain. With continued practice, we lock the new good habit in a brain groove strong enough to compete with and eventually dominate the old bad habit brain groove. This is called neuroplasticity.

To fight addiction, practice any one or combination of the following methods for the rest of your life.

    a. **People**: Find a support network of individuals in recovery from addiction. Tell your story. Receive their guidance and wisdom. Get a sponsor or mentor, one whom you trust. Get some spiritual bodyguards to protect you during vulnerable times.

b. **Activity**: Engage in constructive meaningful activities: school, training, volunteer, work, hobbies, sports, culture, or the arts.

c. **Belief System**: Go to church, synagogue, mosque, AA, NA, or other healing ceremonies.

d. **Affirmations**: Replace junk thoughts with positive thoughts and wisdom pearls. Fill your brain with wisdom first thing in the morning and keep it there. Practice affirmations on overcoming limitation, controlling impulses, and increasing willpower. Apply all of your willpower to positive thought.

e. **Habit Transformation**: Follow the ten steps recommended in *Healing Power, Revised*, pp. 207–19.

f. **Progressive Muscle Relaxation**: Calm the body and mind.

g. **Breathwork**: Relax and heal the body, mind, and soul. Reduces craving.

h. **Contemplation**: Read sacred texts. Find what resonates with you and work with it. Bring this wisdom to realization in your very own consciousness.

i. **Meditation**: In the room of stillness, there is no restlessness, striving, seeking, or craving. Thoughts and feelings calm down. Actions follow suit. The deep peace bred of meditation spreads to every domain of your life.

j. **Prayer**: Effort and grace go together. Put a knee to the ground and speak to God in the language of your heart. *I will do my part, but I can't do this alone. I need your help.* With this surrender, grace comes on its own schedule.

k. **Mindfulness**: Learn how to surf your pain-craving waves without jumping off the board into a destructive habit. As the wave folds back into the ocean, craving ceases.

l. **Practicing the Presence of God**: We would not use drugs in the presence of Jesus, Buddha, Krishna, or the God of love.

m. **Service**: How can you use when you are helping others?

n. **Yoga**: When you practice the yoga of love, service, wisdom, and stillness, craving dissolves.

o. **Transformation of Emotion**: Craving and emotional pain often overlap. When we transform painful emotion into self-knowledge, we gain self-control.

2. Willpower and Perseverance

*   Read *Healing Power, Revised*, pp. 146–50. Here you will find a nine-step method designed to help you quit any addiction. The example given is for cigarettes, but you can apply these steps to any bad habit. Embedded in these steps are some affirmations specifically designed for eliminating bad habits.

*   Set a goal and start your practice.

*   It doesn't matter how much willpower you start out with. Just get started.

- Having said that, we are going to need all of the willpower we can get. See the section on cultivating willpower in *Healing Power, Revised* pp. 142–46. You will find some additional affirmations designed to help you increase your willpower on p. 158.

- Taking on a bad habit often means losing some of the battles. It's okay if you lose a battle. This is par for the course. You don't have to be perfect, but you do have to keep up your effort. If you do the work, power slowly increases. If you don't have enough power to win every battle, that's okay. Pick yourself up, dust off the dirt, and get back in the game.

- Make up your mind that you can do this. Just do your best. Your willpower will slowly increase. Perseverance is the magic of addiction recovery. Victory comes to those who persist.

3. Riding Complex Waves: Craving + Emotion + Body Sensations

- Craving may occur by itself but often combines with painful emotions and bodily sensations, thus creating more complex and confusing waves. It can be frightening and overwhelming.

Riding Complex Waves

- When you feel the craving-emotion-body sensation wave arise, try the following method.

1. Stop

2. Observe: Notice what you are experiencing. Stay with the pain wave as it grows. Ride it to its peak. Don't try to escape. Don't jump off. You may feel like you can't do this or that you are going to break, but you won't. If you ride it out, it will go down. This is the nature of craving. Review the poem by Shakespeare on p. 211 in *Healing Power, Revised*.

3. Breathe: Choose any one of the breathing methods described in the chapter on breathwork. Breathe into the craving-emotion-body sensation wave. Use the breath to steady yourself as you ride the wave, trusting it will naturally subside without any action.

4. Let the story unfold: Observe the medley of thoughts, feelings, and bodily sensations. There may be a story you need to discover. *My girlfriend left me. I am depressed, afraid, humiliated, rejected, alone, ashamed, embarrassed. I don't care. I want a drink.* Let it all come out. This is valuable information.

5. Spiritualize the story: Infuse the story with healing qualities. Love, compassion, understanding, forgiveness, patience, and kindness are water on the fire of reactivity. For more information on spiritualizing the story, review School on pp. 283–86 and Transformation of Emotion, pp. 345–57 in *Healing Power, Revised* and on p. 236-243 in this workbook.

---

4. The Qualities:

- We have one hundred healing qualities. We can cultivate these qualities in response to any bad habit.

- Healing qualities are actual healing powers. There is no limit to their power but we must do the work. The work is practicing PMQ. Throw the switch to power. Roll the wheel.

- When you experience craving (P):
1. Stop.
2. Breathe.
3. Get in the present moment.
4. Choose any method (M).
5. Cultivate any quality (Q).
6. Apply all of your will, thought, and concentration to your method and quality.

---

5. Yoga and Addiction

- We can apply the principles of yoga to the problem of addiction. Review chapter 22, p. 329-243, on Yoga in *Healing Power, Revised* and chapter 30, pp. 227-235 in this workbook.

- When we have a bad habit, our energy goes down and out through the lower three chakras and attaches to the object of our addiction. This down and out force is powerful, magnetic, and seductive.

- We can reverse the flow of energy from down and out to in and up by practicing love, service, wisdom, and stillness. In addition, we can focus at the third eye or spiritual eye. When we focus at the third eye, we are connecting the soul to Spirit. Healing qualities expand. Craving ceases.

---

a. When you experience craving, place all of your attention at the third eye. Make a supreme effort to keep it there. When you notice your attention is no longer focused at the third eye, gently bring it back. If you are in public or working, keep some of your attention there. You don't have to raise your gaze.

b. Notice the battle between craving and peace. When energy goes down and out toward the object of the bad habit, we experience craving. When energy goes in and up to the third eye, we feel calm. This battle—this yo-yo between craving and peace—can go on intermittently for weeks, months, and sometimes years.

c. To get help with your addiction, focus early and often at the third eye. The third eye is a source of willpower, strength, and equanimity.

Chapter 22

Progressive Muscle Relaxation

- When stressed or threatened, the sympathetic nervous system activates a complex response for fight or flight. Part of this response is muscle tension. We carry this tension when we no longer need it. Tension occurs in any part of the body, adds unnecessary suffering, and interferes with optimal functioning.

- To counteract this tendency, practice progressive muscle relaxation. Review chapter 14, *Healing Power, Revised*, p. 223–27.

- This technique relaxes the body and mind and restores balance.

- You might also try practicing passive progressive muscle relaxation or body scanning. This technique is similar to progressive muscle relaxation but is performed without tensing and relaxing the muscles.

Passive Progressive Muscle Relaxation
The Body Scan

- This exercise helps us get connected to what is going on in our bodies.

- We develop both concentration and flexibility of attention. We focus on a body part, become aware of what's there, and then let go. We breathe *into* and *out* from each region a few times and then let go as our attention moves to the next region.

- As you focus on, breath into, and let go of the sensations, thoughts, and images you find associated in each region, the muscles in that region release accumulated tension and relax.

- Remind yourself of the intention of this practice. Its aim is not for you to feel any different or relaxed. This may or may not happen. Instead, the intention is to bring awareness to any sensations you detect as you focus your attention on each body part.

1. You can do this exercise lying, sitting, or standing.

2. Close your eyes.

3. Take a few moments to settle in.

4. Take a few slow, deep abdominal breaths.

5. Feel your body as a whole from the tips of your toes to the top of your head.

6. Now bring your attention to the toes of the left foot. Narrow your beam of attention like a spotlight to your toes. Bring your attention to just this small area of the body. Take note of what is there. Be curious. There is no need to find anything in particular. Soften your awareness, and allow whatever is there to arise: cold, warm, clothing, numbness, tingling,

tension, relaxation, or no sensations. Hold the toes in awareness just as they are. Don't try to push any sensation away. Just sense the body as it is. If you don't feel anything at the moment, that's okay. Observe any changes in sensations.

7. When your mind wanders, gently bring your attention back to your toes.

8. As you focus on your toes, direct your breathing so that it feels like you are breathing into and out of your toes. As recommended by Jon Kabat-Zinn, we can imagine breathing through a hole in the very top of the head, as if we were a whale with a blowhole. We let our breathing move through the entire body from one end to the other, as if it were flowing in the top of the head and out through the toes, and then in through the toes and through the top of the head. Continue this for a few breaths.

9. When you are ready to leave the toes and move on, breathe in all the way down to the toes and, on the out breath, disengage from the left toes and move on to the left foot, left calf, left thigh, pelvis, right toes, right foot, right calf, right thigh, abdomen, lower back, upper back, chest, left fingers, left forearm, left upper arm, left shoulder, right fingers, right forearm, right upper arm, right shoulder, neck, throat, all regions of the face, back of the head, and top of the head. Feel the sensations as you go, direct the breath into and out of each body part, and then let go and move your beam of attention to the next region.

10. When the mind wanders, gently bring it back to the body part you are working with.

11. Move slowly through each region. Maintain your focus on the breath and on the feeling of that particular region. Breathe with and into whatever is there, let it go, and move to the next area.

12. When you become aware of tension or other intense sensations in a particular part of the body, you can breathe healing energy into that part and release the tension on the outbreath. As you breathe into that body part, imagine you are sending healing power and light to that part. With exhalation, imagine you are releasing disease and tension.

13. Acknowledge the presence of whatever comes, and stay with that in the moment. If intense and difficult emotions arise, try to continue the body scan. If you need to look deeper into that feeling, practice an emotional processing exercise as outlined in chapter 31, Transformation of Emotion, p. 236 in this workbook.

14. After you have scanned the whole body, spend a few minutes being aware of the body as a whole.

15. Invoke the witness. Feel the stillness, silence, spaciousness, and serenity that is always there.

Chapter 23

Breathwork

- Review Breathwork, chapter 15, pp. 229–35 in *Healing Power, Revised*. Here you will find a description of several breathing techniques. Following are some additional principles and techniques.

Focused Breathing

- Most of us pay no attention to breathing. Unconscious breathing often leads to breathing habits that create tension. We can change this by practicing focused breathing. Focused breathing stills the restless mind, quiets ragged emotions, and restores the peace. This is the quickest way to induce the relaxation response.

- The breath is always with us, so paying attention to it requires nothing extra. To get centered and calm:

  1. Sit in comfortable position.
  2. Focus on your breath.
  3. Make the breath longer, or just watch it.
  4. Breathe with a relaxed belly.
  5. Make the breath sweet, calm, gentle, and slow.
  6. When the mind wanders, bring it back to the breath.

4:4:6:2 Breathing

1. Inhale to a count of four.
2. Hold at the top to a count of four.
3. Exhale to a count of six.
4. Hold for a count of two.

Mindful Breathing

- Mindfulness is about allowing, welcoming, inviting, accepting, and then letting go.
- We apply this principle to thoughts, feelings, and sensations.
- Use this technique throughout the day when you feel stressed, out of balance, or overwhelmed. It is very effective in reducing reactivity.

1. Breathe: Focus on the breath just as it is or breathe deeply.

2. When thoughts, feelings, or sensations arise, notice, accept, let go, and return to the breath.

3. Thoughts: The goal is not to stop thinking. It is to accept and gently let go. Let thoughts enter and invite them to gently leave. Remember, thoughts are just thoughts. Notice the thoughts that are there and say, "Thinking, thinking." Then let go and return to the breath.

4. Feelings: Notice any emotions that arise. Just observe the feeling and say, "Feeling, feeling." Then let go and return to the breath.

5. Physical sensations: Notice any sensations that arise. Observe the sensation as pleasant, unpleasant, or neutral. Then let go and return to the breath.

6. Sounds: Notice any external stimuli such as sound and say "Sound, sound." Then let go and return to the breath.

Ujjayi Breath, Also Referred to as Victorious Breath and Ocean Breath

- The Sanskrit word *ujjayi* means to conquer or to be victorious. Because of the sound it makes, this technique is also called ocean breath or hissing breath.

- This technique energizes and relaxes the body and mind, reduces emotional reactivity, and restores the peace.

- If you have any medical concerns, particularly a respiratory condition like asthma or emphysema, consult your physician before you begin this practice.

- Start this practice for five minutes and increase to ten to fifteen minutes if you wish.

- Always work within the range of your limits and abilities.

- Stop the exercise if you become faint or dizzy.

1. Begin seated in a comfortable position.

2. In this exercise, you breathe through your nose, gently constrict your throat, and completely fill your lungs.

3. Inhale and exhale deeply through your mouth. Let your inhalations fill your lungs to their fullest expansion. Completely release the air during exhalation.

4. On exhalation, slightly contract the back of your throat, as you do when you whisper. Softly whisper the sound ahhh as you exhale. You will notice your breath sounds like ocean waves, softly moving in and out. Make sure the sound originates from your throat and not from your nose.

5. Now maintain the slight constriction of the throat on your inhalations.

6. When you can comfortably control your throat during the inhalations and exhalations, close your mouth and begin breathing only through your nose. Keep the same constriction

in your throat as you did when your mouth was open. You will continue to hear the ocean or hissing sound as you breathe through your nose.

7. Concentrate on the sound of your breath. Allow it to soothe your mind. It should be audible to you, but not so loud that someone standing several feet away can hear it.

8. Throughout your practice, keep the sound even and the breath steady and smooth.

9. Be careful not to tighten your throat.

Coherent Breathing
Adapted from Stephen Elliott

- For adults, the average rate of breathing is fifteen breaths per minute.

- The ideal is five breaths per minute. This is accomplished with an inhalation of six seconds and exhalation of six seconds. The interval for one complete continuous breath would be twelve seconds. When we stretch the breath to twelve seconds, it becomes slow, deep, continuous, and smooth.

- This is mindful breathing, as it requires conscious effort. To develop your new habit of conscious breathing, it is best to set aside a short time each day for deliberate practice. If at any time you feel pain or discomfort, discontinue this practice. Do only what is comfortable for you.

- Start with just a few breaths and build slowly from there. Stay calm. There should be no strain. Continue for as long as you are comfortable. Then relax and return to your normal breathing rhythm.

1. Begin inhaling for six seconds and then exhaling for six seconds. One complete breath is twelve seconds. Each breath is gentle, smooth, and even. Breathe across the entire interval, inhaling for six seconds and exhaling for six seconds. Both inhalation and exhalation must be smooth and continuous.

2. Continue this practice of breathing at a five-cycle-per-minute rate until you can do it comfortably for one minute, then two minutes, then three minutes, and so forth.

3. Your practice might start with one to two minutes twice daily and build to ten to twenty minutes twice a day.

4. As you breathe, consciously relax, and attempt to let go of any tension you may be carrying.

5. Note any changes in body or mind before and after a few cycles of breathing at the optimal rhythm. Eventually, you will note a distinct relaxation response.

- You can practice conscious breathing at any time throughout the day. Slowly build conscious breathing into your daily program until it becomes your new normal. Continue with your practice until you are proficient at breathing at the twelve-second interval as often as desired.

- With practice, breathing at the target rhythm of five breathing cycles per minute will become commonplace for you. While at rest or activity, make it your objective to breathe at this new rhythm all the time. When you forget, return to the new rhythm.

Memorable Quotes from Classes and Groups

- The full deep belly breath is like magic. It helps reduce mental and emotional reactivity. My higher self and healing qualities take over. I can face my problems and accomplish my goals.

- Breathing and affirmations stabilize my behavior. I can be with people a little bit easier. I throw an affirmation of love in there at any time. This helps me calm down and gets me through. There's a lot of power here. Affirmations become real. I feel like a better person. I am more focused. No matter how tough the scene, I have hope. I am more able to converse with people. This helps every situation that otherwise beats me down. It helps me get back on my feet.

- Don't underestimate the power of affirmations and breathwork. They are like a one-two punch. Sometimes when backed in a corner, this is all we have. They help bring a panic reaction down to size.

- When a negative thing comes in, you can react equally negative, or you can use affirmations and breathing to neutralize it and remain immune. The quality you are cultivating is powerful; it acts like an invisible shield.

- Breathe right into the middle of your pain: resentment, anger, fear, shame. See what is there and breathe into it. Eventually peace takes over.

- Breathing helps you unearth what is there, what you need to face. Breathing also reduces what is already overwhelming. Works either way.

- Bring awareness to breath. Focus on the breath going in and out. No counting or affirmations, just breathe. Later you can add other intentional techniques.

- Use the breath to center all day long. There is a calm center. Focus on peace.

- Add breathwork to your toolbox. It works.

Chapter 24

Contemplation

- Please review chapter 16, Contemplation, pp. 237–43 in *Healing Power, Revised*. Here you will find a six-step technique for contemplation. Following are some additional points and techniques.

- Contemplation is spiritual study. We read, affirm, and integrate wisdom pearls from spiritual books and sacred text.

- A wisdom pearl is not just a positive thought but also a super-positive, deep thought with the potential power to help us heal—not just in the moment but also over the course of a lifetime. Wisdom pearls have the potential to help us in every domain of life, but it takes time to understand them. A deep wisdom pearl can grow throughout our lives and even then not be fully understood.

- It is one thing to sit, read, think, and talk about an idea. But contemplation is not just thinking and talking. It is a deep spiritual practice.

- Pearls of wisdom are useless if they stay in our heads. They must be realized. There must be a change in consciousness, a change in vibration to a higher state.

- Ultimately, we must get beyond words to practice, experience, and transformation. This is very difficult for us. We like to stay with words. Words are much easier than practice. It is a lot of work to get beyond words.

- We apply the idea to our minds, emotions, desires, and egos. That involves a whole other level of understanding and commitment. Wisdom pearls come up against old thoughts and feelings that have to go. There may be discomfort.

- Most are not ready for this. When we are ready, when we see the need and begin our practice, the reward is great. We slowly discover we are the peace, love, joy, power, and wisdom described in sacred texts.

Exercise

1. **Fill Your Brain with Wisdom**

   - Mohammed said one hour of contemplation is greater than sixty years of formal worship.

   - Outer worship in church, synagogue, or mosque points us in the direction of the healing qualities and higher consciousness we want, but the actual change must occur inside the body temple.

     a. Before and after your morning meditation, read from a sacred or spiritual text.
     b. Take a thought from that text and use it as your affirmation for the day.

c. Choose a concept that inspires you to become more than you are, a direction you would like to take, or a quality you want to expand.

d. You might review the list of one hundred healing qualities with corresponding affirmations and quotes on pp. 288-312 and some additional quotes on pp, 358-361 of this workbook. You might like these pearls just as they are. If not, refine them to make them better or create your own.

e. Drop your wisdom pearl into the center of your consciousness. Feel its healing vibrations throughout your system. Send those healing vibrations to others and the surrounding space.

f. During the day, whenever you are not focused on a task, bring in your affirmation. This will help keep your vibration spiritualized. Your mind will be positive, calm, strong, focused, and resilient. You will be ready to help, learn, and enjoy. You will be ready for anything.

- When we do this work, we change the way we think. We reprogram and rewire our brains. We move from the pain story to the healing story.

- Affirm and reaffirm your favorite pearls and qualities. Fill your brain with wisdom the first thing in the morning, and keep it there throughout the day.

2. Sitting with a Saint

- The words of the great ones carry their vibrations. Contemplate their words. They will vibrate you to their presence.

- Focus at the spiritual eye.

- Visualize your favorite saint, sage, guru, teacher, or master: Buddha, Krishna, Christ, St. Francis, St. Theresa, Rumi, or others.

- Invoke the presence of your saint with a quality or affirmation: Buddha's compassion, Krishna's even-mindedness, or Christ's love.

- Open your heart to their wisdom and feeling.

- Realize you are moving in that direction through the power of your love and devotion.

- Slowly, you will absorb the qualities of your saint.

- You might also try visualizing your favorite affirmations, quality, pearl, or any aspect of God that arouses your devotion: light, peace, harmony, the Divine Mother's forgiveness, the Divine Father's wisdom, The Teacher, The Guide, The Protector, The Confidante, The Great Physician, the spiritual warrior's courage, and more. Slowly, you will absorb that aspect.

Memorable Quotes from Students in Class

- At first I wanted to set the abuser on fire. Then I realized I was a slave to him inside. I realized he is sick and that I couldn't help him. I began practicing compassion for him, for others who harmed me, and for myself. Compassion is a healing power. It leads to a greater spiritual infusion and sense of freedom. When I contemplate compassion, I feel safe, secure, and peaceful. Then all I want is good things for him and me. I flipped it through forgiveness.

- I commune with the Creator. It takes me into the safety zone.

- I read, sit with, and embed wisdom in my consciousness. I understand a piece of what is way beyond me. I can see what I am putting into place, another stone in my foundation. I contemplate a new life.

- I take in knowledge and wisdom and release the bad.

- Each time I read, I see new things. The same paragraph speaks differently the next time.

- The words on the page go to my head as an idea and then to my consciousness as a vibrational shift. It's like plucking a magical invisible string. It literally vibrates. Peace and safety become me.

- Omniscient Love permeates the universe. We have a piece of this wisdom and love. We can make it grow. Affirm:

  a. I am a piece of Big Wisdom.
  b. I am a piece of Big Love.
  c. I make my piece grow.
  d. I express it a little bit more each day.
  e. This is my job, every day, every moment.

Chapter 25

Meditation

- Please review chapter 17, Meditation, in *Healing Power, Revised*, pp. 245–66. Here you will review the five stages of meditation and a ten-step meditation technique. Following are some additional principles and techniques.

- You are a house with many rooms. One of the rooms is the room of stillness. It has the greatest concentration of healing power and healing qualities. It is always there inviting us to enter.

- Most of us don't know it is there. We are too busy spending our time in the outer world seeking the little peace, love, and joy we can get from our people, activities, things, and events. However, the Big Peace, Love, and Joy we crave can only be found inside, in the room of stillness. To take advantage of the deep healing available only in stillness, we need to learn how to meditate.

- In meditation, we learn how to reduce and finally stop our thoughts, feelings, and desires. This leads to progressively greater degrees of stillness. In stillness, our restlessness, problems, habits, compulsions, attachments, and ego slowly burn up and are replaced by healing power, healing qualities, and superconscious experience. This is the greatness of meditation.

- When swarmed with problems, it is hard to believe that a room of stillness loaded with expansive healing power is in us. But it is. Go to the quiet room inside. Here there are no problems, just healing qualities. Stillness is the missing element in almost everybody's life. Are you ready to do some work? Try the following technique.

Meditation Technique

- There is a place inside that is completely still no matter what is happening outside. This is the room of stillness. It is filled with healing power, healing qualities, and higher states of consciousness: the peace that surpasses understanding, pure unconditional love, intuitive wisdom, and ecstatic joy.

- The goal of meditation is to enter the room of stillness to experience the deep healing that occurs only there. Following is a ten-step technique designed to help you enter the room of stillness.

Meditation Technique

1. Cast aside all problems
2. Posture
3. Spiritual eye
4. 20 20 20 breathing
5. Tense and relax
6. Prayer, affirmation, visualization
7. Breath or mantra
8. Stillness and expansion
9. Action
10. Repeat

---

1. **Cast Aside All Problems:** For the period of this meditation, use your willpower to cast aside all worldly thoughts, problems, cares, and concerns. Meditation is a time for stillness and expansion. You can work on your problems later. They will be there when you finish your meditation. Take the whole drama—your people, issues, and problems —and leave it in a bundle at the door.

2. **Posture:** Posture is important. Get comfortable, symmetrical, and balanced. Sit with a straight spine and chin parallel to the floor. This helps move energy or *prana* upwards from the lower to the higher centers in the spine and brain where you can experience higher states of consciousness.

3. **Spiritual Eye:** Close your eyes and gently lift your gaze to the point just above and between the eyebrows. This is the third eye or spiritual eye, the gate to higher consciousness and intuitive guidance. With all of your willpower and concentration, bring your mind, consciousness, and energy to the spiritual eye. Leave nothing behind. Practice with intensity but without tension. Check your gaze every so often to see if it is still there. If not, gently bring it back. Feel yourself centered here. This third-eye training will expand your consciousness to higher states.

4. **20 20 20 Breathing:** Inhale to the count of twenty, hold at the top of your inhalation for twenty, and exhale to the count of twenty. Repeat this six to twenty times. You can change the count from twenty to any comfortable number such as eight, ten, twelve, and so forth. Do the count at a pace comfortable for you. 20 20 20 breathing is itself a tremendous technique as it slows down the breath, which in turn slows the mind and body.

5. **Tense and Relax:** Inhale, hold your breath at the top of inhalation, and while you hold your breath, gently tense the whole body for three seconds. Then exhale and relax. Do this four

to six times. Inhale, gently tense, exhale, and relax. Inhale, gently tense, exhale, and relax. Feel all the tension leave your body. Relax the body completely. Feel the peace.

6. **Prayer, Affirmation, or Visualization:** Choose a prayer, affirmation, or visualization that fits your belief system and the need you have at this time.

7. **Breath or Mantra:** The purpose of this step is to cultivate *one pointed, calm, continuous concentration,* a must for stillness and expansion. You can do this by focusing on your breath or mantra.

    - Focus on the breath: Breathe naturally. Watch the breath flow in and out without trying to control it. When the mind wanders, bring it back to the breath. Enjoy the interval of peace between the breaths. Concentrate on the breath and the peace that comes.

    - Focus on a mantra: A mantra is a word or phrase consistent with your belief system: Om, shalom, love, peace, harmony, our Father Who art in heaven, and so forth. Repeat the mantra silently. Keep your concentration exclusively on the mantra. As soon as you notice the mind wandering, gently bring it back to the mantra.

    - Intensity: The best practice position is one-pointed, calm concentration. Bring all of your attention and concentration to your point of focus. Be intense but completely relaxed. We can't get to higher states of consciousness when we are tense.

    - The Yo-Yo Effect: When the mind wanders—and it will for years—gently bring it back to your breath or mantra. This back and forth movement between the wandering mind and the mantra or breath is called the yo-yo effect. It is the natural process of meditation. The yo-yo effect is prominent and can last a long time. However, if you persist in your practice of meditation, you will notice a progressive slowing down of the yo-yo. As the yo-yo slows, stillness increases until stillness is all there is.

8. **Stillness and Expansion:**

    - Now, forget the breath or mantra, and let your body breathe naturally by itself.

    - Keep your body still. Don't move a muscle. Absolute physical stillness helps us get to inner stillness. When you think you need to move, remain still for two more minutes. That is the way to build progressively more stillness into your program.

    - Learn dispassion for the body. There will be some discomfort. Remain still as long as you can. Rise above temperature. If it's too hot or cold and you can change it, go ahead. If you can't, rise above it.

    - Relax, be patient, and don't strain. You can't force your way into the room of stillness. Just show up, be there, and be aware.

    - In the room of stillness, consciousness is deeply alert, but there are no thoughts. The mind is perfectly calm.

    - Stillness itself is a lofty state, but it is a springboard to even higher states of consciousness. In stillness, healing qualities expand and eventually transform into superconscious peace, pure unconditional love, and ecstatic joy. This is the Big Space, the land of Higher Power and higher consciousness, sometimes referred to as nirvana, bliss, or God. This pure consciousness expands to infinity.

- It takes time to cultivate stillness. Don't feel bad if you don't achieve this right away. In the beginning, the mind remains restless despite our practice. We keep thinking about our story and our problems. We've got things to do and people to see. It all seems so important.

- No matter how domineering your mind-drama, just practice a little bit each day. You will see the mind progressively slow down. The more you practice, the further you go, the more still and quiet. You can do this. Just keep going. Eventually you enter the room of stillness.

- As you enter the room of stillness, don't think. Just relax, feel, and absorb the profound healing vibrations of peace, love, compassion, forgiveness, understanding, courage, strength, patience, kindness, sweetness, and wisdom.

- As you focus on these healing qualities, they *slowly expand and permeate* your body, mind, soul, heart, brain, spinal column, spiritual eye, every cell and fiber of your being, and surrounding space.

9. **Action:** As you come out of meditation, allow the expanded peace, love, joy, power, and wisdom cultivated in meditation to permeate every thought, feeling, desire, decision, action, surrounding space, and other people. Give these qualities to all whom you meet.

10. **Repeat:** Repeat this process once or twice a day or more. If meditation is intimidating, start one minute twice a day and increase slowly from there. As with any training, the more you practice, the better you will get.

Additional Tips

- **Regularity:** You may start with a few minutes twice a day and build from there. More is better. Build up to thirty to forty-five minutes twice a day. Make it a regular part of your schedule. However, your schedule may vary. On a busy day, you may only have five minutes. The next day you may have thirty or sixty minutes. Do what you can. Have at least a short meditation daily.

- **Depth:** In the vast stillness of the ocean beneath the surface waves of activity, there is an unlimited supply of healing power. This is the best place to absorb love and its associated healing qualities. First get your meditation on a regular schedule. Then meditate longer and deeper. There is no limit to how long you can practice. The more sweetener, the sweeter it is. Our problem is we don't go deep enough. Make every moment count. Go deep, and then go deeper.

- **Inspiration:** While meditating, give yourself a pep talk. Remind yourself why you are doing this. Tell yourself, *This is good for my physical health. This is good for my mental health. This is good for my spiritual health. This is good for my relationships.* In meditation, the ego shrinks so that the higher self and Higher Power can get in. This is free therapy. Deep healing in the room of stillness; nothing is better.

- **Patience:** In meditation, we want to take advantage of the deep healing available only in stillness. But our restless, problem-focused, desire-plagued, matter-addicted mind will not stop and get out of the way. Thoughts keep coming. The mind races. It hops around like a bunny. Like a pinball machine, thoughts bounce off each other. It's chaos up there. For most of us, building the new brain groove for stillness takes years of patient daily practice. Be patient and persevere. Keep going. Every time you meditate, the brain groove for stillness gets a little bigger.

- **Command the Mind:** To clear the zone at the start or at any time during your meditation, if your mind won't quit, give it a command: *Stop, wait, be still, feel the peace.* By commanding this with maximum intensity—yet doing so calmly and firmly—you can will the mind to stop. Keep doing this. It works. Your mind will respond to your command as you get stronger.

- **Group:** We all need spiritual bodyguards. Meditate in groups. Group meditation enhances your individual meditation. Your individual meditation helps the group meditation.

- **Service:** Meditation and service are another hall of fame power couple. In meditation, we expand love and its associated healing qualities. In stillness, the qualities permeate all of our thoughts, feelings, and desires. When we come out of meditation, the qualities guide our choices and actions. We share the qualities with all whom we meet. This is love in action or service.

Exercises for the Room of Stillness

Following are some additional exercises we can do in the room of stillness.

1. Expand healing qualities.
2. Eliminate problems.
3. Realize the core drive.
4. Explore our relationship with God.
5. Plant wisdom pearls.
6. Negative → positive → stillness → superconsciousness → infinity.
7. Problem solving after meditation.

1. Expand Healing Qualities

- The room of stillness is loaded with healing qualities.

- Go there, absorb the qualities, and send the qualities to all the rooms in your house.

- Permeate all your thoughts, feelings, and actions with the qualities until the entire house and surrounding space is filled with these qualities.

- Share the qualities with all whom you meet.

2. Eliminate Problems

- When we meditate in the beginning, we reduce the significance of our problems. In advanced meditation, there are no problems. Here is how this works.

- In meditation, our thoughts, feelings, and desires progressively slow down. There is less reactivity, more space, and more perspective. Our problems remain, but they are not as significant.

- In advanced meditation, in stillness, there are no thoughts, and therefore no problems. How can you have a problem when you are not thinking?

- With this new perspective, we see the mind as the carrier of our story but not only that. We see how much trouble the mind adds to the story: fear, insecurity, worry, doubt, and more.

- We have all heard "It's all in your mind." When suffering is deep, this is an insult. We have trauma, addiction, replays, egos, and thinking-feeling habit patterns that won't quit for years.

- From the meditative perspective, *It's all in your mind* reflects a deep hidden truth. When we stop the mind and get into the room of stillness, there is no mind, no story, and no worries—only healing power and healing qualities.

- When we slow the mind, we reduce the importance of the problem.

- When we stop the mind, we stop the problem.

- Get out of your mind and into the room of stillness.

- If you can't stop the mind-story, you may have to practice transformation of emotion. Here we let the story unfold and spiritualize the story. Then you can get into the room of stillness. See the exercise on meditation and transformation of emotion on pp. 240-242 in the chapter on Transformation of Emotion in this workbook.

3. Realize the Core Drive

- We want *unlimited* peace, love, joy, and safety, more time, and no pain. This is the core drive. See p. 51 of *Healing Power, Revised*.

- We try to achieve the core drive in the outer world of impermanence, limitation, and suffering, but this is impossible. We can achieve little peace, love, joy, and safety through people, activities, events, and things, but any attempt to get more on the physical plane leads to mental restlessness, overly reactive emotions, excessive material desires, attachments, bad habits, addiction, torment, broken lives, and heart break.

- The saints say the unlimited peace, love, joy, and safety we seek is inside, in the room of stillness.

- Meditate. Enter the room of stillness. Stay there. Wait patiently. Little peace, love, joy, and safety expand to changeless peace, pure love, ecstatic joy, and absolute safety.

4. Explore Your Relationship with God through Stillness and Devotion

- For some, meditation is about the qualities and higher states of consciousness. There is no theology or deity. Others use meditation to explore their relationship with God.

- In meditation, we can cultivate a deep personal relationship with God. God is already there in His/Her Omnipresence. We just have to improve our knowing. "Be still and know that I am God."

- In the room of stillness, practice devotion. Stillness and devotion dissolve the barriers that stand between us and God.

  a. Stillness: Meditate and bring in as much stillness as you can.
  b. Devotion: This is an active part of the process. Bring out your love, yearning, and longing. Talk to God in the language of your heart.
  c. Then stop, wait, relax, open, listen, and feel.
  d. At some point in this still devotional communion, God reveals Her/Himself as the peace, love, joy, light, power, wisdom, guidance, and safety we crave. What a thrill!

5. Plant Wisdom Pearls

- The brain is more plastic, malleable, and receptive during meditation. When we practice affirmations during meditation, we rewire our brain and thinking. We move in the direction of our affirmation. We experience a kind of mental health greater than we have ever known before.

  a. Meditate. Bring in as much stillness as you can.
  b. Then read a portion from your favorite sacred text or saint.
  c. Drop that wisdom pearl in the room of stillness.
  d. Let your pearl vibrate and spread through your entire being and surrounding space. (See the chapter on Contemplation on p. 176)

- Meditation and contemplation are a hall-of-fame power couple for the ages. They work together for advanced healing like no other.

6. Negative → Positive → Stillness → Superconsciousness → Infinity

- Remember this progression. It summarizes the essence of this work.

Negative → Positive → Stillness → Superconsciousness → Infinity

185

- We use our painful problems as a stimulant for the cultivation of healing qualities. For advanced healing, we meditate. When we meditate, we add stillness to our program. Stillness is the doorway to higher and unlimited states of consciousness.

   a. Negative = Painful problems: Healing starts with the identification of any painful problem: physical, mental, emotional, interpersonal, or spiritual.
   b. Positive = Healing qualities: Match your pain with a healing quality, and cultivate that quality in response to your pain by practicing the recommended methods.
   c. Stillness: Build stillness into your program through meditation.
   d. Higher states of consciousness: Stillness is the springboard to superconscious experience: the peace that surpasses understanding, pure unconditional love, and ecstatic joy.
   e. Infinity: There is no end to higher states of consciousness.

   Here is another way to express this healing equation:

   Painful Problem + Love + Stillness → Superconsciousness → Infinity

   f. This is like a chemical formula that works every time. It is combustible.
   g. The magical ingredients are stillness and love.
   h. Bring in as much stillness as you can in meditation.
   i. Add your love though devotion. Devotion is expressing your love by speaking to God in the language of your heart
   j. Now that you're in the room of stillness with love, wait patiently.
   k. Stillness plus love will melt your problem and open the door to higher states of consciousness.
   l. An endless variety of superconscious aspects opens up to infinity.

- For more information and techniques on devotion and stillness, go to pp. 218-221 in this workbook.

7. Problem Solving After Meditation

- It is not a good idea to work on your problems during meditation, as meditation is about stillness.

- It is a good idea to work on your problems after you finish your meditation, as the room of stillness is filled with wisdom.

   a. Bring in as much stillness as you can.
   b. Bring God in, if you have that.
   c. Now, look at your problem from all angles. Consider your options and solutions.
   d. Your best option lies in the still small loving voice within.

Memorable Quotes from Anonymous Students in Class

- Meditation will help you with everything.

- Meditation is an honest keeper. It tricks your body into a luxury state by getting rid of all the craziness.

- Inner silence is the greatest teacher.

- When we're in pain, meditation—rather than self-medication—is one of the most loving things we can do for ourselves. With breathwork and calm quiet reflection, we can illuminate a path that will take us through and beyond our pain. We can do this alone or with others.

- Riding the pain waves propels us towards the room of stillness where we find peace and ecstasy. This can be addicting. It is like a drug high at no charge and without side effects.

- The mind is like a puppy dog at first. You tell it to stay but it won't. Later, with practice and the development of the necessary brain grooves, it will sit and stay when commanded to do so. The mind takes orders but you have to practice.

- Shut out the world and commune with the person inside.

- I connect with my Higher Power. I see that God exists within me.

- In the room of stillness, there are no thoughts, only healing qualities. That's why I like to spend time there. It's free therapy.

- When you stop the mind, the whole package relaxes.

- Meditation: the heart of the matter.

Points to Remember

- When all is said and done, spiritual work is about *stillness and expansion of healing qualities to higher states of consciousness expressed as gentle, humble service to humanity.* Even if we memorize, recite, and understand the greatest scripture and sacred texts, we won't have achieved the goal. All of that good stuff is to stimulate us to do the work of stillness to higher states.

- There are two forms of meditation: (1) concentration: We bring the mind to a single point through concentration. When it wanders, we bring it back to that point of focus, and (2) mindfulness: We let the mind wander, and instead of focusing it right away, we see where it goes. We focus on breath but then look for the messages from the body, feelings, and thoughts. *Where did I go and where am I?* The ultimate goal is the same: stillness and higher states of consciousness.

- Meditation works. We don't have to understand all of the theory for it to work. Just follow the instructions and the technique will do the work for you. It will take you inside, to stillness and healing.

- In the stillness of deep meditation, the ego is reduced, problems dissolve, and love expands. This speeds up our evolution.

- Meditation breeds harmony for our entire being: body, mind, and soul.

- Meditation is training in concentration and attention. This is good for learning and loving.

- Build stillness into your program. This is peace of mind. It helps everything.

- The more you meditate, the more you want to meditate. In the beginning we do not want to sit. Later, we don't want to get up. Then we know we are making progress.

- The greatest experience is in meditation, but you must work for it. Results are slow and cumulative.

- In higher states, there is more space to receive the problems of life. The drama is progressively less important. It doesn't mean you don't care or don't want to do your work. Things are still important but less so.

- In meditation, we cultivate the silent witness, that part of us that is not our body or mind but pure consciousness, pure energy, and pure awareness. You must stop your mind to get there.

- There is no security in this world. Security can only be found inside through meditation.

- Love, service, and meditation; this simple formula is all you need.

Chapter 26

Prayer

- Review chapter 18 on Prayer, pp. 267–73 in *Healing Power, Revised.* This chapter describes some elements that may contribute to the effectiveness of prayer and a six-step technique. Following are a few additional thoughts and exercises.

- There is a lot of God talk here. If you are not comfortable with God, skip these meditations or modify the language to suit your needs. For example, you can substitute Buddha, Tao, universe, consciousness, or mystery for God.

Prayers That Address Specific Needs

- Practice the ten-step universal meditation technique described in the chapter on meditation on pp. 179-182 in this workbook.

- If you have some time left, you may have some specific needs you would like to address.

- Bring in as much stillness as you can.

- With your gaze fixed at the spiritual eye, practice the following affirmations and prayers.

- Concentrate deeply on these words. Convert their actual meaning into experience.

Be Still and Know that I am God

- Very few know anything about stillness. Following are a few key points.

- The goal of spirituality is communion with God.

- Communion with God occurs in stillness.

- There is a place inside that is completely still regardless of the condition of the world or body. God is in that stillness.

- Stillness is the altar of God.

- Stillness is the key that opens the door to God.

- Stillness provides the environment for us to receive the grace of God.

- God manifests where motion ceases.

- God works on us in stillness. We may not be aware of it, as his vibrations are so high (subtle), but in stillness those vibrations change our consciousness.

- In stillness, you will find all of the aspects of God.

    a. Affirm: *Be still and know that I am God.*

b. In stillness, God reveals Herself on Her schedule, through Her grace, as peace, joy, love, light, wisdom, beauty, and guidance. We realize her beauty and power.

c. When meditation is over, we manifest Her love and wisdom through gentle, humble acts of service to humanity.

Guidance and Intuition

- God is Omniscient Love, everywhere present, silently watching, guiding, helping, and inspiring. We can contact this power at the third eye, send our message, and receive a response.

Send a Message

a. Get into the room of stillness. Focus all of your attention at the third eye. There is an inflowing river of love and wisdom there.

b. Ask for guidance.

c. What is Your will for me?

d. What do You want me to do and not do?

e. Where would you have me go?

f. What should I say and not say?

g. What would you have me read, practice, and learn?

h. Ask for wisdom. Is there anything You want me to know?

i. Ask the questions you want answered.

Receive a Response

j. The best guidance is in love and stillness.

k. Listen for the still small loving voice within.

l. Recognize the blessing and the help you are getting.

m. Be aware of the ego. It will take you for a ride in ordinary consciousness and make you think the guidance is coming from a higher order. For more details on intuition and the ego, review chapter 32, pp. 451–58 in *Healing Power, Revised*.

Service

- Affirm and pray: As I begin this day, I offer my body, mind, and soul in loving service to others.

- I will help as many people as I can.

- To do this work, I ask for a healthy body, calm mind, cheerful attitude, and soul filled with peace, love, joy, power, and wisdom.

- All work is sacred when offered to God in loving service.

- No task is too difficult or menial.

- I give everything as an offering to the Divine.

- I love, serve, and give without expectation of reward. This is the highest service.

- I give, give, give, give and then give some more.

The Healing Light

- In the room of stillness, with all of your attention fixed at the spiritual eye, you can send vibrations of peace and harmony to all people and nations of the world.

- God will direct the healing light to those you pray for. You don't have to guide it. Healing power is infinitely powerful and intelligent. It knows where to go and what to do.

- Immerse yourself in the peace and harmony born of meditation.

- Visualize the peace and harmony as light sent from your spiritual eye to the hearts and souls of: friends, family, colleagues, coworkers; social, political, military, and religious leaders; and all people in every city, state, and nation of the world.

- Let these healing vibrations change fear and conflict to understanding and compassion.

A River of Peace Flows through You

- There is a place inside that is absolutely still at all times no matter what the world or body is doing. This is the true self, the permanent peace of the soul. This is not something we can get from the outside. We can find it within. It is already there.

- Be still and know that I am God (Psalm 46:10). The permanent peace of the soul is in the stillness of deep meditation.

  a. Feel the stillness within.
  b. If restless thoughts enter, gently dismiss them and return to the feeling of peace in the room of stillness.
  c. Enjoy the stillness as you go deeper in silent meditation and affirm:
     - I am in the room of stillness.
     - Peace fills my brain and heart, every cell in my body, and surrounding space.
     - Peace is inside, outside, everywhere.
     - Peace spreads through the vast territory of my mind in every direction to infinity.
     - Infinite peace surrounds my life and every moment of my existence.
     - Peace is the embracing language of God within.
     - The soul connected to Spirit is peace itself.
     - I feel each breath take me closer to soul contact with God.
     - I feel God in me now as peace.
     - I absorb myself in the peace of God.
     - God breathes immortal peace through me now.

- I let peace surround, feed, permeate, saturate, spread, and expand through every cell, thought, feeling, desire, decision, action, and surrounding space.

- Peace spreads to every city, nation, earth, planets, stars, galaxies, and cosmos.

- I am in the Ocean of Peace.

- I am peace itself.

- I hold on to the peace I gained from this meditation.

- May your life be filled with the ever-present permanent peace of the soul-Spirit.

Ever-Expanding Love

- When we meditate, our love grows and purifies. When we come out of meditation, we give this refined love to others.

- Place your attention on your heart and feel the greatest love you ever felt for another person.

- Let that love saturate every cell of your body.

- Now expand that to an encircling sphere embracing family, friends, all people, the earth, solar system, galaxies, and island universes.

- Feel yourself merge with the love that permeates all creation.

- Experience everything in the universe floating in this vast sphere of love.

- Bless us that Your love and soothing peace permeate our consciousness and flow through all of our thoughts, actions, and relationships.

God Is Love and So Am I

- The greatest love we can experience is in communion with God in deep silent meditation.

- It is in stillness that we can know God is love and that we are made in that image.
  a. Feel the peace born of meditation.
  b. Let that peace permeate your body and mind.
  c. Enjoy the stillness as you go deeper.
  d. In stillness and peace, affirm:
     - God is love. I am made in that image. I am love.
     - Everything in the world is bathed in love.
     - I am the cosmic sphere of love that holds all beings, planets, stars, and all creation.
     - I am the love that illuminates the whole universe.
  e. Love is always waiting for us inside and out. May our lives be filled with that love.
  f. Hold on to the expanded love from this meditation throughout the day, and give this love to all whom you meet.

Peace-Love-Joy

- I go within to forget my troubles and feel peace, love, and joy.

- Peace is the inner platform upon which love is built.

- Joy dances on the stage of love.

- Peace first, then love, and then joy.

The True Self Is the Soul Connected to Spirit

- The goal of spiritual life is to discover our true self: the soul-Spirit. This is a place inside of pure consciousness and pure awareness. Here there is no world, body, senses, mind, ego, karma-drama, or painful problems. There is no form or story, only the soul tied to God.

- Our current story and identity is temporary. Drop the drama and identify with the true self, the soul tied to God. We are immortal peace, love, joy, power, and wisdom.

- Without meditation, we lose awareness of our true self and get tangled in the ego and the world-body-story. The longer and deeper our meditation, the less we get caught up in tangles.

- After you practice your mantra:
    a. Sit in stillness and enjoy your communion with God as unlimited peace, joy, love, power, wisdom, and light. Remember this is your true nature. Become familiar with this experience. Live in it. Let each breath take you deeper into it.
    b. Go back to this experience again and again until you know it is your true self. You are not your body. You are not your mind. You are not your story. You are unlimited peace, love, joy, power, wisdom, and light.

Gratitude

- Affirm and pray: The blessing is continuous whether hidden or opened.

- I am thankful for everything at all times, even my pain.

- Pain is a blessing as it helps me grow healing qualities and higher consciousness.

- Help me remember Your countless blessings.

- All the power to think, speak, act comes from God.

- I deeply thank You for Your countless blessings, whether hidden or opened.

Receptivity

- God's presence is continuous. Our receptivity is often lacking. To be more receptive:
    a. Stop
    b. Wait
    c. Listen
    d. Feel

e. Recognize the blessing and the help you are getting

Acceptance

- Visualize yourself at the third eye in a state of calm, quiet, patient, waiting.

- Affirm:

   a. Surrender, accept, attune, receive, soft, yield, open, silence, spaciousness, serenity
   b. I work the condition, however long or severe. I wait for You Lord, until You appear.

Bad Habits

Use the following affirmations as coals to build your fire:

   a. I can eliminate any bad habit.
   b. Nothing can stand in my way.
   c. Nothing can stop me.
   d. Nothing can shake my resolve.
   e. My willpower grows stronger every day.
   f. My mind is set.
   g. I will succeed.
   h. No matter how many times I fall, I will rise and conquer.
   i. One by one, I eliminate all bad habits.
   j. I am not my bad habit. My true self is calm and content.

Eliminate Negativity

- Healing qualities are more powerful than any painful problem.

- As soon as you see a trace of negativity:

   1. Stop.

   2. Breathe.

   3. Get in the present moment.

   4. Cultivate love, compassion, kindness, understanding, forgiveness, patience, or any healing quality.

A Date with Big Love

- For the period of this meditation, focus on a love quality and renounce everything else: your roles, work, attachments, worries, karma, restlessness, worldly thoughts, problems, and so forth.

- You have twenty-three hours to work on your stuff but for this one hour, focus on love alone.

- Place all of your will and attention at the spiritual eye.

- Invoke the presence of love, and renounce everything else.

- Let love circulate, surround, feed, permeate, saturate, and comfort you.

- Perform this exercise with any quality: compassion, understanding, forgiveness, courage, strength, peace, balance, harmony, and more.

Even-Mindedness

- Be even-minded under all conditions. What a good idea! But getting there is not so easy. Attachment to outcomes results in a high degree of emotional reactivity.

- We need to watch the movie unaffected. It's a passing show. Don't be overly involved emotionally. We add fuel to the fire when feelings are high.

- Visualize yourself at the spiritual eye remaining even-minded under all conditions.

- Affirm: I watch the Cosmic Movie with calm detachment.

Right Activity and Meditation

- Combine right activity with meditation. There is great power here.

- Right action: during the day practice positive thought, mindfulness, seeing the presence of God in others, and service to humanity. This breeds peace of mind. Then bring this peace to your meditation.

- Meditation: In meditation, peace grows a little bit more. Then bring your enhanced peace from meditation back to your activities.

- Practice right action and meditation diligently, and perfect both. You will see how peace builds and builds.

- Deep inner peace is the goal. Follow these routines day after day. That's how you go deep.

- Eventually you will be able to always stay calm as your energy inside stays still and is not subject to distractions.

- Right activity and meditation: a power couple for the ages.

Perseverance and Unconditional Love

- Affirm: Unconditional love is my goal. This takes time, lots of time. Results do not come overnight. When tests come, I persist in my quest.

- Even if I get beat and pulverized left and right, I never give in to discouragement. Tests and trials are opportunities for expanding love. I persevere.

- I hold on to the consciousness of unconditional love. I continue my practice no matter what life brings. I go on loving and seeking, even if I have a debilitating or fatal illness with terrible pain.

- This is right attitude.

Mind Over Matter

My body takes orders from my mind. Affirm:
    a.   I mentally command my body to be still and relax.
    b.   I consciously feel my body relaxing.
    c.   Love is greater than pain.
    d.   I am love.

Yoga Chakras

- Prana is the life force present in the human body.

- We send prana down the spine and outward toward the world for daily activities and in and up the spine to the higher centers in the spinal cord and brain for God-communion.

- Following is a technique that will help you first become aware of the energy in your spine and then move that energy from the lower centers to the heart center—and from there to the higher centers and spiritual eye. This results in a shift from ordinary material consciousness to higher spiritual experience.

    a.   Sit with a straight spine.
    b.   Bring in as much stillness as you can.
    c.   Chant Aum at each chakra going up and down the spine several times. This brings your awareness to the energy in your spine.
    d.   Now breathe in and imagine your life force flowing upward from the three lower centers into the heart center. Imagine this, and eventually you will feel it. Repeat this several times. Your energy is now focused at the heart center as love.
    e.   Now breathe in, and imagine the love from your heart center flowing to the higher centers of the spinal cord and ultimately to the spiritual eye.
    f.   At the spiritual eye, affirm: Be still and know that I am God.
    g.   Love and stillness expand to infinity.

Devotion

- The purpose of devotion is expansion of love. We bring our little love to God's Big Love, looking to merge.

- Speak to God in the language of your heart: I offer You all the love of my heart. I want only love, nothing else. I love You, Lord. Give me Your love. I want You Lord, only You.

- Bring enthusiasm, zeal, hunger, intensity, and thirst to your practice.

- Use your willpower to cut off any thoughts that pull you back to the world.

- Give your love to God.

- Be still to receive His Love.

- When your little love merges with Big Love, love is all there is.

- Love, love, only love.

Communion

- In communion, we join God in stillness. There is no need to talk. There are no words, thoughts, affirmations, or prayer.

- In this sweet communion, the mind is silenced. There are no questions, problems, or needs—only love.

- Do not think. Just feel.

- Receive Her all-forgiving compassionate embrace.

- Feel Her unfathomable peace.

- Feel Her ecstatic joy.

- Affirm: It is great to be together in love and stillness. I am so happy to be here!

Share

- An anonymous quote: "Early on I had a vending machine version of prayer: money in, chips out. I did a disservice to my relationship with God by asking for petty things I can do for myself. Now I lend more dignity to the relationship. I have a conversation with God."

- Speak truth to God from the deepest place in your heart.

- Share anything.

- Talk to God about your problems, needs, and desires.

- Ask questions.

- Ask for guidance.

- Pray, affirm, or chant.

- I ask for what I need. I pray for it. I work for it. I leave the details to God.

Practice Compassion

- This practice is good for your health and well-being. It gets you out of yourself.

- Think about a good friend. You know your friend suffers from time to time. You don't need to know the specifics of the suffering.

- Visualize your friend's suffering as a dark cloud.

- Inhale: With inhalation, imagine the darkness going to your heart center where compassion resides. In the heart center, compassion transforms darkness to light.

- Exhale: As you exhale, send the compassionate light to your friend. Visualize the light traveling through your whole body and the entire body of your friend.

- Repeat this exercise for yourself, a relative, a neutral person, and an adversary.

- Repeat this exercise for a community of people: Haiti, Egypt, Syria, homeless, impoverished, abused, neglected, starving, war torn, victims of racism, unemployed, refugees, and more. There is no shortage of groups needing relief.

- Take in as much suffering as you can from the whole world. Or you can be more focused, as described in this exercise.

- Practice compassion for everything and everybody. Greet everyone as though they are family.

- At mastery, your compassion will be an unconditional, spontaneous, and automatic habit. Compassion will manifest in all situations without thought. You will run to help people without thinking.

Prayers for Unconditional Love Qualities

The Prayer of an Unknown Confederate Soldier

I asked God for strength that I might achieve. I was made weak that I might learn humbly to obey. I asked for health that I might do greater things. I was given infirmity that I might do better things.

I asked for riches that I might be happy. I was given poverty that I might be wise.

I asked for power that I might have the praise of men. I was

given weakness that I might feel the need of God.

I asked for all things that I might enjoy life. I was given life that I might enjoy all things.

I got nothing that I asked for, but everything I hoped for. Almost

despite myself, my unspoken prayers were answered.

Prayer of St. Francis

Lord, make me an instrument of your peace.

Where there is hatred, let me sow Love.

Where there is injury, pardon.

Where there is doubt, faith.

Where there is despair, hope.

Where there is darkness, light.

And where there is sadness, joy.

O Divine Master, grant that I may not so much seek to be consoled as to console.

To be understood as to understand.

To be loved as to love.

For it is in giving that we receive.

It is in pardoning that we are pardoned.

And it is in dying that we are born to eternal life.

- Annie Lamott wrote a book about three essential prayers: (1) Help, (2) Thanks, and (3) Wow.

- What is your favorite prayer?

- What prayer works for you?

Chapter 27

Mindfulness

- Please review chapter 19 on Mindfulness in *Healing Power, Revised*, pp. 277–99. This chapter discusses the tenets of mindfulness and a suggested practice technique. Following is a review of this material with some additional principles and techniques.

Skillful Pain Management

- Mindfulness training is now provided by most health care clinics and hospitals. Its ever-increasing popularity is the result of its effectiveness. It helps us manage our pain more skillfully. Here is how this works.

Mindfulness Reduces Reactivity

There are two levels to our pain:

1. The inevitable suffering of life that we cannot change.

2. Our reaction to it, which is reversible.
   a. Mindfulness helps us reduce this reactivity.
   b. When we practice mindfulness, we cultivate healing qualities: acceptance, stillness, silence, spaciousness, serenity, love, compassion, understanding, even-mindedness, courage, strength, perseverance and more. These qualities are water for the fire of reactivity. (See illustration on p. 83.)

Three Core Skills

- To practice mindfulness, we need three core skills: concentration, acceptance, and transformation.

Three Core Skills for a Successful Mindfulness Practice

1. **Concentration:** In a pure concentration exercise, we focus on a single point and return to that point when the mind wanders. We pay no attention to the content of our thoughts.

2. **Acceptance:** In a pure acceptance exercise, we see what is going on inside. We pay attention to thought content. We see what is there just as it is but do not try to change it. We ride the pain waves without adding unnecessary reactivity.

3. **Transformation:** This is the same as acceptance with an additional step. We pay attention to thought content and do try to change it. We replace negative thoughts with positive thoughts. We let the story unfold and spiritualize the story. We transform the story with healing qualities and wisdom pearls.

- With the practice of the following exercises, you will:

    a. Improve your powers of concentration, acceptance, and transformation.
    b. Cultivate stillness, silence, spaciousness, serenity, peace, even-mindedness, compassion, love, understanding, courage, strength, perseverance, and more. These healing qualities help us contain, reduce, or eliminate reactivity.
    c. Be a more skillful pain manager. You will control pain so pain does not control you.

Exercises

1. Concentration

- In mindlessness, the mind is unfocused, on automatic pilot, daydreaming, in a trance, hypnotized, floating. We like to float, but when floating becomes our habit, we are not in full consciousness.

- In mindfulness, the mind is focused. We train the mind to be where we want it to be. We focus on one thing at a time. When less prone to distraction, we are better able to work on problems and accomplish tasks.

- We can increase the strength of our concentration muscle by practicing the following exercise. Improving our ability to concentrate helps us succeed in whatever we are doing.

- When you find yourself on the train of thought and you don't want to be on the train:

    a. Focus on your breath.
    b. Breathe naturally or practice any breathing technique you wish.
    c. When the mind wanders, bring it back to the breath.
    d. As thoughts come by, gently return to your point of focus. Pay no attention to thought content.
    e. If it wanders a thousand times, bring it back a thousand times.
    f. Use the breath to center all day long.

g. You can do this same exercise using a mantra, affirmation, or wisdom pearl in addition to the breath as your point of focus.

2. Acceptance

- In a pure concentration exercise, we reduce our focus to a single point. When the mind wanders, we bring it back to the point of focus. We tell the mind, *Get back, stay here.* We pay no attention to content.

- In this acceptance exercise, we pay attention to content. Instead of reducing and focusing to a single point, we expand to include anything or everything in the outside world, our bodies, and inner being. We want to see what is there, but we don't try to change it.

- We accept what is happening outside and inside, even when we don't like it. We accept whatever is there, because it has to be there for that moment. We accept what we cannot change. We create a space for it.

- We leave everything just as it is and detach, create space, reduce reactivity, and importance. Our experience can be negative, positive, or do whatever it does. We just watch it all with calm detachment.

- We don't analyze, judge, or try to change anything. We just breathe, see what is going on in the movie, and observe how we react.

- With practice, we become increasingly attuned to what is going on inside. We see repetitive patterns of thought, feeling, and physical sensations. Most of these are long-term powerful habits that have been around for years.

- By sitting with and feeling everything that comes up—the full range of physical, mental, and emotional discomfort—we get better at allowing these things to be.

- When we get in touch with our reactions and learn how to ride the pain waves, we avoid unhealthy escapes and stay on task.

- When you are uncomfortable and find yourself running, resisting, fighting, and escaping:
  a. Stop.
  b. Breathe.
  c. Get in the present moment.
  d. Observe: Look at outer events and inner reactions.
     - Outer event: What's going on in the movie?
     - Inner reaction: I am anxious. I am angry. My mind is racing. My palms are sweaty.
  e. Accept: Don't try to change or fix anything. Invite and welcome whatever thoughts, feelings, and sensations come up. Completely accept whatever is there.
  f. Let go: There is a place inside that is always still, silent, spacious, and serene. With the breath as your centering device, bring in as much stillness as you can. Relax. Detach. Let go.

g. Act: Each of the preceding steps helps reduce reactivity and slows things down. You have created space and bought some time. Now, even if you are still suffering, you can respond to the world with peace and poise.

- In this exercise, we observe, accept, and let go. We observe the thought, accept the thought, and let the thought go. Content is not important. There are no good or bad thoughts, just thoughts. We welcome and invite them all while we remain calm and gentle with the self.

- You can have a moment of not liking what is there and then accept it. *I don't like it, but it is here. I don't escape. I deal.*

- This is skillful pain management through acceptance, a profound healing quality, one we must cultivate to reduce and eliminate destructive reactivity.

3. Transformation

- With acceptance, we let the story unfold just as it is. We observe, accept, and let go. This is profoundly helpful, but sometimes we need to look into the story and make some changes.

- This is akin to going to school. We study our painful problems and look for the lessons that always have to do with cultivating healing qualities. We get the lessons and qualities we need and move on. This is called *Let the story unfold and spiritualize the story.*

- When you are uncomfortable and find yourself running, resisting, fighting, and escaping:

    a. Stop

    b. Breathe

    c. Let the story unfold. Our pain story carries valuable information about our issues and problems. When you have extracted the necessary information, infuse the pain story with healing qualities.

    d. Spiritualize the story. Review the list of healing qualities. Choose the ones you need for this part of your story. Most of the time we need more love, compassion, understanding, forgiveness, strength, courage, patience, kindness, and humor for ourselves and others. These qualities will reduce and finally dissolve the pain story.

    e. For a more detailed review of this process, review:

    - Transformation of Emotion, in *Healing Power, Revised*, pp. 345–57.

    - School, in *Healing Power, Revised*, pp. 283–86.

    - Surrender, in *Healing Power, Revised*, pp. 152–54.

    - Transformation of Emotion in this workbook, p. 236-243.

4. Staying On or Getting Off the Train of Thought

- In exercises 1–3, you reviewed concentration, acceptance, and transformation. This exercise will help you determine which of these to choose.

- Let's look at anxiety. There are lots of thoughts going on all the time feeding anxiety. Left alone, these thoughts fuel the anxiety and make it worse. Alternatively, we can learn how to contain, reduce, and eliminate anxiety.

- When you become aware that you are on the anxiety train:

  a. Stop.
  b. Breathe.
  c. Get in the present moment.
  d. Decide if you want to get off the anxiety train or stay on it.
  e. Get off the train. If anxiety thinking is an old habit that visits you all too often; if there are no new insights and nothing to learn; or if your ruminations are destructive, painful, and a waste of energy, then by all means get off the train. Shift gears by practicing the concentration exercise above. As you recall, we pay no attention to thought content in this exercise. We just get off the train.
  f. Stay on the train. If you feel there is something to learn from the anxiety, you may need to stay on the train. There may be hidden issues and problems you need to face. The anxiety train is painful but it will take you through some territory you need to explore. You may find yourself ruminating on the same thoughts, but this is okay, because there will be new thoughts and insights that emerge amidst the old ones. If this is the case, choose the acceptance or transformation exercise above.
  g. What trains have you been on?
  h. Is it time to get off or do you need to take the ride?

5. Good Mental Health

- The mind does its best work when it is calm, positive, focused, strong, and resilient. From this position, it can meet any problem, test, or lesson that life presents. It helps us achieve our goals, solve problems, shape meaning, manage our pain skillfully, and pursue happiness, success, harmony, and joy. This is good mental health.

- Unfortunately, the mind does not always work this well. It has a complex bag of tricks that create havoc in our lives. It is often negative, wrong, obsessive, restless, relentless, deceptive, and more. It has a life of its own. We try to control it, but it is slippery and seemingly unstoppable. Thoughts are like glasses. We see the world through them. They determine our reality even when they are wrong or destructive. See *Healing Power, Revised*, pp. 57–59.

- Despite all of this, we seem to be in an unconditional love affair with the mind. We profoundly over-identify with it, no matter how much trouble it gives us. We consider our own thoughts, likes, and dislikes to be the final arbiter of truth. We let it dominate our consciousness, even when it is hysterical or wrong. What to do?

- We have the power to detoxify our negative thoughts. We can take away their power and importance. We can reduce their electricity. We can create more space so they don't cause as much turbulence.

- When the mind is locked in one of its many negative habit patterns, we can bring it back to its power position: positive, calm, focused, strong, and resilient. There are a number of ways we can do this.

- We can take off the negative glasses that distort our world and see the world through our new lenses: healing qualities.

- We can do this by practicing mindfulness or any of the methods described in this work.

- Practice PMQ.

- In this case, the P is restless, negative, distorted thinking.

- We can then pick any one of the fifteen methods to cultivate any one of the qualities.

- All of the methods in this work help bring the mind back to its power position.

6. The Present Moment

- The mind is busy telling stories about the past and future.

- We can't change the past or reach into the future. We can learn from the past and plan for the future, but most of us spend way too much time ruminating on past regrets and future worries and not enough time in the present.

- The more we stay in the here and now, the less stress we have. Mindfulness helps us stay in the present, where we have power and leverage through choice and attention.

- We can choose what we pay attention to. When we place our needle of attention on healing affirmations, we reduce reactivity and create healing vibrations for ourselves and others.

- When you find your mind wandering in the past and future:
  a. Stop.
  b. Breathe.
  c. Get in the present moment.
  d. Affirm.
     - The current moment is the only one I have.
     - The most important moment is now.
     - The most important person is the one I am with now.
     - The most important thing I am doing is what I am doing now.
     - The best way to prepare for the future is to be totally present now.

- Now is the moment that never ends.

- My life is one continuous sacred ritual.

7. Do Not Let Pain Define You

- It's one thing to have pain. It's another thing to let that pain define us, grab us by the throat, and keep us down. Healing qualities can help us with this problem.

- We have unlimited access to a bank of healing qualities. We can use these qualities to help us work through and rise above our pain.

- When pain comes in, takes over, and dominates your consciousness:

  a. Stop.
  b. Breathe.
  c. Get in the present moment.
  d. Refer to the list of one hundred healing qualities on p. 79.
  e. Choose a quality you need for the condition at hand.
  f. Remember, healing qualities are more powerful than any painful problem.

     1. Kindness dissolves cruelty.

     2. Love burns up hate.

     3. Courage defeats fear.

     4. Even-mindedness counters agitation.

     5. Hope replaces despair.

     6. Gentleness dissolves shame.

     7. Choose any painful problem, match it with the quality you need, and go to work.

     8. Affirm your quality, visualize it, feel it, and let it permeate your thoughts and speech.

     9. Let the quality guide your choices and actions.

8. The True Self

- This exercise is designed to help you remember you are not your pain. Your true self is a composite of one hundred healing qualities and higher states of consciousness.

- When you decide your mind is giving you trouble and you want to shift gears:

  a. Stop.
  b. Breathe.
  c. Get in the present moment.
  d. Remember, thoughts are just thoughts. They are not facts, reality, or the true self. They are passing mental events. They have a beginning, middle, and end. They arise, pass through our consciousness, and dissolve.
  e. The true self is healing qualities and higher states of consciousness.

f. Affirm: I have an army of one hundred healing qualities. This is my true self.

g. Affirm: I am still, silent, spacious, and serene.

h. Affirm: I am peace, love, compassion, kindness, understanding, courage, and strength.

i. Affirm the quality of your choice. These are your new lenses.

j. When negative thoughts return, breathe and affirm your quality.

k. With practice, healing qualities slowly contain, reduce, and eliminate negative, restless thoughts. The mind returns to its power position of peace and poise. Then you can enjoy the show and be ready for the next series of classes and tests.

9. The Witness

- The witness is the higher self, true self, or soul. It is the place inside that does not react. It is always calm, no matter what the world or body does. The witness is a powerful antidote to unnecessary reactivity.

- Observe the events of your life and your reactions to these events: thoughts, feelings, sensations, fantasies, judgment, likes, dislikes, and more. When you see you are overreacting:

    a. Stop.

    b. Breathe.

    c. Get in the present moment.

    d. Affirm: stillness, silence, spaciousness, and serenity.

    e. Let these qualities surround, embrace, permeate, and saturate your problem.

    f. Notice the reduction in reactivity and restoration of peace.

10. Riding the Pain Wave (See illustration on p. 106)

- We want *unlimited* peace, love, joy, power, and wisdom, more time, and no pain. But this is not to be. In ordinary consciousness, we are subject to a host of uncomfortable thoughts, feelings, desires, and bodily sensations that will not quit. When we try to resist or escape these painful feelings, we make things worse. We create unnecessary reactivity that adds a great deal of suffering to the inevitable suffering of life.

- "You can't stop the waves, but you can learn to surf" (Jon Kabat-Zinn). To manage our pain skillfully, we need to learn how to ride the pain waves without the add-ons: racing thoughts, highly reactive emotions, excessive material desires leading to attachments and bad habits, hyperactivity, and egotism.

- Practice the following technique. It still hurts, but this way we get the best possible ride. When you feel discomfort of any kind:

    a. Stop.

    b. Breathe.

    c. Get in the present moment.

d. Observe the pain wave as it emerges. Imagine yourself on a board, surfing the wave. Allow the wave to emerge just as it is. It is often our resistance to giving the wave some time and space that gives it even more power.

e. Stay with the wave as it grows. It has a life of its own. Ride it wherever it goes. It may grow, reach a peak, and dissolve quickly, or it may stick around for some time. We cannot control this.

f. But we can steady ourselves on the board with breathwork, healing qualities, and our favorite wisdom pearls. To stay balanced on the board, breathe and affirm the healing quality or wisdom pearl of your choice.

g. Stay with the wave—no matter the size, shape, or duration.

h. When the mind races, return your focus to your breath, quality, or pearl.

i. When your emotions intensify, return your focus to your breath, quality, or pearl.

j. When desires emerge and prompt you to an escape pattern that will ultimately cause more suffering, intend not to act, breathe, and focus on your pearl or healing quality.

k. When any uncomfortable thoughts, feelings, desires, or sensations emerge— be aware, don't judge, be kind and gentle with yourself, and return your focus to your breath, quality, and pearl.

l. Observe your moment-to-moment experience. Stay with it. The process is painful but what you are doing is important. You are getting comfortable with a wider range of experiences.

m. Don't latch on to a particular idea, emotion, desire, or sensation. Just watch what comes and goes.

n. Breathe, observe, accept, and let go.

o. If you fall off the board, get back on.

p. Persevere. Keep on keeping on. This may be your time for the heavy lifting curricula sometimes assigned against our will in the university of life.

q. Remember, effort is progress even if you can't feel it. The qualities are growing beneath the surface waves of pain. Eventually the qualities will become big enough to contain, reduce, or eliminate your pain.

11. Love Is Skillful Pain Management

- When love, compassion, understanding, kindness, courage, strength, perseverance, patience, and forgiveness are in control of our consciousness, we do not overreact. We remain even-minded and calm, even in the face of pain or distress. This is skillful pain management. Love and associated healing qualities are in charge.

- We are either in love or something else. *Something else* is a large variety of negatives: anger, judgment, impatience, irritability, fear, insecurity, worry, and doubt, to name a few. These unnecessary reactions plague us all.

- Love and skillful pain management are the same thing. When you are in pain, mindfully ask yourself:

a. Am I managing this pain skillfully or unskillfully?

b. Am I in love or something else?

c. If you are managing your pain skillfully, the healing qualities or love is in charge. You are in the presence of God or acting mindfully.

d. When you notice you are managing your pain unskillfully, all you have to do is pick the healing quality you need most at the moment and begin breathing and affirming in that direction.

e. Love and skillful pain management are the same thing. Choose love.

12. The Ocean and the Wave

Ocean and Wave

- We can use the Ocean and its waves as a metaphor for life and convert this into a mindfulness exercise.

- The Ocean is the infinite source of all things. It is vast, deep, calm, never-ending, and still.

- Waves are people, activities, events, and things. Waves have a beginning, middle, and end. They come from, exist, and return to the Ocean.

- We are the waves. We belong to the Ocean.

- Most of us focus exclusively on the waves. They command all of our attention. They determine our reality and our identity. A few examples:

   a. We are fascinated and seduced by the drama: our relationships, work, school, training, hobbies, recreation, worries, economic security, and more.

   b. We have powerful reactions to the show. Our restless minds, overwhelming emotions, and excessive material desires lead to attachments and bad habits.

   c. Most of us are hyperactivity junkies, busy from the time we get up in the morning until we go to sleep.

   d. Our bodies give us trouble and take up a lot of our attention.

   e. Our egos ramp up and create unnecessary self-importance and reactivity.

   f. We are unduly concerned with our place in the drama.

- When we focus on surface waves to the exclusion of the Ocean below, we feel insecure and anxious. Everything on the surface of the Ocean is changing and some of these changes are threatening and painful.

- We have little to no awareness of the Ocean underneath the waves. This exercise is designed to help us shift our identity from an isolated wave to a wave connected to the Ocean. The result is an ever-increasing sense of peace. In the end, when the wave merges with the Ocean, we feel the changeless peace of the vast Ocean below.

- When you feel threatened, anxious, or any discomfort:

   a. Stop.

   b. Breathe.

   c. Get in the present moment.

   d. Think *Ocean and wave*.

   e. Notice the waves are in a state of perpetual flux. They are tiny, small, medium, large, or huge and encompass all possibilities: good and evil, pleasure and pain, success and failure, health and disease, praise and blame, wealth and poverty, love and hate, life and death. The goal is to ride whatever waves show up without adding unnecessary reactivity.

   f. Stillness is the antidote to reactivity. The Ocean has an unlimited supply of stillness, waiting to be tapped, free of cost. Begin your practice of identifying more with the Ocean than the wave. Affirm: stillness, silence, spaciousness, and serenity.

   g. No matter the size or shape of the wave, bring in as much stillness as you can.

   h. When a big wave comes in and gets a hold of you, gently label it and work your way back into the deep unchanging oceanic peace just underneath the wave.

   i. If an old, familiar unpleasant wave returns, simply notice its arrival and don't get excited.

   j. The goal is to slowly identify more with the Ocean than with the wave. Affirm: I am one with the Ocean—deep, vast, still, and quiet.

   k. With long-term practice, as your identity shifts from wave to Ocean, you will experience the same waves, but they will have less power. You will react less. The waves will come and go, and you will have room for it all.

13. One Continuous Sacred Ritual

- In mindfulness training, we learn to pay attention to one thing at a time. But what do we pay attention to? There are unlimited options.

- Where we place our needle of attention is monumentally important. Review the mindfulness technique described in *Healing Power, Revised*, pp. 280–92. This technique offers seven options we can use to focus our attention: witness, school, entertainment, service, warrior, ritual, and other.

One Continuous Sacred Ritual

- The Witness: The witness remains even-minded under all conditions.

- School: When difficult or painful, life is school. We enter the pain and extract the necessary lessons.

- Entertainment: When life is entertaining, it's like a movie. We enjoy the show.

- Service: In service to others, we feel peace and joy.

- Warrior: The warrior finds courage in the face of fear and gets ready for anything.

- Ritual: The ritual transforms the ordinary and mundane to magical miracles everywhere.

- Other: Choose any frame, healing quality, or wisdom pearl. Be creative.

- When we bring the unruly mind under control through mindfulness, we gain access to the calm witness, the student in school, the actor in the movie, the servant of humanity, the warrior who is ready for anything, and the magical ritual.

- The key is to mindfully choose the right frame at the right time. This is not easy. We want to stay in the witness, service, ritual, and entertainment. These are the most fun. They bring peace, love, magic, and joy.

- But sometimes we need to be in school. Without school, which is what most people avoid, we lose the full, comprehensive, and deep healing power of mindfulness.

- We can get our lives back at any moment, but we must accept what shows up. Mindfulness teaches us to be in the moment, but we don't want to be in the moment if it hurts. When you feel yourself running, avoiding, or escaping, calm the mind down and face the difficult problem, pain, or conflict.

- The key is to accept pain as the guest teacher. If we do this, we can avoid the pitfalls of unnecessary worry, fear, insecurity, fury, and fantasy, which all come in to steal the moments.

- Breathe, get calm and centered, have fun, enjoy the show, help others, and observe magical miracles everywhere. When pain shows up, go to school. Don't play hooky. Ride the pain waves. Get the lessons and move on to another frame. When we get the frame right, life becomes one continuous sacred ritual, offering up its knowledge and lessons, entertainment and joy, and opportunities to love and serve.

14. Mindful School

- Life is school. There are classes, teachers, subjects, and tests.

- Do you know life is school?

- Do you know what class you are in?

- Do you know the subject?

- Do you know the teacher?

- Have you been in this class before?

- Have you figured out the lessons you need to learn?

- Perhaps you know you are in school, but you think you are more advanced than you are. If this is the case, The Principal of the universal school of life will make the adjustment for you. The right classes, teachers, and subjects will make themselves known to you.

- Perhaps you know you are in school, but you sell yourself short by signing up for classes you have already mastered. That same Principal will guide you to the proper curricula.

- Perhaps you know you are in school and you accept your classes, subjects, and teachers, do the homework, pass the test, and move on. Keep up the good work!

15. Mindful Service

- Gentle, compassionate service to all humanity is the natural consequence of the sustained practice of mindfulness.

- Perform all acts with loving-kindness.

- Remember, the one you are with is the most important person in the world.

- Make your ears so big they touch the ground. Listen, listen, listen with your elephant ears.

- Support and validate. Don't be so quick to give advice.

- Clarify and summarize. Don't try to fix.

- Anonymous, loving, humble service to others without attachment to outcome: such an act is sacred. Connect with people, help them, and let them go.

16. Edit the Tapes

- Look back at a scene in your life you would replay if you could:
    a. Stop
    b. Breathe
    c. Get in the present moment

d. Reframe

- Ask yourself: *What would have happened had I _____?*

- *How would others and I have benefitted if I _____?*

- Review the list of one hundred healing qualities on p. 79.

- Which quality or qualities would help you replay that scene the way you want now?

- Practice your quality now and into the future.

17. Which Wolf Are You Feeding?

- An old Cherokee Indian was speaking to his grandson. "A fight is going on inside me," he said to the boy. "It is a terrible fight between two wolves. One is evil—he is anger, envy, sorrow, regret, greed, arrogance, self-pity, guilt, resentment, inferiority, lies, false pride, superiority, and ego. The other is good—he is joy, peace, love, hope, serenity, humility, kindness, benevolence, empathy, generosity, truth, compassion, and faith. This same fight is going on inside you, and inside every other person, too."

The grandson thought about it for a long minute, and then asked his grandfather, "Which wolf will win?"

The old Cherokee simply replied, "The one you feed."

a. Are you mindful of the battle between the two wolves from moment to moment?

b. Which wolf have you been feeding?

c. When you become aware that you are feeding the bad wolf:

1. Stop

2. Breath

3. Get in the present moment

4. Choose the good wolf—love—a composite of one hundred healing qualities.

5. Often, our only place of power in the story is love. When we get this, we are really moving along.

18. Apply Mindfulness to Everything

- We can apply mindfulness to the simple things of daily life.

- Mindful actions include talking, listening, shopping, cooking, cleaning, walking, chores, playing, working, parenting, eating, showering, driving---any activity, all tasks, all people, everything, and anything. There is no limit to where you can apply mindfulness.

- When the mind wanders or goes on automatic pilot:

a. Stop.

b. Breathe.

c. Get in the present moment.

d. Focus on something positive in the outer world, in your body, or in your inner being.

e. Focus on what you are doing.

f. Focus where you wish. An advanced mindfulness specialist like Rumi uses the entire universe as his palette. You can do this, too. Be creative.

g. Don't miss the magic in the mundane. It is there. Every moment is a sacred moment, every place a sacred place. See *Healing Power, Revised*, pp. 288–90.

h. Affirm: One continuous sacred ritual.

Points to Remember

- You don't have to change your belief system to practice mindfulness. Mindfulness is independent of belief systems, religion, theology, or deity. It is attention training. We learn how to place the mind where we want it to be.

- We can apply mindfulness to any activity: mindful eating, mindful speaking, mindful listening, and more. Life is a string of unlimited opportunities to practice mindfulness. Everything matters: every moment, every level, and every detail.

- We are afraid of suffering, disease, disability, the unknown, and death. This mental distress slows down the healing process and makes our pain worse. With mindfulness, we don't escape from the pain. We face pain just as it is without reacting. When we react less, we suffer less. We slow down and relax. We stay in charge. We get our lives back.

- Pain is both physical and psychological. All pain is experienced in the mind and can therefore be modulated by the mind. The mind often expands and magnifies the pain. With mindfulness, we contain and reduce the pain. We break the locked-in, automatic rapid response between a stressful event and high emotional reactivity. We step back from our thoughts and feelings so they don't trap us or sweep us away. We create space. We go to the calm center within, a place of absolute stillness—no matter the drama of the world or the troubles of the body. This is called the witness. The witness is always still, silent, serene, and spacious. It is packed with healing power and healing qualities.

- With mindfulness, we see things as they are. We bring our complete attention to our experience in the present moment. We accept. We don't judge.

- When we practice mindfulness, we recognize thoughts and feelings as mental events rather than aspects of self or a reflection of reality. This changes our relationship to thoughts and feelings rather than changing the content or meaning.

- The ultimate goal of mindfulness is love. We are either in love or something negative. When negative, shift gears back to love. Everything in this model moves in that direction. Enter anywhere. It's all taking you to the same place: The Love Field.

Chapter 28

Presence of God

- Please review chapter 20, Practicing the Presence of God, in *Healing Power, Revised*, pp. 301–17. Here you will find a six-step technique for practicing the presence of God. Following is a review of this material with some additional principles and techniques.

- This chapter has a lot of God talk. This may be a problem for some people. Remember, there is a cafeteria of options. Higher Power refers to the God of your understanding, higher states of consciousness, higher self, or higher meaning and purpose. One person's traction device is the next person's gag reflex. Nuke offensive language and substitute your own. Take what you need and leave the rest.

- There is a single field with two dimensions: Spirit and matter. Spirit and matter are two sides of the same coin. They overlap. They occupy the same space. We stand between these two worlds, but most of us don't experience Spirit, as the material world has all of our attention. When we practice the presence of God, we reverse this trend. We reduce the power of the material world and make contact with God.

- Following is a brief review of the nature of Spirit and matter and some exercises to help us bring out the spiritual side of the equation.

Spirit

- A singular power inhabits all space, unifying and harmonizing everything in the universe. This power is pure, formless conscious energy. It is at once the source of everything and the link that connects all. It cannot be born, confined, limited, divided, or broken. It is eternal, immortal, changeless, and one. It is inside, outside, everywhere, extending forever in every direction, unifying all things and people.

- The great books and teachers call it the Tao, Buddha, Christ Consciousness, Krishna Consciousness, The Changeless One, bliss, nirvana, God, The Field, Divine Love, The Ocean of Love, omniscient, omnipotent, omnipresent Love, and more.

- We do not enter this field. We are already in it. It is already in us. There is no separation. All is one. We live in this infinite ocean as a fish swims in water. The water is always right here offering peace, love, joy, wisdom, and safety. When we realize our oneness with the ocean, we know we are immortal, indivisible, and connected to all.

- We can have a personal relationship with this omnipotent power. The all-knowing infinite power can mysteriously manifest at our level bearing priceless gifts: guidance, protection, friendship, healing, purification, and expansion of healing qualities—peace, love, compassion, joy, light, and more.

- The Great Healer knocks on the door of ordinary consciousness, but we don't hear it. We have lost our connection to the invisible, subtle, higher vibrations offered by the gracious omnipresent power, stuck as we are in the gross vibrations of material consciousness.

Matter

- This is the material world as we know it in ordinary consciousness. It occupies the same space as spirit. The material world or *maya* commands all of our attention. It makes us think the show on the physical plane is all there is.

- We are addicted to the show with its fascinating stories, alluring objects, and sensual pleasures. Tests and trials come. We get trapped in our thoughts, feelings, desires, habits, attachments, and egos. Separated, mired, and hooked by the limitations of material consciousness, we remain deaf to the Friend trying to help.

Exercises

- We want to get closer to the great God of Love and absorb Her qualities. Instead we experience separation, a gap of sorts. What will help us bridge this gap so we can prove the Friend's existence, explore Her nature, and partake of Her wondrous gifts?

- Review and practice the six-step technique described in *Healing Power, Revised* on pp. 302–12. This will help you tap into the subtle hidden dimension of Omniscient Love just behind the veil of ordinary consciousness.

- Following are some additional ideas and exercises designed to help us find God's presence in all things.

1. Practicing the Presence of God in Activity

- God is not far away, although it feels like it. He is right here, right now, everywhere, in everything. We are in Him, and He is in us.

- Should we decide to pursue the invisible gracious power and receive Her medley of gifts, there are a number of avenues of approach.

- To bring God closer, you might try relating to Her formless form: omniscient, omnipotent, omnipresent Love.

- For those who find Omniscient Love too vague or distant, the following aspects of God may be more approachable and accessible: Father, Mother, Friend, Beloved, Teacher, Healer, Confidante, Great Physician, Grandfather, Creator, Guide, Protector, or Counselor.

- Choose one or a combination of these aspects and begin your practice. For example, you might choose The Beloved Friend.

- The Beloved Friend is everywhere throughout the day no matter what we are doing or what happens to us. He is hiding in every thought, in every cell, in everything within us. He is just behind the veil of ordinary consciousness.

- Talk to your Beloved Friend anywhere, anytime, about anything. Speak to Her in truth from the deepest place in your heart.

- Speak to Her throughout the day. Share your life. Talk to Her no matter what the world or your body is doing. Include anger, elation, silence, everything.

- It doesn't matter whether your problem is tiny, small, medium, large, or huge. You can invoke your special, close, personal, intimate relationship with God as your Beloved Friend and ask for help. Her Love and Wisdom will guide you.

- The Beloved is with us now and forever, inspiring, helping, and guiding. See Her in all people, all creation, all conditions.

- Build a connecting link between you and your Friend that cannot be broken even if the world shatters.

- Use Her as your guide and protector.

2. Practicing the Presence of God through the Qualities

- Some find God accessible through the unified field of pure unconditional love.

- Others get traction by relating to Him/Her as Father, Mother, Friend, Beloved, Counselor, Guide, Protector, Teacher, Creator, Great Healer, Grandfather, and more.

- A third option is practicing the presence of God by cultivating the healing qualities. We can understand God as any one or a combination of healing qualities in unlimited form: love, peace, compassion, courage, strength, patience, kindness, gentleness, and more.

- God = Unlimited Love = Unlimited Healing Qualities. We are made in that image. Our true self is love = the qualities. The qualities are embedded in our consciousness. We can make them grow.

- Choose a quality and practice it throughout the day.

- Use your quality to antidote your restless mind, reactive emotions, excessive material desires, obsessing on problems, egotism, or other negative vibrations.

- Let your quality guide every thought, feeling, desire, decision, and action.

- Give your quality to all whom you meet.

- The qualities grow and eventually expand to the peace that surpasses understanding, pure love, ecstatic joy, and other wonderful superconscious experiences.

- Strive to attune to God's presence. Feel Him. His nature is gentle, compassionate, loving, and wise. He is silently guiding us through these and the other qualities listed in the spiritual alphabet.

3. Practicing the Presence of God in Meditation: Devotion and Stillness

- We can make contact with God in meditation. God is in and just behind the silent darkness. We can coax Her to come out and touch us when we practice stillness and devotion.

- Meditation brings us to stillness.

- In stillness, we practice devotion.

- Stillness and devotion bring out the presence of God as the superconscious love we crave.

- Following is a review of how devotion and stillness work together to bring this sacred, holy experience to you.

- Practice your meditation technique and bring in as much stillness as you can. Then practice devotion and stillness.

- Here is the sequence:

Meditation → Stillness → Devotion → Stillness → Superconsciousness → Service → Repeat → Mastery

Devotion

- Devotion is giving God our unconditional love and gratitude.

- Love is the feeling. The expression of that feeling to the divine is devotion.

- Devotion is active. We knock on the door of God. We ask, seek, and yearn.

- We practice with full attention and intensity. None of this is half-hearted. This is hard, serious work. The mind is awake, on fire.

- Yearning is a part of devotion. It is the magnetic ardor of yearning that draws the grace of God. We must have a fire in our hearts or we won't get a response. A pure call from the heart and He has to respond.

- Our little love is the magnet that draws The Big Love of God. Practice unconditional, one-pointed, steady devotion, and He will come to you.

- Talk to God. Make devotional communion with God an important part of your meditation. Tell Him you want Him. Implore His presence again and again.

- Churn the ether with your love. If you don't feel it, act as though you do and eventually you will.

- Pay no attention to the onslaught of thoughts and drama. Instead, practice one or more of the following devotional heart calls. Seekers use these to create an irresistible magnet that will draw God. You might enjoy practicing these or create your own by speaking to God in the language of your heart.

  - Accept my devotional offering of concentration and attention.

  - Help me calm my body and mind that I might feel Your presence within and without.

218

- With ever increasing intensity, I offer all of my heart, mind, and soul. I want You alone. Nothing else matters.

- I have come to this meditation to experience Your presence. Help me meditate more deeply.

- Awaken in me Your Divinity. Awaken my heart. Awaken my devotion. Let me experience Your Love in this meditation.

- I am Your child, made in Your Love. Open my heart and mind and touch my soul that I may feel Your Love.

- Help me feel Your presence as peace, love, joy, power, and wisdom.

- Help me practice Your presence more continuously in meditation and activity.

- Teach me to feel Your peaceful presence inside and outside, above and below, left and right, all around me.

- May my every thought be saturated with the awareness of Your presence.

- May my every feeling glow with Your Love.

- Help me to know your omnipresence as the peace-love-joy that permeates all things.

- Bathe me, saturate me, permeate me with Your all-forgiving love.

- Lift my consciousness. Immerse me in Your light. Immerse me in the tangible vibration of Your loving presence.

- Be with me now and always. Be my Companion. Give me your gentle joy.

- You are the reality behind all appearance. Bless me that I deeply feel Your presence inside, outside, everywhere, in all people, and in all conditions.

- Bless me, guide me, and be with me always.

- Help me cast aside all burdens.

- Help me be receptive to Your blessings.

- Make Your Love my eternal home.

- Help me remember you are within, without, everywhere—always.

- Lord, Master of the Universe, I will never give up until You talk to me.

- I offer You all of the love of my heart.

- Fill my heart with undying devotion for You alone.

- You are my life. You are my love. You are my only goal.

- Come to me. Reveal Yourself.

- Bathe me, saturate me, permeate me with Your love. Change me forever and forever.

- Help me serve more selflessly and above all love more unconditionally.

- Help me heal myself, our countries, and the earth.

Stillness

- With devotion, we make a sustained intense offering with all of our hearts and will to become one with God.

- After you finish practicing devotion, quietly rest and feel Him in stillness.

- In stillness, God reveals Himself secretly and quietly in a variety of manifestations:

    - A little glimmer of light

    - A feeling of comfort and peace

    - The peace that surpasses understanding

    - Ecstatic joy

    - Pure love

    - Intuitive wisdom

    - A breathtaking and thrilling yet soft and gentle surge of power

    - A soothing embrace

    - A feeling of absolute safety

    - Phenomenon: aura, light, visions, guidance, protection, answered prayers, synchronicity, healing powers

    - Entrance in to the zone: the experience of supreme flow, rhythm, and harmony

    - The unconditional, sweet Love of the Father-Mother

    - Perfect guidance from the Counselor

    - Healing and purification from the Great Physician

    - Training from the Teacher

    - Friendship from the Friend

    - Love from the Beloved

    - Healing qualities expand

    - Our problems burn up

    - Advanced meditators experience samadhi, the ecstasy of complete union with God. We feel him inside, outside, everywhere as unlimited peace, love, joy, power, and wisdom.

- Take note of your manifestation. Embrace it. Capture it. Meditate on it. It will expand.

- Recognize the blessing, guidance, and help you are getting: Affirm: "Beloved Friend, You are with me now, and I am with You."

- When we come out of meditation, we have more space to receive and respond to the suffering of the world with compassionate action. We express our love in quiet, anonymous gentle acts of humble service to all.

The Secret Essence of Spiritual Work

- With devotion, we give God our love.

- In stillness, we receive His love.

- In service, we give love to one another.

- Practice devotion, stillness, and service. This is the secret essence of spiritual work. It will speed up your evolution. Try it. It works.

The Messiah in Disguise: Author Unknown

High in the mountains was a monastery that had once been known throughout the world. Its monks were pious; its students were enthusiastic. The chants from the monastery's chapel deeply touched the hearts of people who came there to pray and meditate. But something had changed. Fewer and fewer young men came to study there; fewer and fewer people came for spiritual nourishment. The monks who remained became disheartened and sad.

Deeply worried, the abbot of the monastery went off in search of an answer. Why had his monastery fallen on such hard times? The abbot came to a guru, and asked the master for advice. The guru said, "I have no advice to give. The only thing I can tell you is that the Messiah is one of you." Then, the guru closed his eyes and remained silent.

The Messiah is one of us, thought the abbott. *Who could it be? Brother Cook? Brother Treasurer? Brother Bell-Ringer? Brother Vegetable Grower? Every one of us has faults, failings, human defects. Isn't the Messiah supposed to be perfect? But, then, perhaps these faults and failings are part of his disguise. Which one? Which one?*

When the abbot returned to the monastery, he gathered all the monks together and told them what the guru had said. "One of us? The Messiah? Impossible!" But, the master had spoken, and the master was never wrong. Which one? That brother over there? That one? Whichever one of the monks was the Messiah, he was surely in disguise.

Not knowing who amongst them was the Messiah, all the monks began treating each other with new respect. *You never know*, they thought. *He might be the one, so I had better deal with him kindly.*

As they contemplated in this manner, the monks began to treat each other with extraordinary respect on the off chance that one of them might be the Messiah. And on the off, off chance that each monk himself might be the Messiah, they began to treat themselves with extraordinary respect.

It was not long before the monastery was filled with newfound joy. Soon, new students came to learn, and people came from far and wide to be inspired by the chants of the kind, smiling monks. For once again, the monastery was filled with the spirit of love.

    a.   Do you see? We are a part of God but don't know it. We are duped into thinking this is not the case.

b. Behave as though you are in the presence of Jesus, Buddha, or Krishna—because you are.

c. God is inside, outside, everywhere. When we awaken to the divinity in all, everything gets better.

Points to Remember

- During the day when you are busy but have a moment between tasks, chant, affirm, pray, or speak to God in the language of your heart. This leads to attunement with the highest vibrations. Then return to your task.

- When we get into the presence and give love, we switch from ego-getting to soul-giving.

- When we practice the presence of God during activity, our meditation is easier. When we practice meditation, we will find God more easily during activity. Meditation and practicing the presence of God in activity compliment each other.

- No matter what the world or your body is doing, Big Love is here, now, embracing, watching, guiding, and inspiring. Be still and receptive so you don't miss the blessing and the help you are getting.

- We stand in between the two worlds, maya and God. These are like two sides of the same coin: the material and the spiritual. Roll the wheel. Practice PMQ. The Invisible Unified Love Field responds with healing and phenomena. Phenomena are part of it but don't have that as a goal. The only desire is for the presence of God as love.

- Let go of the restlessness and separation born of material consciousness, and join the peace-love-joy of God everywhere present.

- Devotion is the overarching magnetic attraction to God. It's what gives meaning to meditation and to all of life.

- The world does what it does, and we respond the way we respond. If we respond with a healing quality, we are already in the presence of God or being mindful.

- In stillness, the door opens. We receive the gift. God appears as the peace that surpasses understanding, pure love, and ecstatic joy. The feeling here is exquisite. Superconscious peace-love-joy is addicting. One taste and we want more. But it doesn't last. God disappears. We return to ordinary consciousness. There is more work to do.

- When God disappears, the separation is ultimately intolerable. We yearn for Her/His return. Yearning brings us closer to God. Yearning is part of devotion. With devotion, we close the gap of separation. This is the romance of God.

- God wants to get married, but we want to play the field—the maya field—so He doesn't show himself. He waits while we learn our lessons. (Maya = the world as we know it in ordinary consciousness.)

- God first, regular meditation, devotional yearning, and service to others. This is the magic of spiritual work.

- Every natural dog sniffs God in the stew. Rumi

Chapter 29

Service

- Please review chapter 21 on Service, in *Healing Power Revised,* pp. 319 – 328. Here you will find some suggestions for a daily routine of love and service. Following are some additional ideas and exercises.

- The purpose of life is to enhance each other's humanity, to make even one life better.

- When you think about a life of greatness, think about a life of service. Love is the currency.

- To be a complete person, you must be in service.

- Service is the expression of love without attachment to outcome. We don't want to slip into conditional love or manipulation.

- Service is like a two-way pill. When I serve you, I heal myself; when I heal myself, I serve you. Be a messenger of peace, love, joy, wisdom, and kindness.

- The size of your service offering does not matter. Small acts of gentle, anonymous, humble service can change the world.

- Do small things with great Love. Mother Teresa

- Service is not about what we get. This is the ego. Service is about what we give. This is the soul.

- It's a simple flip of the switch from what I get to what I give.

- You are a soul sent here for service, joy, and entertainment.

- Service can be informal--whatever shows up--or formal like a volunteer.

- We don't need to be perfect to help others.

- When you love, serve, and give, you are moving closer to God as this is Her nature.

Exercises

1. There is a balance point between helping others and taking good care of yourself.
    - Some do too much for others and not enough for themselves.
    - Some do too little for others and too much for themselves.
    - Some aren't doing for others or themselves.
    - Are you stuck in a pattern?
    - If so, what would it take to find your balance point?

2. Cultivate a consciousness of service and translate that into serviceful action, both formal and informal. Informal service is seeing what comes your way and responding with kindness. Formal would be signing up as a volunteer.

    *   Start out your day by setting up your service intention: to help everybody in little ways.

    *   Practice random, anonymous acts of gentle humble service to all whom you meet.

    *   Keep it small so you don't get overwhelmed.

    *   Help others even when you don't feel like it. This will help you feel better.

    *   Watch others perform random acts of kindness. It is going on but we may miss it if we don't watch.

3. We can't take away other people's pain but we can stand with them while they figure it out on their own schedule. Practice being with others without judgment and without giving advice. Just be there, understand, and validate.

4. There is a dangerous neighborhood in the mind. It shows up against our will. To get some help with this:

    *   Find good people.

    *   Get support.

    *   Fill your brain with wisdom.

    *   Help everyone.

5. *The goal is pure Love and service without attachment to outcome.*

6. I do the best I can in the moment. I give the results to God.

    *   This is tricky, difficult, and sometimes impossible. Operating without our awareness, the ego attaches itself to the outcome. When there is success, it claims victory for itself and feels good. With failure, it feels bad. These reactions are natural but they get in the way and don't go away so easily. The egos works are hidden, subtle, invisible, and sticky. We don't even know it is there.

    *   The antidote to the problem of the ego is the soul connected to God. What matters to the ego, does not matter to the soul. The soul's concern is pure love and service. The story and the outcome are up to God.

    *   Perform your service act with love and leave the consequences to God. At the highest level, God knows what is needed and we don't.

    *   Whether people get better, worse, or stay stuck, our job is the same: serve and help in whatever way we can, however small. The story and outcome are not ours.

    *   When we practice love and service, we learn a kind of detachment that is not intellectual. Our hidden attachments come out and get burned off quickly or they burn us. When

ego attachments burn off, soul qualities expand. We get peace, love, joy, wisdom, courage, and strength and give these to all whom we meet.

- Practice these affirmations:

  a. My job is pure love and service.

  b. The one I serve may go forward, backward, or stay the same. That part is not up to me.

  c. Service in the eternal present is the highest. There is no past or future, just helping.

  d. Immersed in peace, love, and joy, I give what I can.

  e. I do the best I can in the moment. I give the results to God.

  f. I bring my love to brutal reality and serve there.

  g. Pure service is sacred and holy. No one needs to know.

7. In response to your pain, practice love, service, and meditation. This is a powerful variation of the universal healing wheel or PMQ.

- (P) This can be any pain or problem.

- (M) The methods are meditation and service.

- (Q) The quality is unconditional love. There is no attachment to outcomes. We work for--but are not attached to--the results.

- Love, service, and meditation: a simple, powerful formula for dealing with any of life's problems. Try this. It works.

Memorable Quotes from Members

- We are all needed and important.

- Vertical axis methods like meditation get my stuff out of the way. Then I am ready for service on the horizontal axis, the people part.

- The ultimate reward is people.

- The whole is greater than the sum of its parts. In The Living Room, I am bigger. (The Living Room is a drop-in center with groups and activities)

- In service, we connect on a deep level. So much love and joy there.

- In order to keep what you've got, you have to give it away. Help others.

- Hurt people hurt people. We can reverse this trend with service.

- The purpose of life is simple: help others.

- A reality check is very important, as I am so hard on myself. I need to hear that I am not that bad, especially if I am going into my schizophrenic mind.

- When depressed, I get into my head and isolate. It gets worse and worse. This is when I need to find the right people so I can get comfortable and feel safe.

- I can take just a little bit of inner work at a time. When I try to do too much and get overwhelmed, I go to people and tell my story. It helps especially when it starts to feel out of control.

- I can be in the abyss. There is a lot of fear and hurt in my heart. Isolating in my room with cigarettes doesn't work. It will do me in. It is vital to get out of my room. I need to see people every day. If I don't smoke, its much better.

- We get to help each other in any way we can.

- I struggle to go to groups. But I don't listen to the voice that says don't go there. I go. I sit there. Even if I don't feel like it. It's the best place to be.

- My partner gives me unconditional love every day even when I'm in a bad mood. It is so nice to have someone who loves you.

- A friend wanted to drink. I took him to Burnside (a street with many homeless addicts) so he could see where he will be if he drinks. Then to my house. He took a shower. It helped.

- Understanding is the most important thing. Don't jump in with advice. Listen. Try to get me first. Then ask me if I want your advice.

- We can inspire each other with our stories. Take what you need and leave the rest. Eat the chicken. Spit out the bone.

- Helping others is easier than helping myself.

- I would like to pay back my debts and then some.

- I have to focus on myself right now.

- Sometimes we have to serve ourselves by setting boundaries.

- My service work is encouragement.

- Connect with people, help them, let them go.

- Bring your love to brutal reality and serve there.

Chapter 30

Yoga

- Please review chapter 22 on Yoga in *Healing Power Revised*, pp. 329-343. Here you will study four pathways to God: love, service, wisdom, and stillness. Following is a review of these principles and some additional points and techniques.

- Many think yoga is practicing a variety of physical positions on mats. No. This is Hatha yoga, a small part of something much bigger.

- Yoga is a scientific body of principles, steps, tools, and instructions for God-realization and liberation from suffering.

- Review the ten steps on pp. 45-93 in *Healing Power Revised*. Inherent in these steps are the key principles of yoga. Following is a summary of these principles. After that, we will review how to implement these principles in our daily lives by practicing pranayama.

1. **The Ten Steps**

    - Step 1: We have an absolute need for *unlimited* peace, love, joy, and safety. This is called the core drive. The core drive is the motivating force behind all of our actions. It does not shut off. It can't. It is built into the genetic code. We have to have it. We want unlimited healing qualities and higher states of consciousness.

    - Step 2--3: We try to achieve the core drive exclusively on the horizontal axis of people, activities, events, and things but this is impossible. On the physical plane, suffering is inevitable, time is limited, and death wins in the end.

    - Step 4--5: When we persist in our efforts to achieve the core drive on the physical plane, our motor overheats. We get stuck in the mud. We become unnecessarily reactive. The restless mind, highly reactive emotions, excessive material desires, attachments, bad habits, hyperactivity, physical pain, and the ego present an imposing array of problems.

    - Step 6: We see the need to get help. We become seekers.

    - Step 7--10. We discover the teachings of the saints and masters of the great faith traditions. They diagnose our problem: we are trying to achieve the core drive outside. They give us the good news: it can be realized inside. In fact, they tell us, it is already there waiting patiently for our discovery as the true self. They call it the Buddha, Image of God, child of God, the soul, love, or higher self. It doesn't matter what you call it. Just practice love and watch everything improve.

    - In summary, Steps 1--5 describe our pain. Steps 6--10 focus on healing that pain with love.

- Here is the key to understanding Steps 1--10: love is the great healer. It is more powerful than any painful problem. We know how to make it grow. As it grows, our pain is contained, reduced or eliminated.

- Enter yoga, the science that reveals a great hidden truth: *our bodies come equipped with a secret factory that manufactures a very special product, love.*

- The factory knows how to produce love and associated qualities: peace, joy, power, wisdom, and more. Here is how yoga works.

- The definition of yoga is union of the soul with Spirit through love, service, wisdom, and stillness.

- In the first stage of yoga, we make contact with the soul. This is the true self, a composite of healing qualities adding up to love. When we make contact with the soul, we experience expansion of love qualities. We feel better, become better people, and experience higher states of consciousness.

- In the second stage of yoga, the soul merges with Spirit. There is complete liberation from limitation and suffering and we experience the unlimited love of Spirit.

- In effect, when we practice yoga, we take our little soul love and merge it with the Big Love of Spirit.

- Yoga deals with energy or prana. It defines and locates the anatomy and physiology of the energy that corresponds to these principles. Let's take a look at the workings of this inner factory.

2. The Inner Factory: Prana, Pranayama, and the Chakras

- Prana is energy or life force. There are seven centers of concentrated prana in the spine and brain called chakras.

- Pranayama is control of prana by reversing the outward flow of life energy from the world, directing it to the higher chakras in the spine and brain. Energy goes from down and out to in and up.

- Following is a review of how pranayama relates to the ten steps.

- Steps 1--5: Energy goes down and out.

  - In ordinary consciousness, energy travels down the spinal cord and out to the world through the lower three chakras. This corresponds to steps 1--5 described above.

  - We are creatures of habit in thought, feeling, and action. Every thought, feeling, and act has a corresponding flow of energy and consciousness. When our thoughts, feelings, and actions are focused on the outer world, our energy and consciousness flow outward and get attached and habituated to the objects of that world: people, activities, events, and things. This results in material or ordinary consciousness.

- We do get some satisfaction but it is mixed in with the limitations and suffering inherent in material consciousness.

- We get a piece of the love we are looking for but it is mixed in with some undesirables: attachment, addiction, and reactivity.

- Steps 6--10: Energy goes in and up.

  - When we practice pranayama, energy flow is reversed from down and out to in and up, to the higher chakras in the spinal cord and brain. This results in expansion of the little love we can get from the world of people, activities, events, and things to the Big Love we get in superconscious states. This corresponds to steps 6-10 described above.

  - Yoga reverses the flow of energy and consciousness from down and out to in and up the spinal cord and brain where the soul is connected to Spirit. Here we experience Big Love, the superconsciousness we crave.

- There are four key yoga practices:

Four Yoga Practices

1. Bhakti Yoga or love

2. Karma Yoga or service

3. Jnana Yoga or wisdom

4. Raj Yoga or stillness.

- When we practice love, service, wisdom, and stillness, we bring energy and consciousness from the world and body to the higher centers in the spinal cord and brain where it is subjected to a purification process. Karma or debris is burned off. Our consciousness is refined to an ever-increasingly higher grade of peace, love, joy, power, and wisdom that we then give back to the world as evermore useful service.

- Through the patient daily practice of yoga, we slowly and gradually change our long-term thought, feeling, action, and corresponding energy patterns from down and out to in and up.

- We shift the locus of control from the outer world of people, activities, events, and things to the inner world of soul connected to Spirit.

- We learn how to eliminate debris and cultivate a higher grade of peace, love, joy, power, and wisdom in the inner factory of the higher centers in the spinal cord and brain.

- This is yoga, a way of dealing with painful problems through energy control or pranayama.

3. Pranayama Reduces Attachment, Addiction, and Reactivity

- The horizontal axis of people, objects, events, and things is not the cause of our misery. It is our attachment to these that gets us into trouble. When attached, we react. When we react, we are miserable.

- When prana is down and out in the world, we get attached, addicted, and reactive.

- When prana is in and up, we have the qualities in greater measure. We react less. We go through the same experience with less bounce. At mastery, we are even-minded under all conditions.

- Everything gets better when the energy is in and up the spinal cord. Our problems may still be there but we are not reacting as much or at all. This is the whole story of yoga, a story about ever-increasingly skillful pain management.

- Yoga is not easy. Pranayama is work. We can't just turn the boat around because it is a good idea. Our attachment-addiction to the outer world is very strong. Our reactive mind and emotions are powerful habits locked into well-worn brain grooves. Reversing the flow of prana from down and out to in and up takes time and effort. The results are subtle, slow, and cumulative, and sometimes it hurts.

- Sometimes we have to have more pain to have less pain. When we move energy from outer world attachments and habits to higher centers in the cord and brain, we will experience discomfort akin to withdrawal from any habit. We crave a return to our familiar comfort zone. The world as we know it calls: what have you done for me lately? If we answer that call too quickly, we lose the chance to burn off the impurities that keep us from experiencing higher states of consciousness. It is only in the higher chakras in the spinal cord and brain that we can burn off dross and create the more refined and distilled product of the secret inner factory: evermore pure and perfect love. This is the goal of yoga.

4. Pranayama Football

- There are two teams in the pranayama football game: Maya and the room of stillness.

- Maya is the world calling you to familiar habits that keep you from doing vertical axis work.

- Imagine you are in meditation and experiencing a good result. You are in the room of stillness, absorbing the higher vibrations of peace, joy, love, power, and wisdom available only there. You enjoy the experience. You know you are doing good. You resolve to stay in meditation and go deeper.

- Now comes an impulse or idea consistent with one of your well-traveled brain grooves, usually in the form of a person or activity in the horizontal axis: find a friend, watch television, check your e-mail, go for a walk, shop, eat something, and so forth. This is maya calling you to familiar habits, which keep you from doing this work.

- There is some fire here, some heat in the pranayama football game between the refrigerator of life and the room of stillness. Here are a few of the battles.

Maya	Room of stillness
Horizontal axis	Vertical axis
Outer World	Inner World
Energy down and out	Energy in and up
Lower three chakras	Upper four chakras
Ordinary consciousness	Superconsciousness
Little peace, joy, love, power, and wisdom	Big Peace, Joy, Love, Power, Wisdom
Ego	Soul connected to Spirit
Action	Stillness
Locus of control outside	Locus of control inside
Suffering	Transcendence
Fear	Love
Terror at the abyss	Omniscient Love

- In the tug of war between maya and the room of stillness, stay in the room of stillness as long as you can even when you are uncomfortable---*especially* when you are uncomfortable. It is in this heat---this friction---that the magic happens, where dross is burned off, and where consciousness is refined. Sit with this heat. This is the key to yoga.

- Watch this pranayama football game. It's a good game. You win some. You lose some. Persevere and you will win more than you lose. Eventually, your energy locks into the upper four chakras. Stillness takes over. You expand. You feel the unfathomable peace, pure unconditional love, and ecstatic joy of the soul connected to Spirit. You score a touchdown.

5. The Fourfold Pathway of Yoga

- Love, service, wisdom, and stillness are the pathways to God.

- When a yogi is in alignment, these four conditions are met.

  1. Wisdom: Our mind is locked in affirmations of wisdom.

  2. Love: Our heart is immersed in love.

  3. Action: We serve all of humanity without attachment to outcome.

  4. Stillness: Our consciousness is centered and still.

- Place all of your attention on love, service, wisdom, and stillness.

- When you find yourself out of alignment, when you are reacting in an unfavorable way, bring your car to The Shop. The Supreme Mechanic will realign your love, service, wisdom, and stillness wheels. He or She will tell you, "Upgrade your program on the fourfold path of yoga. Everything will eventually fall back into place."

6. The Ultimate Mind Body Technique: Pranayama

- Pranayama is a pain management technique for any kind of pain: physical, mental, emotional, interpersonal, or spiritual. How does this work?

- Pranayama helps us move our energy, consciousness, and mind from our identification and attachment to the world, body, and drama to the soul connected to Spirit.

- The result is a shift from unnecessary reactivity to an ever-increasingly powerful base of peace, strength, courage, compassion, and associated healing qualities within.

- As healing qualities expand, we react less. We may not be able to get rid of the inevitable suffering of life, but reducing and eliminating reactivity is a major stride forward in skillful pain management.

- Moving energy from down and out to in and up is a new way of looking at problem solving. Pranayama is a part of the solution to every problem.

- To become a more skillful pain manager, add pranayama to your tool kit.

7. Yoga Practice in the Moment: Neutralizing The Waves

- A yogi is even-minded under all conditions. We can't do it because of our reactivity, but this is the work of yoga. Our energy is wavy. Yoga neutralizes the waves.

- Watch your reactions.

    a. Are you prone to argument, debate, or defensiveness when stressed or provoked?
    b. Is your mind restless, hyperactive, and have a life of its own?
    c. Do you suffer from excessive fear, worry, insecurity, and doubt?
    d. Are your emotions out of control?
    e. Are you habituated and addicted to the people, objects, places, things, and events of the world?
    f. Are you a hyperactivity junky, constantly running on the horizontal axis, with no time built into your program for contemplation and meditation?

- Yoga neutralizes these waves. It helps us turn it down a notch so we can enter a difficult situation with even-mindedness. When we practice love, service, wisdom, and stillness, we react less. At mastery, we are even-minded under all conditions.

- When you realize you are reacting poorly and want to shift gears:

1. Stop

2. Breathe

3. Present moment

4. Affirm: love, service, wisdom, and stillness.

8. Roll the Wheel

- Review The House on p. 315.

- The first floor of the house is compelling. It captures all of our attention, sucking our entire consciousness into its vortex.

- When we practice yoga, we face everything on the first floor and rise above it to the second floor, soul qualities and third floor, Spirit.

- This is done by rolling the wheel or practicing PMQ.

- P is our pain and problem, whatever is there. M and Q are the means toward transcendence.

- This is a very simple formula, but it's difficult to do. It requires *patient daily practice, moment to moment, for the duration.*

- Everyday we use the circumstances of our life as the springboard for the work. We don't change anything. We just go about our business and roll the wheel. That's it.

- If you do this work, you become a more skillful pain manager, expand healing power, and evolve. You feel better, become a better person, and experience higher states of consciousness.

- PMQ is the essential healing principle or e = mc2 of all psychosocial, spiritual, and religious healing systems

9. Omniscient Love Vs Terror At The Abyss

- The ego has no root or connection. It remains separated, isolated, an island unto itself. It fears even a little change, sensing it might unravel to the abyss, break into a thousand pieces, or be annihilated.

- The soul connected to Spirit is locked in Omniscient Love: safe, secure, and immortal.

- The ultimate battle is between Omniscient Love and terror at the abyss. PMQ is the means of conducting this battle. If we keep practicing M and Q, we slowly move from the world to Spirit, from maya to God, and from fear to safety. See chapter 51, p. 354, in this workbook for more on this topic.

10. Mental Yoga Technique

- Yoga is merging the soul with Spirit through love, service, wisdom, and stillness. Mental yoga is keeping our needle of attention on these four disciplines.

- We can practice mental yoga every day, every moment, at all times, in all situations.

- Practice the following steps in the morning when you get up and any time during the day when you have a moment between tasks.

- We have to focus on our tasks, but we can practice this technique so we will not be totally immersed in the world.

  1. Gently focus your attention at the spiritual eye, the point just above and between the eyebrows. This pulls energy inward and upward.

  2. Open up your heart.

  3. Visualize a saint, a master, light, or any manifestation of Spirit that arouses your devotion. Ask for help.

  4. Affirm love, service, wisdom, and stillness.

Points to Remember

- We want Big Love and try to find it on the horizontal axis of people, activities, events, and things. This is impossible. We can get a little of the love we crave from the outer world, but Big Love can only be found inside. Yoga provides the scientific method for getting inside. The method is pranayama or energy control.

- Pranayama is not just an idea. It is a practice involving the movement of energy. It changes our pattern of thought, emotion, action, and corresponding flow of life force.

- Pranayama is work. It requires discipline. It takes time. When you practice yoga, results are slow and cumulative. Results occur while you think nothing is happening.

- Unconditional love is part of the solution to every problem, but this is not easy. Energy does not necessarily flow in that direction; it contracts, gets tied up in knots, and gets stuck in dark places. Pranayama helps reverse this trend and return the flow of energy to its natural, free-flowing expansive state.

- Attention and concentration are integral to the practice of yoga. We are inundated by sensory input. Our attention is distracted by TV, the Internet, computers, smartphones, and more. Success in all fields come from concentration, which usually stems from deep interest. It's amazing what you can accomplish if you concentrate fully and avoid distraction. Yoga shows us how to develop our attention and concentration muscles.

- The ego is about self-importance, attachment, and consequent emotional reactivity. It keeps us attached to our story and makes everything bigger. The hook is *likes and dislikes or attraction and repulsion*. We want the good and try to avoid the bad and ugly. Both sides keep us in the drama. The physiology and anatomy of this is energy going down and out into the world where it attaches to things and outcomes. Yoga reverses this trend by moving energy in and up the spine towards one unified love.

- Love, service, wisdom, and stillness create heat, a karma-burning furnace of sorts. Love burns karma---mine, yours, and ours. Or, if you prefer, healing qualities are more powerful than any painful problem.

- In the largest sense, we are addicted to the world. Yoga pranayama moves energy from our worldly attachments to the higher centers in the spinal cord and brain where we find the hidden treasure and the secret of all creation: God has hidden Himself as the peace, love, and joy we crave in the body temple itself. Moving energy in and up the spine to the brain and spiritual eye is more holy than any place of pilgrimage.

- The body is the ultimate place of pilgrimage. The spine is the holiest sight. We worship or have respect for saints, masters, stories, and deities but we don't give the same respect to our body temple: our thumb, nose, or heart. But the human body is the ultimate place of pilgrimage and the spinal axis the holiest sight in the body. The higher chakras in the spine and brain correspond to higher states of consciousness.

- I don't care about position or projects. I just want to be in Your heart. I respond with love no matter what the world or body does. This is Bhakti Yoga.

- My mind, my love, and my activity are at Your service. This is Karma Yoga.

- I lock my mind in the wisdom of the ages. This is Jnana Yoga.

- In stillness, my love expands until love is all there is. This is Raj Yoga.

- We need training in the workings of the secret inner factory where the soul connects to Spirit, where little love transforms to Big Love. The Big Love we are looking for is actually in the upper four chakras of the spine and brain.

- The game is Love and Infinity. I am little love seeking Big Love in a romance with the Infinite.

- This entire workbook is yoga in one format or another.

Chapter 31

Transformation of Emotion

- Please review chapter 23, Transformation of Emotion, in *Healing Power Revised,* pp. 345-357. This chapter describes a four-step technique we can use to skillfully manage painful emotions that do not respond fully to the other methods described in this work. Following is a review of this material and some additional points and exercises.

- Most of us do everything we can to avoid emotional pain. We don't know how to ride the pain waves, extract the necessary lessons, and move on.

- Instead we run, escape, hide, minimize, delay, avoid, numb, distract, distance, control, and manipulate.

- We deny and repress our painful problems into the body and subconscious where they are stored in latent form as negative energy waiting for recognition and work.

- We express our unresolved painful problems in destructive and abusive ways toward others.

- We indulge in self-destructive, addictive behaviors: eating, drinking, and drugging ourselves to the brink of mental, emotional, and physical exhaustion time and time again, looking for pain relief but making things worse.

- Painful emotional problems are like hot potatoes. A hot potato lands in our lap. It is too hot to handle so we flip it to our friends, partners, children, strangers, or enemies. They don't like it so they flip the hot potato back to us; most of the time, they add a few of their own. The result: an unnecessary, escalating, destructive fight. Sound familiar? Rare is the person, relationship, or family that does not do this. What to do?

- We need to learn how to stay alone, sit with and ride emotional pain waves, and let them teach. The first step is letting the story unfold. Then we need to spiritualize the story by infusing it with healing qualities.

- Before you proceed, please read the next section on risk.

Risk

- Processing raw emotional pain into self-knowledge is not for everybody. Opening a dialogue with emotional pain can be frightening. When we stand alone and ride the pain waves, there is likely to be considerable resistance. We should never underestimate how frightful this may be. We should never push anybody into such a process.

- Some cannot and should not engage in exploring their pain in such a manner without seeking professional help; it might flood their defenses and cause alarm or panic. In such circumstances, the individual can work with the other techniques described in this work. If you feel that processing emotional pain to gain self-knowledge is too intense, please avoid it at this point and consult with a professional counselor.

Processing Painful Emotion into Self-Knowledge

- This process is reviewed on pp. 351-355 in *Healing Power Revised*. The technique applies to any emotion:

  a. Create a safe healing space.
  b. Ask for help from your Higher Power.
  c. Let the story unfold.
  d. Spiritualize the story.

- Following is a review of some key principles involved in letting the story unfold and spiritualizing the story.

Let the Story Unfold
The Pain Story

- The first phase of healing is letting the pain story unfold. We allow painful emotions to surface so they can tell their story.

- Our stories are a complex mix of great, good, bad, ugly, terrible, right, wrong, distorted, painful, heroic, humor, success, failure, gain, loss, and more.

- The painful part of the story can be tiny, mild, medium, severe, or huge.

- Our pain can start with a seed thought that creates a storm; the pain feeds itself into a ruminative fury.

- It can be chronic, low-grade pain that smolders for years, or for some of us it can go from 0 to 60 in a fraction of a second.

- Emotional pain manifests as anxiety, anger, depression, fear, guilt, shame, embarrassment, humiliation, rejection, loss, resentment, and much more. These feelings can add up, overlap, and overwhelm our best defense, drain our energy, and lock us up. The pain story can be fierce. What to do?

- "You cannot stop the waves, but you can learn to surf." Jon Kabat-Zinn

- The first step in healing the pain story is acceptance. We ride the pain waves just as they are. We accept and validate it all.

- Surfing or riding emotional pain waves is not easy. A pain wave has its own way and time, a kind of natural rhythm to it. When we let a feeling have its playing time, it is in control and we are not. The waves come, have their way with us, and go on their own schedule. We can't successfully make it go faster, slower, or not go at all. We don't like this arrangement, but often the quickest way to get rid of it is to enter the feeling at its very center. We are afraid of this kind of surrender. However, by accepting and riding the pain wave, we get crucial information, messages, and even wisdom.

- Emotions are packed with meaning and purpose, story and self-knowledge, lessons and qualities. We need to extract this knowledge and move on. If we don't do this work, emotional pain waves may get bigger and cause even more trouble.

- While it is good to find out what our pain is about, we don't want to identify with it, ruminate on it, and get stuck there. When you have completed the first phase of healing, let the story unfold, switch gears to the second phase of healing: spiritualize the story. We transform the pain story to a healing story by infusing it with healing qualities.

Spiritualize the Story
The Healing Story

- The first phase of healing is let the story unfold.

- The second phase of healing is spiritualize the story. In this phase, painful emotions are reduced and replaced by strength, courage, endurance, love, compassion, understanding, forgiveness, peace, harmony, and a host of other Love-qualities.

- The healing story trumps the pain story, takes over the dominant position in consciousness, and determines our true identity as peace, Love, joy, power, and wisdom manifested as serene and compassionate service to humanity.

- Healing qualities are the spiritual solution to any pain, problem, conflict, symptom, disease, or disability. Guided by healing qualities, the story unfolds in the direction of love.

- When we let the story unfold and spiritualize the story, the emotional pain wave has a half-life and ultimately disappears, leaving in its wake, the love-qualities we need.

- The degree to which love is in charge of our story will determine our direction, the quality of our interactions, and the quality of our experience.

- Bear in mind that transformation of emotion will not eliminate the inevitable suffering of life---illness, old age, the unknown, and death---but it does help us contain, reduce, and eliminate unnecessary mental restlessness and emotional reactivity.

Exercises

1. **Self-Knowledge**

   - Review pp. 354-5 in *Healing Power Revised*. Here you will find an example of how to transform painful emotion into self-knowledge. Although Joe's problem may be minor compared to many, we can apply the same principles to more severe problems.

2. **Balance the Pain And Healing Story**

   - When we ride the pain waves and let the story unfold, we discover where we need to do some work. We find our issues, problems, weaknesses, and flaws. There is a risk however of dwelling too long in the pain story. We can get stuck in rumination or negative cyclical thinking. It isn't helpful to commune with our pain when all we are doing is repeating the same thoughts.

- How will you know when you have finished letting the story unfold and are ready to spiritualize the story?

- Watch your thoughts as you journal or take your emotional pain out for a walk. There will likely be a lot of repetitive thoughts, but interspersed with these repetitions, will be some new insights. As long as there is new information coming through the repetitions, there is likely a need to continue letting the story unfold. When there is no new information coming through, you are probably at the end of that round or layer of work. Then you can spiritualize the story. If there is another layer of work buried in the subconscious but not ready to come out now, it will come out later.

- In summary, when pain is telling your story, there will be a lot of new thoughts. When you have completed the pain story, there are no new thoughts, only ruminations. Then move to the healing story.

- Getting the right balance between the pain and healing story is not easy, and sometimes it's impossible.

- Some dwell too long in the pain story and get stuck in rumination or negative cyclical thinking. All of us know people who are stuck in their pain story and unable to get out. All you hear from them is the problem and painful side of their story.

- Others move too quickly into spiritualizing the story and miss finding some of the negativity that needs to be dug out. We have all met people who are "very spiritual," but filled with tension and darkness. They have spiritualized their story but have not spent enough time letting the story unfold. Consequently their subconscious problems, flaws, and conflicts weigh them down and interfere with the love they profess. This is easy to do. No one wants to go to the dentist. Yet here we are our own mental dentist, drilling into the dark hidden recesses of our consciousness, looking for problem areas that need work. This hurts. It's much more fun to spend time with the healing qualities: patience, kindness, compassion, love, and so forth.

- There is a tension between letting the story unfold, where we give our emotional pain time and space, and spiritualizing the story where we shift gears and focus on a healing quality. We need to swing in and out of both. This is an ongoing process. Just look for and try to approximate the right dose of each.

- We can trust the intelligent healing power inside. It will let us know if we are dwelling on the pain too much and need to move to the healing story. On the other hand, if we are avoiding pain and need to continue working with the inner dentist, this too will make itself known. Listen to the still small loving voice within.

    a. Analyze your pain and healing stories. Observe how they interact.
    b. Are you stuck in your pain story?
    c. Does your story have enough healing qualities?
    d. Do you need to practice the two phases of healing?

1. Let the story unfold

2. Spiritualize the story

3. Meditation And Transformation Of Emotion

- The goal of meditation is stillness, but sometimes, when we try to meditate, all we experience is our problems. Bad habits, hard feelings, conflicts with others, the need to forgive, insecurity, worries, resentment, and a host of other problems beg our attention and recognition. We can try to meditate but sometimes these problems require work, which must be done before we can get into the room of stillness.

- If this is the case, we may have to switch gears from meditation to transformation of emotion. We may have to let the story unfold and spiritualize the story. Then we can meditate and get into the room of stillness.

- For example, it is difficult or impossible to achieve stillness when we are angry and harbor resentment against those who have done us wrong. We may need to sit with our pain and let the story unfold to discover who remains in our inner prison. Then, if we choose to do so, we can spiritualize the story, in this case applying forgiveness to these individuals, thus liberating them from the inner prison. Then we can get into the room of stillness and absorb the deep healing vibrations that reside only there.

- When you try to meditate but find yourself ruminating on your problems, try the following method.

  a. Stop
  b. Breathe
  c. Get in the present moment
  d. Let the story unfold
     - Observe. See what is there.

     - Note the medley of thoughts, feelings, and bodily sensations. Embedded within these sensations, there may be a story you need to discover, lessons you need to learn, or tests you need to pass. *I am afraid of loss, humiliation, and rejection. I feel a pit in my stomach. I am not sure I can do this. I don't care. I want a drink. I am angry at my girlfriend.*

     - Ride any pain wave that shows up. Stay with the wave as it grows. Ride it to its peak. Don't try to escape. Don't jump off. Let it all come out. See the illustration on p. 106

     - Breathe into the pain. Use the breath to steady yourself as you ride the pain wave, trusting it will naturally subside if you stay with it.

     - You may feel like you can't do this or that you are going to break, but most of the time, if you ride the pain wave and get the necessary lessons, it will dissolve.

- If you are new at this and feel overwhelmed, it may be wise to seek professional help.

e. Spiritualize the story

- When you have extracted the necessary information, infuse the pain story with healing qualities.

- Review the list of healing qualities on p. 79. Choose the ones you need for this part of your story.

- Most of the time we need more love, compassion, understanding, forgiveness, strength, courage, patience, kindness, or humor.

- These qualities will reduce and finally dissolve the pain story.

f. Now we can meditate, enter the room of stillness, and participate in the deep healing that occurs only there.

- See the diagram on p. 242. Meditation and transformation of emotion are very powerful tools. Together they help us transform painful problems into ever-increasing peace, love, joy, power, and wisdom expressed through quiet acts of humble service to all humanity.

Transformation Of Emotion And Meditation

Let the story unfold

↓

Spiritualize the story

↓

Meditation

↓

Room of stillness

↓

Expansion

↓

The Big Space

↓

Let the story unfold

↓

Repeat

↓

Ever-increasing peace, joy, love, power, and wisdom

↓

Ever-increasingly useful service to all of humanity

---

4. Release Negative Energy from its Subconscious Prison

- When we repress our problems, they take up residence secretly in the subconscious mind and body. They occupy space, tie us in knots, create tension, and make us gloomy. This repressed energy wants to be released from its subconscious prison to join the free flowing river of peace, love, joy, power, and wisdom.

- Stop running, resisting, and repressing, all of which perpetuate trouble, increase tension, and magnify rumination.

- You have the intelligence to understand and the power to overcome. Trust the healing power within. It knows what to do. Armed with this knowledge and faith:
  a. Face your pain.
  b. Gently name it.
  c. Relax into it.
  d. Be a compassionate, nurturing presence for the pain.

e. Breathe into it and affirm the following: *soft, yield, open, surrender.*

f. If you are afraid, pray. Ask for help and grace so you can stare down the monster and reduce its power.

g. Talk to a friend, partner, family member, or counselor.

h. Journal, draw, walk, or dance.

i. Go to AA, church, synagogue, mosque, or other healing ceremonies.

j. Create a ritual to honor your feelings.

k. Practice progressive muscle relaxation or do a body scan.

l. Practice affirmations.

m. Contemplate wisdom pearls from sacred texts.

n. Meditate.

o. Practice mindfulness.

p. Practice yoga.

q. Work, volunteer, or help others.

r. Eat popcorn and watch TV.

Points to Remember

- The mind is like a jukebox. It plays a record sometimes at our request and sometimes against our will. Most of the time when a record plays against our will, it is because there is unfinished business in that domain. If we let the story unfold and then spiritualize the story, we bring the story under our control and lay down a record that can now be used for wisdom and power when we need it. Instead of the record playing against our will, we play the record when we choose to do so.

- In ordinary consciousness, a problem is like a big fish in a small pond. It creates lots of waves. As you advance, after you have done some deep inner work, you enter the ocean of ever-expanding space where the same sized fish has less---and ultimately no---effect on you. At some point, you will be ready for anything: pain, change, the unknown, and death.

- You have completed your review of the fifteen methods. In the next chapter, you will learn how to create a balanced healing program.

Chapter 32

A Balanced Healing Program

- Please review chapter 35, A Balanced Healing Program, in *Healing Power Revised*, pp. 481-488. Following is a review of the principles from this chapter with a few additional points to remember.

- This work describes fifteen methods that help us manage the inevitable suffering of life and our reaction to it. These are the methods we can turn to when doctors and other health care professionals cannot solve the problem.

The Methods

Horizontal Axis: external work

1. People
2. Activities
3. Belief systems

Vertical Axis: internal work

4. Affirmations
5. Habit transformation
6. Progressive muscle relaxation
7. Breathwork
8. Contemplation
9. Meditation
10. Prayer
11. Mindfulness
12. Practicing the presence of God
13. Service
14. Yoga
15. Transformation of emotion

- These methods are described in detail in *Healing Power Revised* and elaborated on in this workbook.

- Following is a brief review of the fifteen methods.

- Remember, these methods work no matter the size, shape, or complexity of your problem.

- For chronic, severe problems, we will need to practice these methods in a variety of combinations for years.

Horizontal Axis: External Work

1. People

- When we are in pain, we instinctively turn to trustworthy loved ones, friends, family, or counselors. We tell our story seeking understanding, validation, comfort, and relief.

- We have a deep inherent need to give and receive love, compassion, understanding, patience, kindness, and humor. These qualities are the healers and pain managers.

- The idea is to have the best possible network of like-minded, warm, wise, and compassionate people: the right people, at the right time, at the right dose.

- Find a support network of like-minded people.

- Tell your pain story to a counselor, mentor, sponsor, trusted family member, or friend.

- Be understood, validated, and supported.

- Give and receive love.

- Spiritualize your relationships.

  a. Do you have enough support?
  b. Who is in your life you can really talk to?
  c. Do you spend too much time with people?
  d. Are you codependent?
  e. Is your *people dose* too high or too low?

2. Activities

- Constructive, meaningful activities contribute mightily to pain management and healing.

- We need a variety of such activities: school, training, volunteering, work, hobbies, culture, exercise, martial arts, sports, the Internet, TV, radio, music, culture, reading, the arts, and more.

- We can spend too much or not enough time in activities.

  a. What is your day like?
  b. Do you have enough to do?
  c. Is your *activity dose* too high or too low?

3. Belief System

- It doesn't matter whether your belief system is secular, spiritual, fixed, or opened as long is it gives meaning, purpose, and positive thought. We need a strong, healthy belief system rooted in love qualities expressed as service to humanity. This is monumentally important for pain management and healing.

    a. How do you understand the meaning and purpose of life?
    b. Do you have a way to understand the things that happen?
    c. Do you have a spiritual program or philosophy of life?
    d. Do you get support and wisdom from church, synagogue, mosque, a twelve-step program, DBT (dialectical behavior therapy), or other healing ceremonies?
    e. Do you have a service project that helps other people and benefits your community?

- Many people make the mistake of trying to solve all of their problems on the horizontal axis of people, activities, and belief systems. Some problems can only be resolved by doing some inner work.

- When you have done everything you can in the world of people, activities, and belief systems, and you are still in pain, there are twelve additional methods you can use to help you with your painful problem. Methods 4--15 describe the work we can do internally. These are the methods of the vertical axis.

- When we learn how to balance external and internal practices, we become more skillful pain managers. Healing qualities expand. We evolve at maximum speed.

Vertical Axis: Internal Work

4. Affirmations

- The mind has great power to do harm or good.

- The science of healing affirmations teaches us how to apply the inherent power of thought for healing and pain management.

- Thoughts impact disease and healing.

- Practice affirmations for healing body, mind, and soul.

- Fill your brain with powerful positive thoughts and wisdom pearls.

- Keep your mind locked in affirmations rooted in the healing qualities.

- Let healing qualities be your guide during good and difficult times.

5. Habit Transformation

- All of us have a mix of good and bad habits.

- For full recovery and deep healing, we must release the energy captured by bad habits and transfer this power to new good habits.

- Cultivate the habits of a seeker: the fifteen methods.

- Cultivate the habits of a sage: one hundred healing qualities.

6. Breathwork

- Breath is always available.

- We can use it to get centered and calm.

- Breathwork helps dissolve painful emotions, curb addiction and craving, and convert mental restlessness to peace of mind.

- Practice any one or a combination of breathing techniques.

7. Progressive Muscle Relaxation

- Progressive muscle relaxation calms the body and mind through tensing and relaxing the muscles.

- In addition, when the body and mind are relaxed, it is easier to practice other methods such as contemplation, meditation, and mindfulness.

- Progressive muscle relaxation helps reduce stress, anxiety, fear, panic, depression, insomnia, and fatigue.

- You might also do a body scan.

8. Contemplation

- We do not need a Higher Power or religion to practice contemplation. All we need is some quiet time and our favorite wisdom.

- The wisdom can come from any source, secular or spiritual.

- Learn how to crack open the shell of a wisdom pearl to release its hidden secrets and soothing healing powers.

- Learn how to "fill your brain with wisdom" and how to "sit with a saint."

- Convert such great qualities as compassion---or any other healing quality or idea---from the surface superficiality of mere words to feeling, experience, and action.

9. Meditation

- Right now, there is a place inside of us that is absolutely still and serene but our mental restlessness bars us from entering. Meditation is the solution to this problem.

- When we learn how to meditate, we learn how to slow down the mind, replace negative with positive thought, and eventually get into the room of stillness.

- The experience of peace in the room of stillness surpasses understanding. Here you will find unfathomable beauty, joy, compassion, light, energy, power, elation, and ecstasy.

- In meditation: Negative → Positive → Stillness → Higher Consciousness → Infinity

- Learn how to meditate. Experience deep healing in the room of stillness. This doctor charges no fee.

10. Prayer

- Ask for help from your Higher Power.

- Ask for courage, strength, humility, acceptance, forgiveness, perseverance, self-control, transcendence, wisdom, and more.

11. Mindfulness

- Mindfulness is paying attention in the here and now to one moment at a time.

- Here you will learn how to stay in the present and ride the pain waves just as they are, without adding unnecessary reactivity.

- This technique has four steps:
    a. Stop
    b. Breathe
    c. Present moment
    d. Reframe to The Witness, Warrior, Service, School, Entertainment, or Ritual.

- When we rotate these frames, life becomes one continuous sacred ritual, offering up its knowledge and lessons, entertainment and joy, and opportunities to love and serve.

12. Presence Of God

- This is the same as mindfulness for those who have a personal relationship with God.

- Practice the presence of God as peace, courage, strength, perseverance, compassion, love, understanding, or any one of the healing qualities you need at the moment.

13. Service

- In service to humanity, we discover who we really are and what really helps.

- We come to know love as the power that heals the self first and then others. As we change ourselves, we change the world.

- The healing power of love is a magnet that draws all good things to it.

- It is not what you do but how you do it. Add love to every action.

- The way is small acts of gentle, humble service without attachment to outcomes.

- When we help others, we help ourselves. Healing power grows. We evolve.

14. Yoga

- Yoga is union of the soul with Spirit through:

  1. Love: Bhakti Yoga
  2. Service: Karma Yoga
  3. Wisdom: Jnana Yoga
  4. Stillness: Raj Yoga

- We can know God or Brahma through love, service, meditation, and wisdom but not until we reduce the restlessness and excesses of the body, mind, emotions, desires, and ego by practicing one or a combination of these four yogas.

- The science of yoga teaches us to still the waves of mental restlessness, excessive material desire, and emotional reactivity in both meditation and activity.

- Practice love, service, wisdom, and stillness.

15. Transformation Of Emotion

- Emotions are a rich source of information. If we are able to experience sadness or anger without excessive use of alcohol, drugs, food, gambling, sex, or violence, we may discover why we are experiencing these feelings in the first place.

- Painful emotions are a part of the normal, natural, intelligent healing process. When we learn how to process emotion into self-knowledge, we gain strength and peace.

- Emotions tell a story with lessons having to do with the cultivation of healing qualities. When we finish the story, it will stop coming up.

- Learn how to:
  a. Let the pain story unfold.
  b. Spiritualize the story: infuse the pain story with healing qualities.

LOCUS OF CONTROL

- If you spend most of your time in methods 1–3, your locus of control is primarily outside. Most of us start here.

- When life presents overwhelming problems, it is often necessary to do some inner work. As you begin to practice methods 4–15, healing qualities such as courage, peace, and strength slowly grow.

- As the qualities grow, your locus of control gradually shifts to your inner self. You become less dependent on the outer world of people, activities, events, and material things when you find inner peace, security, and contentment.

- At mastery, when your locus of control is deeply rooted inside, you will be even-minded under all conditions.

- For most of us, even-mindedness under all conditions is an affirmation, not a reality. On the way there, we can have fun with the challenge.

- Following are some exercises designed to help you create an individualized balanced healing program.

Exercises

1. The Keys to Skillful Pain Management

- When we do all the right things and it still hurts, it may be helpful to remember some key points. Please review chapter 13, Roll The Universal Healing Wheel, on p. 97 in this workbook. Here you will find key principles and exercises designed to help manage any painful problem skillfully. *These dynamics apply no matter the size or shape of our problem.* We need to understand and practice these principles even more when confronted with our biggest problems. Topics covered are:

  a. Roll The Wheel
  b. Hold PMQ in the same space
  c. Four stages of growth
  d. What to do when pain does not go away
  e. Embrace the gap: getting comfortable with the uncomfortable
  f. Find your power in the story
  g. Ride the pain wave
  h. A mindfulness exercise: two doors
  i. Learn to trust the process
  j. Deep suffering and deep healing: how far are you prepared to go
  k. Start slow and build to one continuous sacred ritual
  l. How to manage a backslide
  m. Physical healing and spiritual healing
  n. Pain and healing: a marriage of wisdom
  o. Saints are skillful pain managers

p.   A palette of colors

2. Balance Horizontal and Vertical Axis Options

Horizontal Axis: Action and Distraction

- We always want to get rid of our pain in the easiest possible way, usually by engaging our family, friends, work, sports, hobbies, entertainment, nature, and possessions. This is good.

- Action and distraction in the outer world of people, activities, events, and things have their time and place. It works. Our pain is contained, reduced, or eliminated.

- Often however, this is not enough, doesn't work, or makes things worse.

Vertical Axis: Sit with the Pain and Go In

- Sometimes we need to sit with the pain as the teacher and stimulant for the growth of healing qualities.

- When we do this, the pain may get worse before it gets better. This is hard to accept and even harder to do, but the reward is great.

- When we practice transformation of emotion, affirmations, prayer, meditation, contemplation, and other vertical axis methods, we gain peace, power, strength, compassion, love, understanding, humility, wisdom, and more.

Balance

- There is tension between finding something positive like a person, activity, event, or thing on the horizontal axis and giving space and time for inner being work on the vertical axis. We need to swing in and out of both.

- Balanced healing occurs when we find the correct ratio of time on the horizontal and vertical axes.

- How do we know when to distract ourselves through action or sit with the pain?

- If we try to use the horizontal axis to solve problems that must be resolved internally, we become frustrated, angry, depressed, and anxious. Some people develop codependency, bad habits, and unhealthy attachments. Many become hyperactivity junkies, immersing themselves in activities from morning to night, trying to avoid the work that must be done inside.

- Some use vertical axis options like meditation and spiritual study as a way to escape painful issues needing work on the horizontal axis.

- Over time we can learn through trial and error how to navigate our way through and balance horizontal action-distraction and vertical axis options.

- The balance point varies according to our stage of life and responsibilities. If you are a parent with young children or in medical school, there will be very little time for meditation and contemplation. However, one can always practice mindfulness, breathwork, and affirmations.

- Choose the method that fits your need at the moment. Balance horizontal and vertical axis methods. Practice these methods until they become your new mental habits locked in brain grooves that will not quit.

- Doctors try to prescribe the right medication, at the right dose, at the right time. The fifteen methods prescribed here are similar but you are the doctor. You prescribe the method and dose.

- Pay attention to the dose. When the dose is too low, we don't get the full effect. When we get too much, there are side effects. Through trial and error, we can discover the right method, at the right dose, at the right time.

3. Abyss Pain vs Time Release Pain

- In exercise 2 above, we discussed action-distraction versus sitting with the pain.

- We want to be able to sit with our pain and learn from it. Sometimes we can do this, but sometimes life presents complex and overlapping problems that overwhelm our defenses and bring us to the abyss.

- Abyss pain is dark, scary, and overwhelming. We are afraid of being swallowed, breaking into a thousand pieces, and being unable to put it together again.

- What is the best way to manage abyss pain or severe pain of any kind?

- When pain is very intense, we can balance methods in two categories:
  a. Methods that distract, soothe, and comfort.
  b. Methods that may cause the pain to get worse before it gets better.

- For the most part, soothing methods are people, activities, church, synagogue, mosque, AA meetings, other healing ceremonies, progressive muscle relaxation, breathwork, contemplation, prayer, affirmations, mindfulness, the presence of God, service, and yoga.

- Methods that may cause the pain to get worse before it gets better are meditation, habit transformation, and transformation of emotion.

- The combination of techniques we need on any particular day may vary depending on how we feel.

- When we feel strong and ready to take on some pain, we might schedule an hour for transformation of emotion. If an overwhelming pain wave emerges while doing deep inner work, we can shift gears and turn to more soothing methods: TV, popcorn, friends, twelve-step meetings, breathwork, and affirmations---until we are ready to go back inside.

- Although some might profit from scheduling an hour, others may prefer a less formal approach. For example, we can practice transformation of emotion and meditation for as long as we wish or until the pain is too intense, at which point we can shift to more soothing actions, like being with friends or going to the gym.

- We can move from emotional processing to being with a friend for dinner, to emotional processing, to watching television and eating popcorn, to prayer and meditation, to physical exercise, to going to a meeting, and so forth.

- With this balanced approach, we can learn how to:

  a. Move into pain we do not know.
  b. Release some of the pressure without breaking apart.
  c. Ride increasingly bigger pain waves.
  d. Control pain so pain does not control us.

- You will find more information on this topic in chapter 51, Omniscient Love and Terror at the Abyss, p. 354.

4. A Block of Marble and the Chisel of Wisdom: Chip, Chip, Chip (see illustration p. 254)

- Pain has a purpose: the cultivation of healing qualities and higher states of consciousness. This is a lot of work. Change is slow, painful, and difficult. It may seem overwhelming.

- Try the following metaphor. We start with a big marble block and the chisel of wisdom.

- The marble block is the sum total of our being. We are a combination of problems and the Image of God or Buddha.

- The chisel of wisdom is the methods (M) and qualities (Q).

- *Chip, chip, chip.* Begin the process of carving out the image. The image is The Buddha = The Image of God = one hundred healing qualities and higher states of consciousness.

- When we practice the methods, the qualities get bigger and our problems get smaller.

- Having fifteen methods is an advantage. One day you might practice breathwork and affirmations; the next day, mindfulness, the presence of God, or prayer.

- Choose the method that works for you in the moment. Change methods according to your need and feeling.

- Work your way through the fifteen methods in any combination, and go around again.

- Throw the PMQ book at your problem, and be patient.

- Give yourself time to heal.

- Be patient, disciplined, and persevere.

- Don't put a schedule on how long the pain will last.

- Hang in there. Work the condition, however long or severe, and wait for the qualities to appear.

- Don't identify with the pain or problem. Identify with the qualities. This is your true self.

- Practice peace no matter what.

- Practice positive thought no matter what.

- Practice the qualities no matter what.

- Forgive yourself no matter your mistakes or problems.

- Forgive others.

- Practice compassion for others.

- Practice compassion for yourself.

- Get some momentum and keep going.

- At some point, you will see the Image of God or Buddha manifesting as ever-expanding love qualities and higher states of consciousness.

A Block of Marble and The Chisel of Wisdom

5. David and Goliath

- The phrase *David and Goliath* denotes an underdog situation, a contest where a smaller, weaker opponent faces a much bigger, stronger adversary.

- All of us have David and Goliath moments. Problems seem too big, overwhelming, frightening, even terrifying.

- Remember this: the universal healing wheel applies to any problem: tiny, small, medium, large, or huge. The rules are the same for big problems. It just takes longer.

- We can practice PMQ for the most severe, complex, long-term, deeply embedded problems: chronic illness or disability, brutal reality, the cave of darkness, or the dark night of the soul.

- Big tests require more work, time, patience, and discipline. When we do the work, the reward is even greater: healing qualities expand until they become unconditional. The soul merges with Spirit. Big Love takes over. We experience the peace that surpasses understanding, pure love, ecstatic joy. How grand!

6. Go to Your Room

- Sometimes, we have had enough. We get frustrated, irritable, angry, depressed, or anxious. There is no room in the inn. All the rooms are filled. We have no space. What to do?

- The best thing to do at a time like this is:
    a. Go to your room.
    b. Read "The Guesthouse" by Rumi, in *Healing Power, Revised*, p. 345.
    c. Practice transformation of emotion and meditation. These two powerful techniques clear the zone and create more space. See exercise 3 in the chapter on Transformation of Emotion in this workbook, p. 240-242.

7. Shifting the Locus of Control

- Please review chapter 8, Shifting the Locus of Control, *Healing Power Revised*, pp. 115--123.

- Following are some additional points to remember.

- Through a series of painful lessons, life teaches us that the unlimited peace, love, and joy we seek in the outer world, can and must ultimately be found within.

- This necessitates a shift in the locus of control from outside to inside.

- This model presents fifteen methods, three on the horizontal axis and twelve on the vertical axis.

- How much work we do on each axis is personal and individualized.

- Most of us do most of our healing and pain management work on the horizontal axis of people, activities, and belief system. This is good.

- The horizontal axis does give a little of the peace, love, and joy we crave, but the unlimited peace, love, and joy of the core drive, can only be found inside.

- For deeper healing, we need to do progressively more work on the vertical axis.

- Readiness is key. We are not ready for a deeper level of vertical axis work until we are ready for a deeper level. For example, no one is going to meditate in a consistent way until the timing is right.

- We must be motivated, comfortable, and ready for the next step in vertical axis work.

- This model attempts to speak to you at your current spot on that spectrum, recognizing your experience is universal.

- It hopes to receive you just where you are: at the brink between the outer world and the inner true self.

- It receives you at the doorway where the shift occurs and guides you to your inner being as the very thing you have been looking for the whole time.

- But you must be ready, and ready means *saturated with the world* to some degree. If not, you will go back again and again until you finally figure out what it will give you and what it won't give you.

- When you have finally had enough suffering, when you have a passionate desire to change, and when you are ready to do some work, you can upgrade your vertical axis practice. But you must be ready, world saturated, and hungry. Otherwise, the world or maya will have the predominance of your attention.

Points to Remember

- We want *Big Peace, Love, Joy, and Safety*, more time, and no pain. This is the core drive. We try to achieve the core drive in the outer world of people, activities, events, and things. This is impossible. On the physical plane, suffering is inevitable, time is limited, and death wins in the end.

- We can achieve little peace, love, joy, and safety in the outer world, but any attempt to get more on the physical plane leads to attachment, addiction, and reactivity.

- The saints bring us the good news: the *Big Peace, Love, Joy, and Safety* we seek is inside, waiting patiently for our discovery as the true self, Buddha, or Image of God. We can prove this to ourselves through direct personal experience when we practice vertical axis methods.

- You may not be able to control outer events, but you own the space within. It is your house. All the rooms belong to you. You can choose the furniture and the decorations. Why not fill your house with the attributes of love? Practice outer and inner methods in a healthy balance. You will see love fill the rooms of your house and surrounding space.

- Here is a quote from a member: "I don't do big pain alone. I thought I could do it myself. I can't. I do horizontal and vertical axis methods."

- Do the work on smaller problems now so when bigger ones come later, you will be ready.

- As you build your external world of people, activities, events, and things, you can also build an inner world of peace, power, strength, courage, and wisdom.

- Balance healing with horizontal and vertical axis methods. Cultivate love, compassion, acceptance, humility, faith, understanding, and forgiveness in response to your problems. Do this for years and decades. Love grows and takes new shapes and forms. We learn how to serve in ever-increasingly useful ways. There is no limit to love's creative powers.

The next section elaborates ten healing qualities in detail. You will study love, peace, humility, faith, courage, forgiveness, truth, intuition, oneness, and healing.

Part 4
Qualities

Chapter 33

Love

- Please review chapter 25 on Love in *Healing Power Revised*, pp. 363-382. Following is a review of this material with some additional points and exercises.

- *The essence of religion is the triumph of Love over pain.*

- We share a seemingly infinite variety of painful problems that we manage either unskillfully or skillfully. When we manage our problems unskillfully, we get stuck or go backwards. When we manage our pain skillfully, we hold our ground and move forward. When we respond to our problems with love, we are skillful pain managers. Love itself is the skillful pain manager.

- Love is greater than pain. To put this profound principle into practice, we need to define our terms and a means to carry it out.

- In this work, the pain can be any kind of pain or problem: physical, mental, emotional, interpersonal, or spiritual.

- Love is defined as one hundred healing qualities and higher states of consciousness.

- When we practice the recommended methods, we can hold love and pain in the same space. When we hold love and pain in the same space, love contains, reduces, or eliminates the pain and guides us through what is left. We do this by practicing PMQ or rolling the universal healing wheel.

- We turn the tables on our pain and make it work for rather than against us. We do this by using every painful problem---whether tiny, small, medium, large, or extreme---as a stimulant to expand our love until it is pure and unconditional. Love and pain alternate, overlap, and coexist throughout our lives but love wins in the end.

Exercises

1. Definition of Love

- In this work, Love is one hundred healing qualities and higher states of consciousness or superconsciousness.

- Superconsciousness is an unmistakable shift in consciousness sometimes described as the peace that surpasses understanding, pure love, ecstatic joy, unfathomable stillness, intuitive wisdom, a feeling of oneness with everything, and other wonderful expressions of Spirit. These experiences may last from a few minutes or hours to several days, but there is inevitably a return to ordinary consciousness unless one is a spiritual master.

- What is your definition of love?

- Have you ever had a superconscious experience. What was it like?

2. Love is a Diamond with Many Facets

- Omniscient Love is Infinitely Creative. There is no end to its variety of manifestations. Let Her in. Watch Her play throughout your day in an endless variety of ways.

- See *Healing Power Revised*, pp. 374-77 for a description of thirty ways to practice love.

- What would you add to this list?

3. The Love Field and the Material Field

- In this exercise, we will look at two overlapping fields: the material field and the love field.

- The material field and the love field occupy the same space and compete for our attention.

- Please review the following table. Here you will find some key characteristics of the two fields.

The Material Field	The Love Field
Many	One
Form	Formless
Visible	Invisible
The human condition: good, bad, ugly, great, and terrible	The Qualities and Higher States of Consciousness
Limitation, impermanence, suffering	The Changeless One
Duality and brutal reality	Safety, Security, and Immortality
Ordinary consciousness	Superconsciousness
Body	Soul
Reactivity	The Qualities
Limited peace, love, joy	Unlimited Peace, Love, Joy
Human love	Divine Love
Conditional love	Omniscient, Omnipotent, Omnipresent Love
Attraction and repulsion	Equanimity
Likes and dislikes	Love everyone equally
Separation	Oneness
Maya	God

- **The Material Field**

  a. This is the world as we know it in ordinary physical plane consciousness.
  b. It includes our people, activities, places, events, and things.
  c. It is the entirety of the human condition: good, bad, ugly, great and terrible.
  d. It has most or all of our attention.
  e. Our energy is trapped and addicted to this layer of reality.

- **The Love Field**

  a. The Love Field is a singular omnipresent power of pure, formless conscious energy.
  b. It inhabits all space, unifying and harmonizing everything in the universe.
  c. It is at once the source of everything and the link that connects all.
  d. It cannot be born, confined, limited, divided, or broken.
  e. It is eternal, immortal, changeless, and one.
  f. It is inside, outside, everywhere, extending forever in every direction, unifying all things and people.
  g. We do not enter this field. We are already in it. It is already in us. There is no separation. All is one.
  h. We live in this infinite ocean as a fish swims in water. The *water* is always right here offering peace, love, joy, wisdom, and safety.
  i. When we realize our oneness with the ocean, we know we are immortal, indivisible, and connected to all.

- The Love Field is also referred to as The Big Space, The Ocean, The Tao, Bliss, God, The Great Gift, The Pearl of Great Price, The True Secret.

- The Love Field is omnipresent. It occupies the same space as the material field. We are immersed in both fields at the same time.

- The two fields are like magnets. They pull us in opposite directions. Our consciousness is caught in the middle of this tug of war. We have a choice. Which magnet do we follow?

- We want to stay in The Love Field at all times no matter what the world or body is doing. This is equivalent to practicing unconditional love. This is difficult and sometimes impossible; there are a host of intruders on the physical plane that cause reactivity.

4. **Reactivity**

- Reactivity is the culprit. It throws us out of The Love Field. Like a magnet, it captures our attention and energy, pulling our consciousness out of The Love Field into the material field.

- For a detailed review of how reactivity operates, see step 5, Tools Become Barriers, in *Healing Power Revised*, pp. 56-66.

- Step 5 describes six power tools that help us achieve our inner and outer goals: thought, feeling, desire, the body, activity, and ego. However, in response to stress, the tools spin out of control, adding an additional layer of pain called reactivity.

- The six tools out of alignment are a universal problem. This misalignment pins us to the mat of the status quo. This is the root cause of much of our suffering. These are the add-ons to the inevitable suffering of life. These are the elements that pull us out of the Love Field:

  a. The restless mind
  b. Reactive emotions
  c. Excessive material desires, attachments, and bad habits
  d. Problems of the body
  e. Hyperactivity
  f. The ego

- The answer to the problem of reactivity can be found in The Love Field. The Love Field is always right here, everywhere present, inside and out, offering its gifts of unlimited healing qualities: peace, love, joy, power, wisdom, courage, strength, perseverance, and more.

- When we are thrown out of the Love Field by reacting to a provocative stressor, we get back to love as soon as we can. We do this by rolling the wheel.

  a. Practice PMQ: We see the problem, in this case, reactivity, pick a method and quality, and go to work.
  b. We work the quality until it reduces and replaces reactivity. Then we are back, comfortable and secure, in the Love Field.
  c. When thrown out again, we roll the wheel again.
  d. This back and forth yo-yo between two magnets---the reactivity of the material field and the healing qualities of the Love Field---results in ever-expanding love until love is all there is.

5. How Can You Know if You Are in the Love Field?

- We cannot escape the material field. Our job is to live in it and respond with love, to remain in the Love Field as much as possible. How can you know if you are in the Love Field? Ask yourself:

  a. Are my thoughts, feelings, desires, and actions permeated with love or something else?
  b. Is my mind restless or peaceful, positive, poised, and focused?
  c. Are my feelings out of control or am I calm and centered?
  d. Am I compelled by material desires, attachments and bad habits? Or am I content with what I have?
  e. Am I locked in a negative reaction, or are the healing qualities in charge: patience, kindness, compassion, understanding, forgiveness, humor, and more.

f. Do I love everyone equally, or am I favoring some over others on the basis of body type, personality, race, religion, nationality, sexual identity, economic class, educational level, politics, or other sources of division and separation?

g. Is the person I am with the most important person in the world?

h. Can you think of other criteria?

6. God's Will is Love

- God's will is always right here, right now, everywhere present, in The Love Field.

- Think of love as a powerful magnetic energy field with a will of its own, pulling and drawing us. Follow that direction. It is God's will.

- God's will is the love in every moment, detail, scene. Ask yourself, "What would love do?"

7. Human And Divine Love

- Please review pp. 364-368 in *Healing Power, Revised*. Here you will find a discussion of the connecting link between human and Divine Love. Following is a review of that material.

- Religions preach and masters teach Divine Love as the goal of human life. This exercise describes the process of using human relationships as a starting point for the cultivation of Divine Love. Here you will find a description of how to *expand and purify love* through horizontal and vertical axis methods. This is a difficult and sometimes painful process involving purification and transformation. The result, however, is profound and worth the struggle: ever-expanding healing qualities and superconscious love.

- We have an insatiable drive for unconditional love. We must have it. In the beginning, we look to family, friends, and lovers to satisfy our craving for this perfect love. We all start here. However, human love can only satisfy a part of this need. Divine Love is the only experience that is completely fulfilling.

- When we look to people for pure love, we fail; human love is imperfect. We all have egos, flaws, attachments, and bad habits. These barriers impede our ability to manifest perfect love. When our need for unconditional love remains unmet, we get anxious. In frustration, we desperately seek love in all the wrong places. We end up with codependency, multiple partners, addiction, and other such bad habits. The solution lies in the transformation of human love to Divine Love.

- We can achieve this change through a process of purification. This requires discipline, effort, and ego reduction. It takes time and it hurts, so we are slow to enter the process; even when we start, we resist its completion. However, this is the purpose of life. *We are here to learn how to love when we do not.* Until we begin transforming human to Divine Love, there will be restlessness, frustration, and dissatisfaction. To eliminate this unnecessary suffering, we must expand our love until it is unqualified.

- We can use our current relationships as a starting place. In our lives, we give and receive love in a variety of roles: parent, child, sibling, coworker, friend, neighbor, or romantic partner. In the daily grind of these relationships problems inevitably emerge. Rather than be dismayed, we can use these as opportunities to expand and purify our love. We can do some interpersonal work to improve communication and problem solving. However, the transformation of human love to Divine Love is ultimately about self-reform and self-mastery. It is not about others' behavior. It is about our response.

- Instead of looking to others, we bring love from within. Instead of trying to control and change others, which usually causes resistance, we learn how to be content and comfortable inside. There is no expectation, demand, or need for others to behave in a certain way. We give love, no matter what. This higher love gives complete satisfaction while setting up the condition for others to change when they can.

- Divine Love is omnipresent, always available as the universal balm for any problem or pain. We can tap into Divine Love at any time; it is already with us, implanted in the body temple as the soul, or Image of God. We already have the superconscious love we are looking for. It is always inside, regardless of our outer condition.

- Through mindful introspection, we can identify any flaw that impedes the free flow of love. Then we can apply a vertical axis method such as mindfulness or meditation to cultivate the love that is already there. We leave no stone unturned, working to remove all traces of negativity, however long that might take.

- To summarize, when we have an interpersonal conflict:

  a. We do some work on the horizontal plane: communication, problem solving, negotiating unmet needs, and so forth. (see Interpersonal Problem Solving Discussion, pp. 140-143 of this workbook). This works, but often our problem will not immediately dissolve. We are still in pain. This is good as it allows us to practice surrender or acceptance.

  b. We accept pain as the teacher and stimulant for the cultivation of higher love through the practice of vertical axis methods. Pain is the teacher. The lesson plan is cultivation of unconditional Divine Love through the methods described in the great books: meditation, mindfulness, spiritual study, breathwork, yoga and so forth.

  c. When we do this work, love grows on the vertical axis. Then we give that higher more refined love to all whom we meet on the horizontal axis.

  d. Connect human or horizontal axis love and Divine Love or vertical axis love in a continuum with movement slowly to vertical over time. As we learn how to grow and balance love on the horizontal and vertical axes, there are fewer bumps. The ride is smoother and then smooth.

  e. In the end, love is one. There is no division between God, self, and others and no vertical or horizontal axes---only Love. It takes a long time and a lot of work to get to this exalted state of consciousness. It is reserved for the masters. On the way, there is a slow and subtle increase in peace, strength, harmony, and balance with an occasional glimpse of ecstasy. Later, there is ever-new joy.

- What is the difference between conditional love and unconditional love? How are they connected?

- Create yourself as a character in a story whose center is unconditional love.

Quote from Groups and Classes on Love

- Love makes it all happen. It opens and calms you.

- Only love can change others.

- I tell my pain story to God in meditation. Then I sit there and wait for Big Love to come in and help me manage it skillfully, because I can't do it alone.

- Your power in the story is always love. When you find love, you find your power.

- Love is in the details. It is in small things like tone of voice, facial expression, passing actions of hospitality, in showing concern to some kid on campus who you don't know but who you caught out of the corner of your closely observant ear or eye. Maybe this is another way of saying, 'Good is in the details.' There are good people everywhere and it is worth observing them carefully, because in the end it is those small things we see done with care that influence over the course of a lifetime. Everything else is abstraction. Stephen G. Post

- Everything that counts is for love. It is the engine of life.

- Compassion is a muscle. It needs exercise.

- Always connect to the heart first.

- It's all about love. Start your climb.

- Listen to the voice of love, inside and out.

- Love is not an emotional sentiment but the ultimate truth at the heart of creation.

- Live from love within while you pursue your outer goals.

- Focus on giving love instead of all the bad stuff coming in. Love works better than any strategy.

- When there is no love, you can be the Love that is missing. Create the love you are not feeling.

- Talk to people. Befriend them.

- Unconditional Love unties the knot of every problem, small or large.

- Love is my medicine. I take love pills every day and PRN (as needed). I take it IV slow drip for long-term problems and IV push for crisis. The one thing I know, I always need more.

- Compassion is a tough taskmaster.

- Be kind whenever possible. It is always possible.

- Love is the general in charge. The qualities are the soldiers.

- The answer to the cosmic puzzle is unconditional love. Cultivate that and see everything fall into place.

- Get out there and let love kick you around.

- Some saints practice radical compassion = compassion under all conditions even at risk of losing life or enlightenment.

- Every painful problem, whether tiny, small, medium, large, or extreme, is a stimulant to expand our Love until it is pure and unconditional. To accomplish this lofty goal, we need help from the God of Love. Love is the God of the universe, the Healer of healers, the Power of powers. She is stronger than even the most brutal of realities. With our efforts and Her grace, we can transform the inevitable suffering of life into peace, strength, and wisdom.

- Use any method you wish to cultivate love in response to your pain and you will evolve. It doesn't matter what pain does. Just keep coming back with love. Love and pain alternate, overlap and coexist throughout our lives. Love wins in the end.

Chapter 34

Peace

- Please review chapter 26 on Peace in *Healing Power, Revised*, pp. 383-392. Following are some quotes about peace and additional points to remember.

- Peace is difficult to attain for those whose minds are centered on the body. Nityananda

- Peace is a costly privilege—to be fought for, attained, and won. It comes only from a conquered mind. Paul Brunton

- Like water, we are truest to our nature in repose. Cyril Connolly

- Never be in a hurry; do everything quietly and in a calm spirit. Do not lose your inward peace for anything whatsoever, even if your whole world seems upset. Francis de Sales

- That man attains peace who, abandoning all desires, moves about without longing, without the sense of mine, and without egoism. Bhagavad-Gita

- God is peace. His name is peace, and all is bound together in peace. The Zohar

- When everything is in its right place within us, we ourselves are in balance with the whole work of God. Henry Amiel

- From the cradle to his grave, a man never does a single thing which has any first and foremost object save to secure peace of mind, spiritual comfort, for himself. Mark Twain

- If you really want peace of mind and inner calm, you will get it. Regardless of how unjustly you have been treated, or how unfair the boss has been, or what a mean scoundrel someone has proved to be, all this makes no difference to you when you awaken to your mental and spiritual powers. Joseph Murphy

- Slowly, painfully, I have learned that peace of mind may transform a cottage into a spacious manor hall; the want of it can make a regal park an imprisoning nutshell. Joshua Liebman

- I was glad I was born, glad I suffered so, glad I did make big blunders, glad to enter peace. Vivekananda

- Each one has to find peace within. And peace to be real must be unaffected by outside circumstances. Mohandas Gandhi

- Peace of mind is worth any price it demands. Gayatri Devi

- Peace cannot suddenly descend from the heavens. It can only come when the root causes of trouble are removed. Jawaharlal Nehru

- Five great enemies to peace inhabit us: avarice, ambition, envy, anger, and pride. If those enemies were to be banished, we would infallibly enjoy perpetual peace. Petrarch

- Peace of mind is that mental condition in which you have accepted the worst. Lin Yutang

- When a man finds no peace within himself, it is useless to seek it elsewhere. Francois La Rochefoucauld

- Perfect peace can dwell only where all egotism has disappeared. Gautama Buddha

- Peace is the most priceless possession of man. It is the sign of a virtuous character. Sathya Sai Baba

- Our work for peace must begin within the private world of each of us. Dag Hammarskjold

- The peace which results from social comfort, passing gratification, or worldly victory is transitory in nature, and is burned up in the heat of fiery trial. Only the selfless heart can know the Peace of Heaven. James Allen

- The first rule is to keep an untroubled spirit. The second is to look things in the face and know them for what they are. Marcus Aurelius

- If you only knew the peace there is in accepted sorrow. Madame Guyon

- Everyone thirsts for peace, but few people understand that perfect peace cannot be obtained as long as the inner soul is not filled with the presence of God. Anandamayi Ma

- There can never be peace between nations until there is first known that true peace which is within the souls of men. Black Elk

- To win true peace, a man needs to feel directed, pardoned, and sustained by a Supreme Power. Henri Amiel

- No matter how turbulent the storm might be, there is an 'eye' at the center of the hurricane where all is calm and still. Donald Curtis

- Inner peace is not found by staying on the surface of life, or by attempting to escape from life through any means. Inner peace is found by facing life squarely, solving its problems, and delving as far beneath the surface as possible to discover its verities and realities. Peace Pilgrim

- Discord is rife in the outward world, but unbroken harmony holds sway at the heart of the universe. James Allen

Chapter 35

Humility

- Please review chapter 27 on Humility in *Healing Power, Revised*, pp. 393-405. Following are some quotes about humility and additional points to remember.

- Humility is the mother of all virtues. It is in being humble that our Love becomes real, devoted, and ardent. If you are humble nothing will touch you, neither praise nor disgrace, because you know what you are. If you are blamed, you will not be discouraged. If they call you a saint, you will not put yourself on a pedestal. Mother Theresa

- Every healing quality has humility as a part of it or it wouldn't be a healing quality.

- The spiritual ego awaits our success at every turn. We make some progress and already walk with swag. No. School is still in session. Just because we pass a test doesn't mean we pass the course, let alone the next grade, let alone graduate. Enjoy recess, float in the playground, have fun, but expect class to resume momentarily. Be humble. Know your place. The light is still dim.

- Humility is getting right sized.

- Humility must always be doing its work like a bee making its honey in the hive. Without humility all will be lost. Teresa of Avila

- Go and sit in the last place and then you will be invited to take the first. Jesus

- All streams flow to the ocean because it is lower than they are. Humility gives it its power. Lao-tzu

- The nail that sticks up will be hammered down. Japanese proverb

- The richest pearl in the crown of graces is humility. John Good

- The more you are reduced, the more powerful you become. In humility there is greatness and power. John Panama

- Lowliness is the foundation of loftiness. Lao-tzu

- True humility is not an abject, groveling, self-despising spirit. It is but a right estimate of ourselves as God sees us. Tryon Edwards

- God can do great things through the man who doesn't care who gets the credit. Robert Schuller

- Where there is humility and patience, there is neither anger nor vexation. Francis of Assisi

- No need to discount yourself in order to achieve humility; neither can you attain humility by overestimating what you are. Humility is your correct weight; no more, no less. Fred Van Amburgh

- Teach the tongue to say "I do not know," and thou shalt progress. Maimonides

- If two angels were sent down from heaven--one to conduct an empire and the other to sweep a street--they would feel no inclination to change employments. John Newton

- The most powerful weapon to conquer evil is humility. For evil does not know at all how to employ it, nor does it know how to defend itself against it. Vincent de Paul

- Be willing to be a beginner every single morning. Meister Eckhart

- If you cannot be the sun, then be the humble planet. Tibetan proverb

- Of myself I can do nothing. The Father that dwells in me, He does the work. Jesus.

- Life is a long lesson in humility. James Barrie

- In heaven, an angel is nobody in particular. George B. Shaw

- Be humble, that you may not be humbled. The Talmud

- The tree laden with fruit always bends low. Ramakrishna

Chapter 36

Faith

- Please review chapter 28 on Faith in *Healing Power, Revised*, pp 407-416. Following are some quotes about faith and points to remember.

- One doesn't discover new lands without consenting to lose sight of the shore for a very long time. Andre Gide

- Faith is a dynamic power that breaks the chain of routine. Helen Keller

- If man wishes to be sure of the road he treads on, he must close his eyes and walk in the dark. John of the Cross

- Faith is on-again, off-again rather than once and for all. Faith is not sure where you're going but going anyway. Frederick Buechner

- Maybe you are searching in the branches, for what only appears in the roots. Rumi

- Faith supplies staying power. Anyone can keep going when the going is good, but some extra ingredient is needed to keep you fighting when it seems that everything is against you. Norman V. Peale

- Faith begins as an experiment and ends as an experience. W.R. Inge

- Fear knocked at the door. Faith answered. Irish proverb

- The whole course of things goes to teach us faith. We need only obey. There is guidance for each of us, and by lowly listening we shall hear the right word. Ralph W. Emerson

- Faith can grow only by long cultivation and careful attention. Sathya Sai Baba

- Faith is a simple childlike belief in a Divine Friend who solves all problems that come to us. Helen Keller

- The man of faith must burn his boats behind him every day of his life. Indeed, he needs no boats, because he walks on the sea of experience upheld by invisible forces. Henry Hamblin

- God never fails his devotees in the hour of trial. The condition is that there must be a living faith and the uttermost reliance on Him. The test of faith is that having done our duty we must be prepared to welcome whatever He may send---joy as well as sorrow, good luck as well as bad. Mohandas Gandhi

- I do not pray for success. I ask for faithfulness. Mother Teresa

- Life is God's novel. Let Him write it. Isaac Bashevis Singer

- Faith is the wire that connects you to grace, and over which grace comes streaming from God. Anonymous

- Faith and Truth are the same thing. God's side is Truth. Our side is Faith. Bernadette Roberts

- Learning to be men and women of faith is like being trained as an athlete. We have to be tested, and our training made more severe, so that our strength and powers of endurance are increased progressively. Every time of testing prepares us for greater adventures in faith. Henry Hamblin.

Chapter 37

Courage

- Please review chapter 29 on Courage in *Healing Power, Revised*, pp. 417-424. Following are some quotes about courage and additional points to remember.

- We can use our tests and trials to develop the qualities we need. Win every battle---every test of the world and test of the body---by never losing your courage. Be strong. Persevere. Ask your Higher Power for help.

- Every painful problem (P) has only one purpose: to go deeper into our method (M) and quality (Q). The bigger the pain (P), the bigger the (M) and (Q) have to be. Every painful problem is an opportunity to expand love and associated qualities.

- Courage is the price life extracts for granting peace. Amelia Earhart

- The weak in courage are strong in cunning. William Blake

- A hero is no braver than an ordinary man, but he is brave five minutes longer. Ralph W. Emerson

- Courage and perseverance have a magical talisman, before which difficulties disappear and obstacles vanish. John Quincy Adams

- Talk courage, think courage, act courageously. The opposite course will surely cause you to have more mental burdens than you can carry. Fred Van Amburgh

- When there is no adversary, what avails thy courage? Rumi

- Courage is like a muscle, strengthened by use. Ruth Gordon

- We must build dikes of courage to hold back the flood of fear. Martin L. King, Jr.

- You cannot discover new horizons unless you have the courage to lose sight of the shore. Anonymous

- I always remember this truth when I mentally try to find a way to escape from something that seems too hard for me. I think then: *I am escaping, not overcoming.* Sri Gyanamata

Chapter 38

Forgiveness

- Please review chapter 30 on Forgiveness in *Healing Power, Revised*, pp. 425-438. Following are some additional principles and exercises.

1. Seven Times Seventy

- How many times do we have to forgive? Jesus said, "Seventy times seven."

- Forgiveness is a long-term process with many layers. We forgive until forgiveness is all there is.

- For some, this is the deepest suffering. It feels like a salmon swimming upstream. But the deepest suffering requires the deepest healing. Strength, peace, and wisdom result from this deep inner work.

2. Let the Story Unfold and Spiritualize the Story

- Forgiveness involves letting the pain story unfold and spiritualizing the story.

- Letting the pain story unfold is your truth, and it is good. It is part of the healing process but don't stay there, as truth in this form---at some point---is no longer helpful. It repeats itself against our will and keeps the fire of destructive reactivity burning. Forgiveness is the water we need to put out the fire.

- If we let the story unfold and then spiritualize the story, we bring the story under our control and lay down a record. The stored record emanates peace, power, strength and wisdom. We play that record when we need it rather than have it play against our will.

3. Sin-Guilt-Punishment

- One member saw his illness as a punishment.

- Another felt like a very bad person since he heard voices commanding him to kill himself.

- A third member committed a very bad crime and could not forgive himself even though he believed God is love and he saw Jesus as his savior.

- The core belief is these cases was sin-guilt-punishment. These individuals felt they could never change, that they had been given a life sentence of suffering.

- We can work against this by rolling the wheel.

- Practice any one or a combination of methods, including affirmations, service to others, and prayer. Ask for help from your Higher Power.

- The pain may last for a while but *chip, chip, chip.*

- Continue your PMQ practice.

- While you may not experience immediate relief, just keep going. At some point, you will.

4. Gentle Compassion

- When a negative person elicits a negative reaction in you, practice gentle compassion for the negative person and for yourself.

5. Prayer for Forgiveness

- Teach me to forgive others.

- Forgive me for my faults.

- Forgive me when I forget that I owe my health, life, soul, everything to You, the source of all good and beauty.

Chapter 39

Truth

- Please review chapter 31 on Truth in *Healing Power, Revised*, pp. 439-450. Following are some quotes about truth and additional points to remember.

- There are very few human beings who receive the truth complete and staggering by instant illumination. Most of us acquire it fragment by fragment, on a small scale, by successive developments, cellularly, like a laborious mosaic. Anais Nin

- There are many truths of which the full meaning cannot be realized until personal experience has brought it home. John S. Mill

- Truth is the pearl of great price. One cannot obtain truth by buying it—all you can do is strive for spiritual truth and when one is ready, it will be given freely. Peace Pilgrim

- Sit down before fact as a little child, be prepared to give up every preconceived notion, follow humbly whatever and to whatever abyss nature leads, or you shall learn nothing. Thomas Huxley

- Truth is a diamond that scratches every other stone. Shantidasa

- To live in the presence of great truths and eternal laws—that is what keeps a man patient when the world ignores him and calm and unspoiled when the world praises him. Honore de Balzac

- The deepest truth blooms only from the deepest Love. Heinrich Heine

- Though the sages speak in diverse ways, they express one and the same Truth. Srimad Bhagavatam

- I arrived at Truth, not by systematic reasoning and accumulation of proofs but by a flash of light which God sent into my soul. Al-Ghazali

- Hard are the ways of truth and rough to walk. John Milton

- The measure of a man's truth is the measure of his Love, and Truth is far removed from him whose life is not governed by Love. James Allen

- The greatest friend of truth is time, her greatest enemy is prejudice, and her constant companion is humility. Charles Colton.

- We forget that Truth is self-sufficient, self-sustaining, and does not require human hand to protect it. Paramananda

- Whoever undertakes to set himself up as a judge in the field of Truth and Knowledge is shipwrecked by the laughter of the Gods. Albert Einstein

- There is no negotiation with truth. Ferdinand Lassalle

- Truth is not to be found by anybody who has not got an abundant sense of humility. If you would swim on the bosom of the ocean of Truth, you must reduce yourself to zero. Mohandas Gandhi

- To love God and love the truth are one and the same. Silvio Pellico

Chapter 40

Intuition

- Please review chapter 32 on Intuition in *Healing Power, Revised*, pp. 451-458. Following are some quotes about intuition and additional points to remember.

- To get beyond ordinary reason and the senses to intuition, get into the room of stillness.

- Intuition is in the room of stillness where love resides in pure form. It is only in love and stillness that we get the pure message.

- Intuition can't come through when we are restless or reactive. Whatever degree of turmoil is there, so too is that message contaminated with egoistic deception. That is okay. We just have to know it is contaminated.

- We need to get calm and centered before we can even approach intuition. This may take hours, days, weeks, or months. It cannot be hurried. It shows up on its own schedule. Be patient and work your way to love and stillness. Listen to the still, small loving voice within. Here you will find the best possible advice.

- Clear your mind of dogmatic theological debris; let in the fresh, healing waters of direct perception. Attune yourself to the active inner Guidance; the Divine Voice has the answer to every dilemma of life. Though man's ingenuity for getting himself into trouble appears to be endless, the Infinite Succor is no less resourceful. Yogananda

Chapter 41

Oneness

- Please review chapter 33 on Oneness in *Healing Power, Revised,* pp. 459-467. Following are some additional points to remember.

- There is a unified field of Intelligent Consciousness, an Omnipotent Power that underlies and unites all. The great books and teachers call it the Tao, Buddha, Christ, or God. It is omniscient, omnipresent, omnipotent Love. This power is inside, outside, everywhere, extending forever in every direction, uniting all things and people. We do not enter this field. We are already in it. It is already in us. There is no separation. All is one. We are always in the Changeless One, even as a wave is part of the ocean.

- Because of maya however, we experience ourselves as isolated waves, separate from the ocean. Maya refers to the power inherent in ordinary consciousness that makes us think we are separate from the Creator, creation, and other creatures. Under the influence of maya, we experience the division, separation, limitation, impermanence, and suffering of ordinary or worldly consciousness.

- Maya is powerful and seductive. It is responsible for our hook to the physical plane. It tricks us into thinking we can achieve peace, love, and joy by focusing on the little wave of our life to the exclusion of the ocean. Under the spell of maya, we focus on our soap opera, possessions, and bodies while we exclude the Changeless One from our consciousness.

- We love maya, the physical plane, despite the limitations, impermanence, and suffering it imposes. However, in order to contact the Changeless One, we must reduce the power of maya as it has captured all of our attention. The Omnipresent Giver of Peace and Love exists just behind the ever-changing world of people, events, and things. When we contact the Giver, we can draw from Her miraculous healing powers and qualities.

- The shift from maya to higher consciousness is not easy. To find the Changeless One behind the veil of ordinary consciousness, we need help. This work describes a variety of methods designed to help us do this work. With persistent practice of these techniques, we can experience our little wave as a part of the Infinite Ocean below.

Exercises

1. The Big Space

Every affirmation, pearl of wisdom, quote, and technique in this work is an aspect of or doorway to The Big Space: a space filled with healing qualities and higher states of consciousness.

- Roll the universal healing wheel, the essence of each technique, to enter this unified field of healing energy.

- With persistent practice of the recommended techniques, we can experience a profound shift of consciousness from separation to oneness.

- Then we know we are eternally safe and protected.

2. Maya and the Room of Stillness

- The seductive world of maya is always calling, "I am people, activities, places, events, and things. Come out here and play with me."

- The God of Love in the room of stillness is always calling, "I am love qualities and superconsciousness. Come in here. Be with me. Don't lag behind in this seductive world that tricks you into thinking it is so important."

- We stand between these two seemingly contradictory worlds, but there is no conflict when we lead a balanced life of meditation and service.

- Practice love and service on the horizontal axis, and expand and purify your love with vertical axis methods; then you will experience progressively greater degrees of oneness until oneness is all there is.

- When we stand between the two fields, matter and Spirit, and roll the wheel, the Love Field responds with ever-expanding healing qualities and higher states of consciousness. This principle applies whether your problem is tiny, small, medium, large, or huge. You can prove this to yourself through direct personal experience when you practice PMQ.

3. From the Karma Drama to Love and Oneness

- Under the spell of maya, we focus on our soap opera, possessions, and bodies while we exclude the Changeless One from our consciousness.

- We are addicted and attached to our story by the ego, which creates self-importance, attachment, and associated emotions.

- The hook is likes and dislikes, attraction and repulsion. We like the good and dislike the bad. Both sides keep us locked in the drama.

- This heightened state of reactivity corresponds to our energy going down to the lower three chakras and out into the world where it gets attached to people, activities, events, and things.

- When we practice love, service, and meditation, energy goes in and up to the higher centers in the spinal cord and brain. There is a corresponding movement from the emotions of the karma drama to love and stillness. There is less reactivity and more peace. Our service is evermore refined and evermore useful. We see that love and oneness are one and the same.

4. Maya and God in the Same Space

- Maya and God exist in the same space.

- In ordinary consciousness under the influence of the ego, we experience the apparent division, separation, and impermanence of maya.

- In spiritual consciousness, under the influence of the soul, we experience the Changeless One.

- It's a matter of vibrations. Love is the key. When our consciousness and vibrations are freed of dross, when our love is pure and unconditional, we will be one with the Changeless One, the energy that permeates and flows through all things including us.

- No matter what the world and your body are doing, you can get help from the omniscient, omnipotent, omnipresent Love that is always right here, right now.

- We can mindfully remember to bring this Love to every thought, feeling, and action.

5. Simplicity

- The mind of ordinary consciousness divides everything up; we see complexity and multiplicity.

- When we meditate and get into the room of stillness, we see the oneness and simplicity of Love.

- Bring that Indivisible Love to the complexities of your world. Everything improves with this simplicity.

6. Immersed in the Field of Oneness

- No one goes through life without joy and pain, triumph and sorrow. But the unified field of healing energy is everywhere present and cannot be broken. We can tap into this field to get help with any pain or problem.

- We can immerse ourselves in the field of oneness, a field loaded with healing qualities and higher states of consciousness.

- May we never leave it and may it never leave us.

- May this love, compassion, forgiveness, strength, courage, and humor guide our every thought, feeling, desire, decision, and action.

- May we give this to all whom we meet.

7. Affirmations

- We are the same being in different disguises.

- Every person is an extension of the same Spirit.

- I look through the lens of oneness. In this field, every one is equal.

- I give myself a one-word command: oneness.

- Oneness is Love.

Chapter 42

Healing

- Please review chapter 34 on Healing in *Healing Power, Revised*, pp. 469-478. Following are some additional exercises.

1. Spiritual Chiropractor

- We want to reduce reactivity, the pain we add on to the inevitable suffering of life. We can locate this reactivity in the six tools that become barriers described in step 5 in *Healing Power, Revised*, pp. 56--68.

- When the tools are in alignment, they are our best friends, powerful allies that help us achieve our goals. The tools in alignment:

    a. Mind: positive, calm, focused; brilliant at solving problems and shaping meaning
    b. Emotion: a source of self-knowledge
    c. Desire: for health, prosperity, and success
    d. Body: engages life, the doer of all of our activities, the source of our potential liberation and enlightenment
    e. Activity: work, recreation, sports, culture, hobbies
    f. Ego: establishes our place in the world of work and relationships

- When the six tools are out of alignment, they become our worst enemies, a source of unnecessary and often profound suffering. Tools out of alignment = reactivity

    a. Mind: restless, relentless, a life of its own
    b. Emotion: high emotional reactivity
    c. Desire: excessive material desire leading to attachments and bad habits
    d. Body: heavy, tired, hurts, disability, death
    e. Activity: hyperactivity
    f. Ego: separation, selfish, territorial, self-important

- Think of the six tools as our spiritual backbone.

- When the tools are out of alignment, we become our own spiritual chiropractor.

- To get our spiritual backbone back in alignment, we give it a whack with a method and quality.

- This is the day-to-day, hand-to-hand combat, grind-it-out spiritual work.

SPIRITUAL CHIROPRACTOR

Tools out of Alignment

Mind: restless, relentless, a life of its own

Emotion: high emotional reactivity

Desire: excessive material desire leading to attachments and bad habits

Body: heavy, tired, hurts, disability, death

Activity: hyperactivity

Ego: separation, selfish, territorial, self-important

Tools in Alignment

Mind: positive, calm, focused; brilliant at solving problems and shaping meaning

Emotion: a source of self-knowledge

Desire: for health, prosperity, and success

Body: engages life, the doer of all of our activities, the source of our potential liberation and enlightenment

Activity: work, recreation, sports, culture, hobbies

Ego: establishes our place in the world of work and relationships

METHOD & QUALITY

2. **The Ocean and the Wave** (See illustration p. 209)

   *   Think of life as an ocean.

   *   On the surface of the ocean are its waves. The waves are sometimes calm and safe, other times choppy, turbulent, stormy, or dangerous.

   *   In this metaphor, the waves represent the human condition: the good, bad, ugly, great, and terrible. Love is there, in the waves, but it is contaminated with a variety of negatives.

   *   Beneath the surface, the ocean is deep, vast, still, and immutable. Consider the deep part of the ocean as pure, unconditional, unlimited love.

   *   We want to get off the surface waves of suffering into the ocean of infinite love below.

   *   Stillness is the way.

- In meditation, when we calm the waves, we enter the deep part of the ocean and absorb Her nature.

- In the stillness and silence of deep meditation, love qualities slowly expand until love is all there is. Here we experience absolute safety and protection from the problems of the body and the problems of the world.

- When we come out of meditation, we give that love to all whom we meet.

3. The Resentment Prison

- When hurt, rejected, or abandoned, we feel resentment.

- Resentment is seductive, difficult to shake.

- Resentment is like a prison. We keep the provocateur behind bars and throw away the key. Resentment saps energy, adds weight, and feels bad. Who wants to be the warden of such a prison? What to do?

- Make a list of the inmates in your resentment prison.

- In a meditative state, visualize the inmates in their cells.

- Now fill those cells with respect and understanding, compassion and gentleness, tolerance and forgiveness, kindness and spaciousness, mercy and light.

- Notice how these healing qualities dissolve the bars and walls of the prison thus liberating the inmate and the warden from the bondage of resentment.

- Love qualities heal the inmate and the warden. Visualize yourself and those released in harmony and peace.

- What warden? What inmates? What prison?

In the next chapter, Fill Your Brain with Wisdom, you will find one hundred healing qualities with associated wisdom pearls.

Chapter 43

Fill Your Brain with Wisdom
One Hundred Healing Quality Pearls

Important Points about the Qualities

- You have an army of one hundred healing qualities.

- Everyone has every quality. They are in the genetic code = the inherited wisdom of the body.

- They are not just words but actual healing powers.

- We can deploy them in response to any pain or problem.

- They are more powerful than the painful problem.

- We know how to make them grow.

- Grow one and the others grow with it. They are interconnected.

- USA: unconditional, spontaneous, automatic. The goal is to make them USA.

- As they become USA, the locus of control shifts from outside to inside.

- We always need more of all of them but from moment to moment some stand out as more important than the others.

- When you expand the qualities, you feel better, become a better person, and may experience higher states of consciousness.

- The growth of healing qualities is the goal of all psychosocial and spiritual work.

- The most important question: are the qualities growing?

Suggested Homework

- Below is a list of one hundred healing qualities with corresponding affirmations and quotes. You might like these pearls just as they are. If not, refine them to make them better or create your own.

- Drop these healing quality pearls into the center of your consciousness, feel their healing vibrations throughout your system, and then send those healing vibrations to others and surrounding space.

- Fill your brain with wisdom the first thing in the morning and keep it there throughout the day by affirming and reaffirming your favorite pearls and qualities.

- You can use these pearls to stimulate discussion in groups, classes, and individual therapy sessions.

Acceptance:

- The cure for the pain is in the pain. Rumi

- When you are in pain and can't get out, accept pain as the teacher and stimulant for the growth of healing qualities.

- Life is school, pain is the teacher if we open to its lessons, and the lessons always have to do with expansion of healing qualities.

- We get the easiest possible ride when we accept the pain we cannot change by cultivating the qualities. This mature wisdom takes time and practice.

Appreciation:

- Acceptance + understanding + appreciation = love

- Appreciate others and let them know about it. Compliment at least one person every day.

- Appreciate the passage of time, and the slow accumulation of wisdom it affords.

- Appreciate the miraculous in the common, the sacred in the ordinary.

- My expectations were reduced to zero when I was twenty-one. Everything since then has been a bonus. Stephen Hawkings

Balance:

- Balance meditation with service. In meditation, you expand healing power and healing qualities. When you come out of meditation, you can give your enhanced peace, love, joy, power and wisdom to all whom you meet.

- Love and safety is the goal. Am I loved? Am I safe? We look outside and get what we can through people and activities. But saints say the Buddha or Image of God inside is love and safety itself. "Go in," they say. We do. Now we do both outer and inner work to get love and safety. Can it be balanced perfectly? Sometimes we get it right and sometimes we miss, but we can always intend that goal and do our best.

Beauty:

- Moon and evening star do their slow tambourine dance to praise this universe. The purpose of every gathering is discovered: to recognize Beauty and to Love what's Beautiful. Rumi

- In your light I learn how to Love. In your beauty, how to make poems. You dance inside my chest where no-one sees you, but sometimes I do, and that sight becomes this art. Rumi

- When you look for ugliness, you will find it everywhere. When you look for beauty, you will find that everywhere. Narayan

- It is wisest and best to fix our attention on the beautiful and the good and dwell as little as possible on the evil and false. Richard Cecil

- There is no physical barrier to experiencing yourself as beautiful, only your belief. Harold Bloomfield

- Let the beauty we Love be what we do. Rumi

Belief:

- Belief consists in accepting the affirmations of the soul, unbelief in denying them. Ralph W. Emerson

- Why crawl with beliefs when with a little more effort you can soar by knowing? Shantidasa

- Right now, you have more healing power than you are using. You can tap into that power through mindfulness and positive thought. Positive thoughts are healing powers. Drop these down to the center of your consciousness and send them to every cell, tissue, organ, and system in your body, to surrounding space, and other people. This reduces stress and stimulates healing power for yourself and others.

Changelessness:

- There is a part of our consciousness that never changes. It remains still, silent, spacious, and serene no matter what happens. This superconscious state has many names: the Big Space, nirvana, ecstasy, God, Truth, The Way, Cosmic Consciousness, and more. Here you experience absolute safety, security, and immortality. You cannot be cut, burned, hurt, or wetted. You can experience this in deep meditation when you transcend the world, body, senses, and mind. This is a high state of consciousness reserved for those who persist in meditation, love, and service to humanity.

Cheerfulness:

- Cheerful service to humanity is catching. Start an epidemic.

Clarity:

- Fill a glass of clear water with mud and stir it up. The water is now uniformly muddy. After some time, the mud settles down and the water is clear. When we sit in meditation at first, our consciousness is clouded with restless thoughts. Many people give up at this stage thinking they are not succeeding in meditation. Wait patiently. Continue to meditate. In time, all thoughts will settle and your consciousness will clear of all restlessness. Then you will know the peace that surpasses understanding.

- Clear eyes, full hearts, can't lose. Coach Taylor in Friday Night Lights

Community:

- When many people live together and each one cares for the rest, there is one mind. Shining Arrows, Crow

- You have an army of one hundred healing qualities you can call up at any time. Realize these qualities for yourself and share them with your friends, family, neighbors, and all people. This creates a community that will not quit.

- Join others in group meditation. The sum is greater than the parts.

Compassion:

- Love and compassion are necessities, not luxuries. Without them, humanity cannot survive. Dalai Lama

- Be kind, for everyone you meet is fighting a battle you know nothing about. Anonymous

- No one has ever become poor by giving. Anne Frank

Confidence:

- You have an army of 100 healing qualities. This is your true self. You are unlimited peace, Love, joy, power and wisdom. Learn to stand alone, secure in your own virtues and self-worth.

Contentment:

- There is a basket of fresh bread on your head, yet you go door to door asking for crust. Rumi

- You wander from room to room, hunting for the diamond necklace that is already around your neck. Rumi

- Acceptance + humility + love = contentment and joy

Courage:

- A test is there to heal you. A test will hurt. It must hurt. You must walk through a test to find your power in the story. To be spiritual is not to escape. Face all your tests with courage and strength. A spiritual warrior is not a spiritual cream puff.

- Courage is the bridge between fear and peace. Face your fears with courage.

- Courage in the morning. Gratitude in the evening.

Creativity:

- The Intelligent Power that runs the universe is infinitely creative. There are billions of forms and stories. Nothing repeats twice. We are here to participate. Merge with this force. Get to the edge. Step into the unknown. Think outside of the box. Make your contribution.

Desirelessness:

- You go from village to village on your horse asking everyone, "Has anyone seen my horse?" Rumi

- We chase ephemeral worldly pleasures like a dog chases the bunny at the racetrack. No matter how fast the excited dog runs, he or she never catches the bunny. When you discover the fountain of peace-joy in the stillness of deep meditation, you have no desire to go elsewhere. Go inside. Meditate. Find the room of stillness. Here you experience the ever-new satisfaction and undying contentment that can only be achieved within.

Devotion:

- Devotion is a feeling of intimacy with the inside of the cosmos. Enter the inner circle of the heart to find that Love Supreme. Who can resist feeling the power of the current in that stream?

- Tonight we go to that place of eternity. This is the wedding night---a never ending union of lover and Beloved. We whisper gentle secrets to each other, and the child of the universe takes its first breath. Rumi

- Convert emotion to devotion. Be on fire for God, good, or service.

Endurance:

- The inevitable suffering of life can be mild to extreme. We don't know what we are going to get. We have no control over this. We need to be ready for anything, all of it. This is where endurance comes in. No matter your tests, you are not too weak to fight. You can do this work. Learn how to endure with courage when you don't get your way. When you learn how to ride the pain waves, you will find your power in the story.

Energy:

- Where the mind goes, energy flows. Ernest Holmes

- Scientists conclude the universe and everything in it is made of energy. In yoga, this energy is called prana and control of the energy is pranayama. Yoga teaches us to reverse the flow of energy from going down the spinal column and out to the world for daily activities to inward and upward to the higher chakras in the spinal column and brain in meditation. This results in a shift in consciousness from ordinary and mundane to ever-expanding peace, love, joy, power, and wisdom. We then bring that refined consciousness to every thought, feeling, and action.

- Practice pranayama. Everything gets better. Painful problems slowly disappear and we have more control over those that remain. Pranayama is a part of the solution to every problem.

Enthusiasm:

- Set your life on fire. Seek those who fan your flames. Rumi

- Deep self-healing work is slow, difficult, and sometimes painful. To start and maintain a practice, we need motivation, discipline, and patience. If we don't have enough motivation, we are likely to quit when the going gets rough. Here are a few one-word affirmation coals you can use to stoke your fire: zeal, hunger, intensity, thirst, yearning, longing, crying, and craving.

- How much enthusiasm do you have? More is better. What lights your fire?

Equality:

- The earth is our mother. She nourishes us. All living things are connected and we share an equal relationship with the earth and all her creatures. It is from this connection that we come to understand the power of nature and the importance of living in harmony with the earth and one another. Native American Wisdom

- Show respect to all men but grovel to none. Tecumseh, Shawnee

- On the spiritual plane, we are equal. Here our true identity is the healing qualities. We are peace, joy, love, power, wisdom, and the other wonderful qualities listed in the spiritual alphabet.

Eternity:

- The universe is infinite, eternal, and immortal. There is no beginning or end to the infinitely intelligent, omnipresent power that runs the show. We are a part of that consciousness. We can realize this consciousness through the practice of yoga. Yoga means union of the soul with Spirit. When we practice yoga and merge the soul with Spirit, we know ourselves as infinite, eternal consciousness.

Even-mindedness:

- Coaches train athletes to remain even-minded despite the ups and downs of a game and the season. Yoga teaches even-mindedness no matter the condition of your life or body. Practice meditation and mindfulness. You will see a steadiness grow no matter your tests and trials.

Faith:

- Faith supplies the staying power. Anyone can keep going when the going is good, but some extra ingredient is needed to keep you fighting when it seems everything is against you. Norman Vincent Peale

- To leap across an abyss, one is better served by faith than doubt. William James

- Faith is the bird that sings when the dawn is still dark. Rabindranath Tagore

- In the midst of winter, I found within me an invincible summer. Albert Camus

- Fear knocked at the door. Faith answered. Irish proverb

- I do not pray for success. I ask for faithfulness. Mother Teresa

- Faith can only grow by long cultivation and careful attention. Sathya Sai Baba

Fearlessness:

- Keep walking, though there's no place to get to. Don't try to see through the distances. That's not for human beings. Move within, but don't move the way fear makes you move. Rumi

- Fearlessness is a long-range goal, difficult to achieve for most. Start by facing your fears with courage. Persevere and you will slowly move in that direction.

Forbearance:

- Don't turn away. Keep your gaze on the bandaged place. That's where the light enters you. Rumi

- No matter who you are or what your problems are, you can do this work. Effort is progress even if you can't see it. Keep on keeping on. Never give up.

Forgiveness:

- Everyone has faults. We all make mistakes. Getting upset and angry about this is natural but staying there is unhealthy. Learn to forgive. Opportunities to do this present themselves throughout the day. Jesus said, "Forgive seven times seventy." Be understanding, compassionate, kind, and gentle with yourself and others repeatedly until forgiveness is all there is.

Freedom:

- The degree of freedom from unwanted thoughts and the degree of concentration on a single thought are the measures to gauge spiritual progress. Ramana Maharshi

- It is in living life simply, that we gain the greatest freedom. David Cunliffe

- What lies behind me and what lies before me are small compared to what lies within me. Ralph Waldo Emerson

- If you want to move on with your life, you must let go.

- A secret freedom opens through a crevice you can barely see. Rumi

Friendship:

- I looked for my soul, but my soul I could not see. I looked for my God, but my God eluded me. I looked for a friend and then I found all three. William Blake

- Friendship with oneself is important because without it one cannot be friends with any one else in the world. Eleanor Roosevelt

- Friends are like stars. You may not always see them, but you know they are there.

- I get by with a little help from my friends. John Lennon

- Those who bring sunshine to the lives of others cannot keep it from themselves. James Matthew Barrie

- Give your love to $1 \rightarrow 2 \rightarrow 4 \rightarrow 16$. It's nuclear.

Fun:

- Now that You live here in my chest, anywhere we sit is a mountaintop. Rumi

- When healing qualities grow, life becomes more enjoyable.

- Compassion + Love + understanding = liberating joy.

Generosity:

- There were two rooms, each with a number of people, a pot filled with enough good food to go round and some ridiculously long spoons. In the first room was hell. A group of angry and frustrated people were trying to feed themselves and finding it impossible. As the door to the second room opened you heard gales of laughter as people together coped with the difficulties of feeding each other on opposite sides of the table.

- Are you jealous of the ocean's generosity? Why would you refuse to give this joy to anyone? Fish don't hold the sacred liquid in cups! They swim the huge fluid freedom. Rumi

- Share your inner and outer resources. Give it away to keep it. Let it go and see what comes back.

Gentleness:

- Gentleness corrects the offensive in our nature. It trumps bitterness and cruelty. Be gentle with yourself and others. Touch everything lightly.

Gratitude:

- Wear gratitude like a cloak and it will feed every corner of your life. Rumi

- Hear blessings dropping their blossoms around you. Rumi

- There are a thousand ways to kneel and kiss the earth. Rumi

- Can you find another market like this? Where, with your one rose, you can buy hundreds of rose gardens? Rumi

- If the only prayer you ever say in your entire life is thank you, it will be enough. Meister Eckhart

- Gratitude is the way to stay connected to the countless blessings we miss.

Harmony:

- To be in harmony with all things, you must be in harmony with yourself. Lakota Proverb

- Harmony is always present but sometimes it is hidden. We have to go deeper to find it. Add more Love to the equation. Hidden harmonies appear.

- Meditation + Service → Harmony

- Meditate in the morning. Love and serve during the day. Meditate in the evening.

- A balanced life of meditation and service is the quickest route to harmony.

Healing:

- I am a patient of love, you are like medicine for me. Rumi

- Love is the great healer. It breaks into one hundred healing qualities that will help you in every domain of your life. These qualities are in the genetic code but they will not grow without your attention, work, and discipline. When you practice yoga, meditation, mindfulness, breathwork, and affirmations, healing qualities expand. You become a more skillful pain manager. You feel better, become a better person, and experience higher states of consciousness.

Honesty:

- The purpose of honest self-inquiry is not humiliation but rather to find your power in the story. Be kind, gentle, and compassionate with yourself.

- When you speak truth to others, be sure it is necessary and be kind.

Hope:

- There is a secret medicine given only to those who hurt so hard they can't hope. Rumi

- Hope opens the door to expanded healing power.

Humility:

- I have been driven to my knees many times by the overwhelming conviction that I had no place else to go. Abraham Lincoln

- Sometimes you fall down because there is something down there you are supposed to find.

- Pride goes before destruction, a haughty spirit before a fall. Proverbs 16:18

- All streams flow to the ocean because it is lower than they are. Humility gives it its power. Lao-Tzu

- When humility marries equality, wisdom blooms.

- We are all of equal value.

- Go and sit in the last place and then you will be invited to take the first. Jesus

- Humility is the mother of all virtues. Babaji

- Humility = being right sized.

Humor:

- Don't take yourself so seriously. Reduce your self-important ego to discover lighthearted joy.

Immortality:

- Life is not separate from death. It only looks that way. Blackfoot proverb

- Energy cannot be created or destroyed. There is a part of us that cannot be born or die. We send out energy that never quits.

Infinity:

- Your heart is the size of an ocean. Go find yourself in its hidden depths. Rumi

- There is no beginning or end to the power and wisdom of the universe. That power runs through you.

Integrity:

- Place your feet carefully on the earth for the faces of coming generations are looking up from the earth. Oren Lyons, Onondaga Nation

- Live a good life. If there are gods and they are just, then they will not care how devout you have been, but will welcome you based on the virtues you have lived by. If there are gods, but unjust, then you should not want to worship them. If there are no gods, then you will be gone, but will have lived a noble life that will live on in the memories of your Loved ones. Marcus Aurelius

- I am not bound to win, but I am bound to be true. I am not bound to succeed, but I am bound to live up to what light I have. Abraham Lincoln

- Every man must decide whether he will walk in the light of creative altruism or in the darkness of destructive selfishness. Martin Luther King

- Do right always. It will give you satisfaction in life. Onondaga proverb

Interconnectedness:

- And while I stood there, I saw more than I can tell and I understood more than I saw; for I was seeing in a sacred manner the shapes of all things in the spirit, and the shape of all shapes as they must live together like one being. Black Elk

- Humankind has not woven the web of life. We are but one thread within it. Whatever we do to the web, we do to ourselves. All things are bound together. All things connect. Chief Seattle

- We are connected to everything and everybody, all life in the cosmos. We create waves that keep going. We carry vibrations from each other. You are always having an impact. Practice this interconnectedness.

Introspection:

- Yesterday I was clever, so I wanted to change the world. Today I am wise, so I am changing myself. Rumi

- There is a Wise Counselor inside. Contact the Counselor in meditation. He of She will help you answer these questions. How did the day go? What went well? Could I do better? Did I hurt someone? What do I need to learn? What do I need to do? What qualities do I need most right now to help manage my problems?

- The goal of introspection is purification of consciousness, strengthening the good and eliminating junk. Get the negative out of there before it hurts you and others. Make introspection a part of your daily meditation.

Intuition:

- Intuition is direct knowledge of the truth through the sixth sense. Listen to the still small loving voice within.

- We may not be able to decipher our ego-driven will from God's will. But we can always bring our actions in alignment with the higher order of the universe with love and stillness.

Joy:

- If you knew yourself for even one moment, if you could just glimpse your most beautiful face, maybe you wouldn't slumber so deeply in that house of clay. Why not move into your house of joy and shine into every crevice! For you are the secret Treasure-bearer, and always have been, didn't you know? Rumi

- Wherever you are and whatever you do, be in love. Only then can you know the highest joy.

- Self-acceptance → peace → love → joy

Justice:

- It may not happen right away. It may not make sense right away. But negative and positive seeds are planted and eventually come to full blossom. What goes around, comes around.

Kindness:

- The world can be harsh and negative, but if we remain generous and patient, kindness inevitably reveals itself. Something deep in the human soul seems to depend on the presence of kindness. John O-Donohue

- Send loving-kindness thoughts to yourself first, then to those you like, then strangers, then enemies.

- When you send loving-kindness thoughts to others, your consciousness expands but don't stop there, do for them.

Knowledge:

- If we wonder often, the gift of knowledge will come. Arapaho proverb

- Knowledge is inherent in all things. The world itself is a library. Chief Luther Standing Bear

- You can be exposed to the finest thinking available, but it won't do you or anyone else any good if you don't cook it on your own stove. Anonymous

- Give me knowledge so I may have kindness for all. Lakota proverb
- Your true self is love and its one hundred companion healing qualities. Go deep. Bring this knowledge out. You will heal.

Laughter:

- The funny edge of the world makes a bid for your attention. Go there to heal.
- What soap is to the body, laughter is to the soul. Yiddish proverb
- Don't forget the recipe of making three people laugh every day. Edgar Cayce
- Always go to other people's funerals; otherwise they don't come to yours. Yogi Berra
- Laughter is the shortest distance between two people. Victor Borge
- If everything goes wrong, just laugh! Just let it have its fling, and let it go. But keep your vision upon God, and know that all will come right. White Eagle
- A person without a sense of humor is like a wagon without springs—jolted by every pebble in the road. Henry W. Beecher
- A person who knows how to laugh at himself will never cease to be amused. Shirley MacLaine
- Laughter is a tranquilizer with no side effects. Arnold Glasgow
- Never trust a God who doesn't dance. Friedrich W. Nietzsche

Light:

- The wound is the place where the Light enters you. Rumi
- Ring the bells that still can ring. Forget your perfect offering. There is a crack in everything. That's how the light gets in. Leonard Cohen
- Seeing cosmic light is one of many superconscious experiences. It is an actual light you can see and feel. It comes with the peace that surpasses understanding, unfathomable stillness, and ecstatic joy.
- Visualize the love-light healing everyone and everything, within and without, above and below, in front and behind, everywhere.

Listening:

- If you are to be a leader, you must listen in silence to the mystery and the Spirit. Leaf Dweller, Kaposia Sioux
- Talk less. Listen more. Everything gets better.

Loyalty:

- Remain loyal to love and its one hundred associated healing qualities. This is your higher self. Stay with the qualities when the going gets rough. There is no love without loyalty.

Mercy:

- Suffering is a gift. In it is hidden mercy. Rumi

- Resentment is like taking a poison and waiting for the other person to die. Forgive yourself and others. Without mercy, there can be no peace, love, or joy.

Mindfulness:

- In every moment, some element of our loving self is at stake. Ed Bacon

- Instead of letting the mind wander aimlessly, focus your attention on a healing method and healing quality. You will feel better, become a more skillful pain manager, and evolve to higher states of consciousness.

Mystery:

- A Japanese master received a university professor who came to inquire about Zen. The master served tea. He poured his visitor's cup full, and then kept on pouring. The professor watched the overflow until he no longer could restrain himself. "It is overfull. No more will go in!" The master said, "Like this cup, you are full of your own opinions and speculations. How can I show you Zen unless you first empty your cup?"

- The illiterate of the twenty-first century will not be those who cannot read and write, but those who cannot learn, unlearn and relearn – Alvin Toffler

- In the beginner's mind there are many possibilities; in the expert's there are few. Shunryu Suzuki-roshi

- Deep in the heart, every mystery of Spirit is hidden. Only from soul can soul draw its secrets, not from any page or eloquent speech. The heart of the matter is soul, nothing else. Rumi

- Knowledge is learning something every day. Wisdom is letting something go every day. – Zen Proverb

- If you could get rid of yourself just once, the secret of secrets would open to you. Rumi

- The infinite mysterious unknown can be frightening, a call to adventure, or both. Where do you stand?

Non-attachment:

- Chop wood, carry water. Love and serve all. Let everything else go.

- Attachment feeds the fire of reactivity. Love without attachment is water for the fire.

Non-injury:

- An eye for an eye will make the whole world blind. Do no harm to yourself and others.

- Permeate every thought and act with patience, kindness, sweetness, tenderness, gentleness.

Oneness:

- All religions, all this singing, one song. The differences are just illusion and vanity. The sun's light looks a little different on this wall than it does on that wall, and a lot different on this other one, but it's still one light. Rumi

- Now be silent. Let the One who creates the words speak. He made the door. He made the lock. He also made the key. Rumi

- In truth everything and everyone is a shadow of the Beloved. And our seeking is His seeking. And our words are His words. We search for Him here and there, while looking right at Him. Sitting by His side, we ask: 'O Beloved, where is the Beloved?' Rumi

- Even when tied in a thousand knots, the string is still but one. Rumi

- All in one and one in all → supreme Love → ecstatic joy.

Openness:

- Don't put blankets over the drum! Open completely. Let your spirit ear listen to the green dome's passionate murmur. Rumi

- I know you're tired, but come. This is the way. Rumi

- These pains you feel are messengers. Listen to them. Rumi

- You are so weak. Give up to grace. The ocean takes care of each wave till it gets to shore. You need more help than you know. Rumi

Order:

- In seemingly empty space there is one link, one life eternal, one way of life flowing through everything, animate and inanimate, unifying everything in the universe, a oneness of life, a unity and harmony so vast, so perfect, breathtakingly perfect, that it automatically breeds reverence and humility. Yogananda

- Make this your mantra for a day: balance, rhythm, harmony, order.

Patience:

- When you go through a hard period, when everything seems to oppose you, when you feel you cannot even bear one more minute, never give up. Because it is the time and place that the course will divert. Rumi

Peace:

- I am poor and naked, but I am the chief of the nation. We do not want riches but we do want to train our children right. Riches would do us no good. We could not take them with us to the other world. We do not want riches. We want peace and love. Red Cloud

- For peace of mind, resign as general manager of the universe. Larry Eisenberg

- Peace comes not from doing but from undoing; not from getting, but from letting go. Satchidananda

- There is a calm center within that our hyperactive culture cannot reach. Learn how to meditate. You will find new healing powers in the room of stillness.

Perfection:

- How will you know the difficulties of being human, if you're always flying off to blue perfection? Rumi

- Advanced sages describe perfect peace, Love, and joy when the soul merges with Spirit, an impossible goal for anyone but a master. While it is good to strive for this elusive goal daily, don't be a compulsive perfectionist and drive yourself crazy when you come up short. Be understanding, compassionate, forgiving, and gentle with yourself and others. Relax. Be human. Have fun with it.

Perseverance:

- Winds may blow strong in my face, yet I will go forward and never turn back. I will continue forward until I have finished. Teedyuscung, Delaware

- Your legs will get heavy and tired. Then comes a moment of feeling the wings you've grown, lifting. Rumi

- Perseverance is the magic of spiritual work. Make the effort. Never give up. Get in there and fight. Eventually you will breech the barrier and then another.

- Walk the spiritual path, say little, love much, give to all, judge no one, aspire to all that is pure and good, keep on keeping on.

- I may not be there yet, but I am closer than I was yesterday.

- I fall; I get up. I fall; I get up.

Play:

- Good work and joyous play go hand in hand. When play stops, old age begins. Play keeps you from taking life too seriously. George Byron

- Knowledge that is acquired is not like this. Those who have it worry if audiences like it or not. It's a bait for popularity. Disputational knowing wants customers. It has no soul. The only real customer is God. Chew quietly your sweet sugarcane God-Love, and stay playfully childish. Rumi

- There is one way of breathing that is shameful and constricted. Then, there's another way: a breath of Love that takes you all the way to infinity. Rumi

- What a fun game to play, this training in love and Infinity.

Positive thinking:

- Fill your brain with wisdom the first thing in the morning and maintain it throughout the day. There is tremendous healing there.

Power:

- There is a fountain inside you. Don't walk around with an empty bucket. Rumi

- Gamble everything for love, if you are a true human being. If not, leave this gathering. Half-heartedness doesn't reach into majesty. Rumi

- Right now, at this very moment, you have more power than you are using. Tap into that power and use it to do the work of self-healing. Focus all of your powers on the cultivation of love.

Practicality:

- If all you can do is crawl, start crawling. Rumi

- Think cosmic thoughts while you tie your shoes.

Pure awareness:

- There is a place in your consciousness that is not your body or mind referred to in yoga as the soul connected to Spirit. Since there is no body there, you cannot be hurt, cut, wetted, or burned.

Pure consciousness:

- And don't look for me in a human shape. I am inside your looking. No room for form with Love this strong. Rumi

Purity:

- Purify your eyes, and see the pure world. You life will fill with radiant forms. Rumi

- Everyone sees the unseen in proportion to the clarity of his heart, and that depends upon how much he has polished it. Whoever has polished it more sees more—more unseen forms become manifest to him. Rumi

- To enter higher states, we have to clear out the negativity that keeps us down and replace it with healing qualities. Healing is a process of purification, sometimes purification by fire. When consciousness is purified, we discover our heritage: ecstatic joy!

Receptivity:

- To experience superconsciousness, we need to become aware of more subtle vibratory frequencies than can be detected by the five senses and ordinary mind. This occurs in meditation when we learn to stop the world, body, senses, and mind.

- Be still and know that I am God. Psalm 46-10

Reverence:

- Will you ever begin to understand the meaning of the very soil beneath your feet? From a grain of sand to a great mountain, all is sacred. Yesterday and tomorrow exist eternally upon this continent. We natives are guardians of this sacred place. ~ Peter Blue Cloud, Mohawk

- Reverence is right attitude, when everything and everyone is sacred.

Rhythm:

- In the mob of I's inside, which one is me? Hear me out. I know I'm wandering, but don't start putting a lid on this racket. No telling what I'll do then. Every moment I'm thrown by your story. One moment it's happy, and I'm singing. One moment it's sad, and I'm weeping. It turns bitter, and I pull away. But then you spill a little grace, and just like that, I'm all light. It's not so bad, this arrangement, actually. Rumi

- The universe dances to the beat of its own drum. It's a complex dance, unpredictable, ever-changing, difficult to follow. We can't always get it right but we can get the beat more often when we are quiet.

- I am a drunkard from another kind of tavern. I dance to a silent tune. I am the symphony of stars. Rumi

- Sometimes we have to go deeper in Love to find the inner harmony always there.

Safety:

- At the heart of the cyclone tearing the sky is a place of central calm. Edwin Markham

- I learned it is possible for us to create light, sound, and order within no matter what calamity may befall us in the outside world. Helen Keller

Security:

- Each one has to find his peace from within. And peace to be real must be unaffected by outside circumstances. Mohandas Gandhi

- Perfect peace can dwell only where all egotism has disappeared. Gautama Buddha

Self-control:

- There is only one corner of the universe you can be certain of improving: your own self.

- We must have discipline on the spiritual path. Learn to behave. You can't rob a bank in the morning and see God at night.

Service:

- Be a lamp, or a lifeboat, or a ladder. Help someone's soul heal. Walk out of your house like a shepherd. Rumi

- There should be less talk; a preaching point is not a meeting point. What do you do then? Take a broom and clean someone's house. That says enough. Mother Theresa.

- Help everyone and let everything else go. The more you give, the more you receive.

- I'll get by with a little help from my friends.

Silence:

- Silence is the language of God; all else is poor translation. Rumi.

- In silence there is eloquence. Stop weaving and see how the pattern improves. Rumi

- The still mind of the sage is a mirror of heaven and earth—the glass of all things. Chuang Tse

- If the mind can get quiet enough, something sacred will be revealed. Helen Tworkov

- Silence gives us a new way of looking at something. Mother Teresa

- Retreat. Turn off the radio, TV, computer, and Internet. Practice contemplation and meditation. You may be anxious at first but soon you will learn how to be alone and comfortable. Wonderful experiences occur in stillness and silence that cannot be had in any other way.

Simplicity:

- The simplified life is a sanctified life, much more calm, much less strife. Oh, what wondrous truths are unveiled. Projects succeed which had previously failed. Oh, how beautiful life can be, beautiful simplicity. Peace Pilgrim

- There is nothing to chase after. We can go back to ourselves, enjoy our breathing, our smiling, ourselves, and our beautiful environment. Thich Nhat Hanh

- We are happy in proportion to the things we can do without. Henry David Thoreau

- Happiness is not what you have but who you are. You are already who you need to be. Diogenes

- Nothing is more simple than greatness; indeed, to be simple is to be great. Ralph W. Emerson

- Simplicity is the nature of great souls. They live and serve as incense burners. Papa Ramdas

- Simplifying breeds peace and harmony. Progressively simplify your life. Plain living and high thinking. What is better?

Sincerity:

- Sincerity is the key which will open the door through which you will see your separate parts, and you will see something quite new. You must go on trying to be sincere. Each day you put on a mask, and you must take it off little by little. G. I. Gurdjieff

- Sincerity is an openness of heart; we find it in very few people; what we usually see is only an artful dissimulation to win the confidence of others. La Rochefoucauld

- Sincerity is impossible, unless it pervade the whole being, and the pretense of it saps the very foundation of character. James Russell Lowell

- Sincerity is the way to heaven. Confucious

Spaciousness:

- Christian, Jew, Muslim, shaman, Zoroastrian, stone, ground, mountain, river, each has a secret way of being with the mystery, unique and not to be judged. Rumi

- When you feel overwhelmed it is as though "there is no room in the inn." This is a time to create more space. You can do this in meditation. Advanced sages have it. They say it is like an ocean. Ordinary consciousness is like a small pool. When you have more space, the same pain or problem makes a much smaller wave than when the pool is small. In the ocean, even big problems create barely a ripple.

Stillness:

- Put your thoughts to sleep, do not let them cast a shadow over the moon of your heart. Let go of thinking. Rumi

- We need to find God, but we cannot find Him in noise, in excitement. See how nature, the trees, the flowers, the grass grow in deep silence. See how the stars, the moon, and the sun move in silence. Mother Teresa

- Nothing in all creation is so like God as stillness. Meister Eckhart

- The only language able to express the wholeness of truth is silence. Silence is our eternal speech. Silence is ever speaking. It is a perennial flow of language, which is interrupted by speaking. Ramana Maharishi

- The most important thing is silence. We cannot place ourselves directly in God's presence without imposing upon ourselves interior and exterior silence. Mother Teresa

- Silence is the language God speaks. Everything else is a bad translation. Thomas Keating.

- You do not need to leave your room. Remain sitting at your table and listen, wait, be quiet, still, and solitary. The world will freely offer itself to you, to be unmasked, it has no choice, it will roll in ecstasy at your feet. Franz Kafka

- Any trial whatever that comes to you can be conquered by silence. Abbot Pastor

- In the room of stillness, healing qualities abound. It doesn't matter if you make mistakes, are misunderstood or abandoned on the outside. In the room of stillness inside, you are forgiven, understood, and cherished.

- Make contact with the Beloved Friend by quieting the restless mind in meditation. The still small loving voice within is always there.

- The more you talk about it, the more you think about it, the further from it you go. Stop talking, stop thinking, and there is nothing you will not understand. Seng-Ts'an

- Stillness is the doorway to higher states of consciousness. Enter the room of stillness in deep meditation and stay there as long as you can. Eventually you will know the peace that surpasses understanding.

Strength:

- What hurts you, blesses you. Darkness is your candle. Rumi

- Brother, stand the pain. Escape the poison of your impulses. The sky will bow to your beauty if you do. Learn to light the candle. Rise with the sun. Turn away from the cave of your sleeping. That way a thorn expands to a rose. Rumi

- Strength is not only physical, it is also mental. Fundamentally it is Spiritual. The source of our strength comes from the guiding principles we receive from the Creator. The greatest of these is that we are all related. Native American Wisdom

- Peace and strength are on the other side of every painful problem. Learn to endure with courage and you will find your power in the story.

- There are great reservoirs of strength even at your weakest moments. Surrender to find it. The darkest hour can be just before the light. Persevere.

Success:

- Even more important than worldly success is the cultivation of healing qualities inside. This is spiritual success.

- We can do anything we want to do if we stick to it long enough. Helen Keller

- To laugh often and much. To win the respect of intelligent people and the affection of children. To earn the appreciation of honest critics and endure the betrayal of false friends.

To appreciate beauty. To find the best in others. To leave the world a bit better. To know even one life has breathed easier because you lived. This is to be successful. Ralph W. Emerson

Surrender:

- If you are irritated by every rub, how will your mirror be polished? Rumi

- There is a necessary dying and then Jesus is breathing again. Very little grows on jagged rock. Be ground. Be crumbled, so wildflowers will come up where you are. You've been stony for too many years. Try something different. Surrender. Rumi

- Sometimes the only thing on the menu at the Brutal Reality Café is a big hot plate of *damned if you do* served with a side of *damned if you don't*. For most of us, this is a hard meal to swallow. Choosing to bear our suffering instead of pigging out on self-destruction often means a long wait for dessert. Fortifying ourselves with patience and faith gives us the strength to endure the wait until our reward arrives. Tim Casebeer

- Here are a few one word surrender affirmations: accept, attune, receive, soft, yield, open, stillness, silence, spaciousness, and serenity. Apply these affirmations to a problem that won't go away and you will reduce your reaction to that problem. Some problems dissolve. The problems that remain create less of a stir.

Sweetness:

- When the heart has seen the sweetheart, how can it remain bitter. Find the sweetness in your own heart, that you may find the sweetness in every heart. Rumi

- Close your eyes, fall in love, stay there. Rumi

Tenderness:

- Love has taken away my practices and filled me with poetry. A mountain keeps an echo deep inside itself. That's how I hold your voice. Why should we grieve that we've been sleeping? It doesn't matter how long we've been unconscious. We're groggy, but let the guilt go. Feel the motions of tenderness around you, the Buoyancy. Rumi

- Be kind and gentle with everyone and everything. Be sure to include yourself.

Thoughtfulness:

- Listening is thoughtfulness. Talk less and listen more.

- Think about others and be aware of their needs. We can't always figure it out and sometimes forget or miss the mark but keep trying and don't forget; small gestures mean a lot.

Tolerance:

- Do not judge your neighbor until you walk two moons in his moccasins. Cheyenne

- We are equal and one yet different. Create some space and enjoy the diversity show.

Trust:

- Your pain is the route to healing. Learn to trust this principle by rolling the universal healing wheel or practice PMQ. You will see that it works. As you feel better, become a better person, and experience higher states of consciousness, your trust in the healing process grows.

- Once the seed of faith takes root, it cannot be blown away, even by the strongest wind. Now that's a blessing. Rumi

Truthfulness:

- O' Great Spirit, help me always to speak the truth quietly, to listen with an open mind when others speak, and to remember the peace that may be found in silence. Cherokee Prayer

- Fight for truth but only with love in your heart.

- Tell yourself the truth. Do a searching and fearless inventory. Find and remove all traces of negativity but always remain compassionate, gentle and forgiving towards yourself.

Unconditional Love:

- This love is the rose that blooms forever. Rumi

- Love is the great solvent of all difficulties, all problems, all misunderstandings. White Eagle

- If only you could love enough, you would be the happiest and most powerful being in the world. Emmet Fox

- To love means never to be afraid of the windstorms of life. Elisabeth Kubler-Ross

- Love is an incurable disease. No one who catches it wants to recover, and all its victims refuse a cure. Ibn Hazim

- Love is a medicine for the sickness of the world, a prescription often given, too rarely taken. It cures those who give it and it cures those who receive it. Karl Menninger

- Love is the only sane response in an otherwise insane world. Corbett Monica

- A thousand half-loves must be forsaken to take one whole heart home. Rumi

- You can't force a person to grow. Just provide the right conditions. People respond on their own schedule.

- God loves you just as you are and too much to leave you there.

- I love myself just as I am and too much to leave me there.

- Love is the supreme goal of life, the ultimate experience, the salvation of man. Nothing is better.

Understanding:

- Be grateful for whoever comes, because each has been sent as a guide from beyond. Rumi
- Practice this daily: Understanding → respect → compassion → forgiveness → peace → love → joy

Unity:

- Lovers don't finally meet somewhere. They're in each other all along. Rumi
- They say there is a doorway from heart to heart, but what is the use of a door when there are no walls? Rumi
- You are not alone, separate or isolated. You are part of the cosmic whole. Connect yourself to everything through love, the great unifying force in the universe.

Usefulness:

- Find ever-new creative ways to love and serve without attachment to outcome.

Warmth:

- Raise your words not voice. It is rain that grows flowers, not thunder. Rumi
- Be soft like a pillow.

Will:

- Choose a healing quality such as compassion, love, understanding, forgiveness or courage. Focus on it with calm, continuous, intense concentration. You will see an increase in that quality. This is the greatest use of your willpower.
- Use will and thought to accomplish your goals every step of the way.
- My mind is set, my will is strong. I can change. I will change.

Wisdom:

- You will not have wisdom until you have self-knowledge. Strength, understanding and peace are found only through a journey within. By learning how to live, we bring meaning to our lives and to those we touch. Native American Wisdom

- You are a volume in the divine book. A mirror to the power that created the universe. Whatever you want, ask it of yourself. Whatever you're looking for can only be found inside of you. Rumi

- If you keep open your eyes of wisdom and calmness, you will see there is a lot of enjoyment in this world—just as though you are watching a motion picture. Paramahansa Yogananda

- Use the healing qualities in your everyday life for protection and guidance. With this wisdom, everything improves.

Witness:

- The Witness is the place inside that is completely still, silent, spacious, and serene. Go to the witness early and often. There you will find the wise counsel of the still small loving voice within.

Other:

Part 5
Miscellaneous

Chapter 44

The House

- In the next four chapters, you will review *the house, the movie, school, and the car.* These metaphors are designed to help us understand self-healing and skillful pain management.

- Imagine we live in a three-story house. The first floor is our story. The second floor is our higher self. On the third floor, there is a Higher Power. (see illustration on p. 317)

A Three Story House

- The first floor of the house is ordinary human consciousness. It is under the control of the ego. This is where our individual and collective stories play out. As the story unfolds, we see the entire human condition: beauty and goodness, triumph and tragedy, humor and sadness, trials and tests, the good, bad, ugly, terrible, and great.

- The second floor of the house is filled with unlimited healing qualities. (See p. 79) This is the higher self or soul. We can go there for solace and comfort. No matter the problems we face on the first floor, the second floor offers peace, safety, harmony, and strength.

- The third floor is the land of Higher Powers.

- The goal is to infuse powerful second-floor healing qualities into the first-floor story. When we add patience, kindness, love, understanding, compassion, forgiveness, strength, courage, and humor to the story, everything gets better. This is called spiritualizing the story or skillful pain management. The story and problems are the same but there is less reactivity and therefore less pain. The goal is to work with anything that shows up on the first floor and remain even-minded, patient, kind, and calm.

- Our imperfections preclude our ability to succeed at this 100 per cent of the time but what a wonderful goal. Go to the second floor of your house and bring healing qualities down to the first floor to help you manage your pain and problems. How do we do this?

- The steps to the second floor are the practices recommended in *Healing Power, Ten Steps to Pain Management and Spiritual Evolution Revised.* There are fifteen steps or methods to the second floor. The methods are (1) people, (2) activities, (3) belief systems, (4) affirmations, (5) habit transformation, (6) progressive muscle relaxation, (7) breathwork, (8) contemplation, (9) meditation, (10) prayer, (11) mindfulness, (12) presence of God, (13) service, (14) yoga, (15) transformation of emotion.

- If you practice these methods and the qualities become strong enough, they can no longer contain themselves. They inflate by nature. Gradually, they take over the first floor and expand through the ceiling of the second floor to the third floor of the house. Here there are no walls, no ceiling, and no roof. This is the Big Space, the land of Higher Power and higher consciousness, sometimes referred to as nirvana, ecstasy, or God. Here you may experience a superconscious state: unfathomable peace, pure unconditional love, and ecstatic joy. This pure consciousness expands to infinity. Blow off the second story ceiling with your ever-expanding compassion and love. You will see the stars, then touch them.

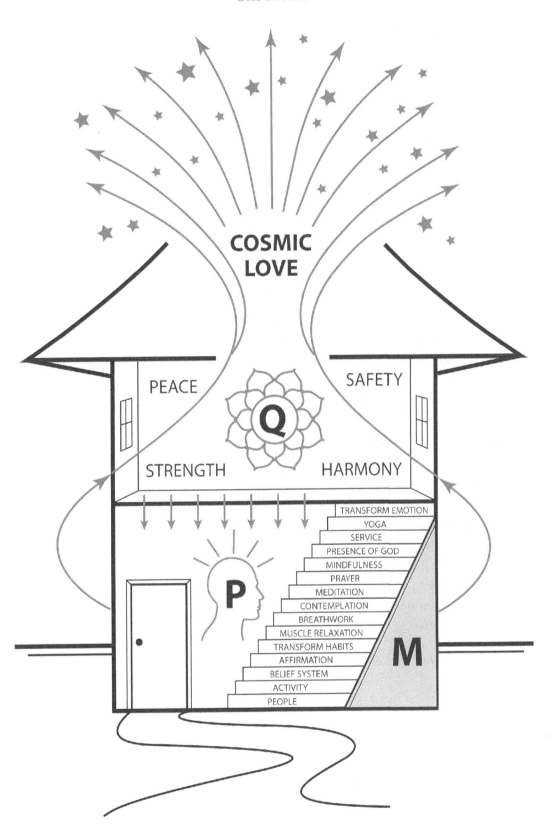

Exercises

1. How does the three-story house apply to your life?

2. Do you have a second and third floor philosophy?

3. What is your belief system?

4. Do you have a higher self and/or a Higher Power?

5. What are your practice methods?

6. **Pain Has a Purpose**

   • Our pain is important but not as important as how we respond.

   • We can turn the tables on our pain and make it work for rather than against us. We can make medicine out of our pain.

   • No painful experience is wasted on the first floor. We can always use our pain to propel ourselves to the second and third floor.

   • Every painful problem---all tests, trials, tribulations, temptations, character defects, ego, pride, emotional reactivity, anger, resentment, guilt, shame, anxiety, and more--- has but one purpose: to get us to grow the qualities. Use the pressure of the problem on the first-floor to push yourself in the direction of expanded second-floor healing qualities and third-floor superconscious states.

7. **Transforming Problems Into Invited Guest Teachers**

   • In this exercise, we transfer the healing power of second floor qualities to the first floor to help us manage our painful problems.

     a. Introspection
     b. Guest-teachers
     c. Healing and purification
     d. Action
     e. Repetition
     f. Mastery

   a. **Introspection**

     • The first floor represents the physical plane. This is where we struggle with issues, problems, flaws and symptoms. Some of these we can fix. Others do not respond so easily.

     • All of us have problems that take up residence on the first floor of our home against our will. We do everything we can to eliminate them. However, no matter what we try, some problems will not budge. We cannot fix them or evict them. On the contrary, the more we struggle, the more upset and agitated we become.

- Make a list of problems you are unable to eliminate from the first floor of your house. For example, you might choose highly reactive emotions.

b. Convert Problems to Invited Guest Teachers

- When agitated, it is often because we have not created enough space for the problem. We have treated the problem as an uninvited guest. When we find ourselves in this dilemma, we can accept the problem in our home as a resident instructor.

- Go to the second floor of your magical house where there is unlimited space. Bring a portion of that space down to the first floor, and create a guest room for your problem. Fill the room with an atmosphere of acceptance, thus making the uninvited problem a guest-teacher.

- We can create as many rooms as we need. There is an infinite supply of space on the second floor of this magical house. We can do this with all of our problems, so that on the first floor all we have are invited guest teachers in the school of life.

- This sets the stage for healing and purification.

c. Healing and Purification

- When we respond to first floor painful problems with second floor qualities, we heal and purify.

- The atmosphere on the second floor is still, silent, spacious, and serene. Here there is unlimited love and associated qualities. The goal is to bring these qualities to the first floor to help us manage our painful problems.

- Go back to the second floor to get whatever qualities you need to manage your problem. We have one hundred qualities to choose from up there!

- The steps to the second floor are the recommended methods: affirmations, mindfulness, meditation, loving service, and more. When we practice these methods, we climb to the second floor where we draw from an unlimited supply of space and healing qualities.

- Practice meditation, mindfulness, service to humanity, or any other methods that you enjoy, and absorb the qualities you need to skillfully manage your first floor problems.

- For highly reactive emotions, you might choose peace, even-mindedness, and patience. Permeate all of the rooms in your house and their invited guest teacher problems with these qualities.

d. Action

- Bring your expanded peace, even-mindedness, and patience to all of your thoughts, feelings, desires, decisions, and actions.

- Give these qualities to all whom you meet.

e. Repetition

- All first floor problems are teachers with the goal of helping us expand healing qualities until these qualities are unconditional.

- Repeat this process of healing and purification until the qualities become unconditional.

f. Mastery

- In the end, we become patient, peaceful, and even-minded under all conditions.

8. Spaciousness

- When we practice spiritual disciplines, we expand the space in our house so it will be big enough to hold our problems. When we have a lot of space, problems can show up with barely a ripple.

- What happens if we do not have enough space in our house to hold our problems?

- Did you know you can create more space and make your rooms bigger?

- Did you know you can fill the rooms with love, light, and any of the other one hundred healing qualities?

- Is your house big enough?

- What will you do to create more space?

9. Right Attitude

- *Right attitude* is when our thoughts, feelings, decisions, and actions are aligned with the healing power of love and associated qualities.

- Bring love, compassion, understanding, forgiveness, courage, strength, perseverance, and other second floor healing qualities to your first floor problems.

- With right attitude on the first floor, knots are untied. Problems melt. Balance and harmony result.

- Cultivate right attitude for first floor problems.

10. Who Owns This House?

- We cannot get rid of all of our problems but we can learn how to live with and above them.

- We can do this by learning how to live on the three floors of the house at the same time.

- Painful problems are on the first floor.

- Unlimited healing qualities are on the second floor.

- The third floor is Higher Power or Spirit.

- Find your problems on the first floor, but don't identify with them. They are invited guest teachers but they do not own the house. Welcome these guests into your home but not as permanent residents.

- Instead, identify with the second and third floor. This is the soul connected to Spirit. This is your best self, higher self, and true self. Focus there as you work with your first floor realities.

- While we face everything on the first floor, we transcend and rise above it by getting to the second and third floor.

- Remember, your problems are teachers, helping expand your healing qualities until these qualities are unconditional.

- Call up your army of one hundred healing qualities from the second floor of your house, and send them down to the first floor to take charge of the story.

- When your pain or problem persists, never forget this is not who you are. You are not your problems. Problems are guests. The owner of the house is love. You are love itself.

- Affirmations:
  a. I am not my problem, defect, illness, or symptom. These first floor identifications need to be managed but are not who I really am.
  b. It doesn't matter what the world or my body does. I am the serene and compassionate space within and without.

11. The Compelling Nature of the First Floor

- The first floor is the human condition.

- The second floor is love.

- The third floor is infinity.

- There are many layers on the first floor: the world story, our personal story, our roles, relationships, responsibilities, personalities, attachments, and problems.

- The first floor story is compelling and magnetic. It grabs all of our attention, sucking into its vortex our entire consciousness. It is important but we make it too important. It consumes all of our attention and energy.

- Don't let the first floor story define you. Cast off these layers by spiritualizing the story with the love qualities from the second floor and contact with the Infinite One on the third floor.

- Affirm:
    a. I hold all of my problems in a compassionate space.
    b. I hold all of your problems in a compassionate space.
    c. I will work with this condition, however long or severe. I respond with love.

12. Our True Identity

- Problems are on the first floor of the house where we live in ordinary consciousness. But we are not our problems. We need to face our problems and work on them, but they are not our true identity. Never, even for a moment, assume the identity of the problem. There is something deeper: the soul and Spirit.

- Our true self is second floor healing qualities and third floor higher states of consciousness.

- The higher self is unconditional peace, joy, love, wisdom, courage, strength, warmth, harmony, balance, beauty, and a host of other healing qualities listed in the spiritual alphabet. At some point the qualities expand into superconsciousness: the peace that surpasses understanding, pure love, and ecstatic joy.

13. Soul and Ego

- The ego is in charge of the first floor.

- The soul is in charge of the second floor.

- The goal is to have the soul take over the first floor. This is going to take some time. The ego resists the soul's attempts to take over. They fight with each other.

- Continue your practice. Persevere. Keep going. Soul qualities slowly grow and replace the trickster ego. Eventually, the soul takes over the first floor.

14. Reactivity

- We may not be able to fix or eliminate all first floor problems but we can reduce reactivity by infusing the first floor with healing qualities: love, compassion, forgiveness, understanding, acceptance, and more.

- When we find ourselves overreacting, there is a shortage of healing qualities on the first floor. When we have enough healing qualities on the first floor, we do not overreact.

- Go to the second floor. Here you will find an additional supply of any one or a combination of healing qualities you need. Decorate every room on the first floor of your house with the beautiful and loving healing qualities of the second floor.

15. Provocative People

- Make a list of people who provoke you.

- In a meditative state, visualize each one of them in a room with plenty of space.

- Then permeate the room with understanding, respect, compassion, forgiveness, patience, tolerance, kindness, light, and love.

- Picture yourself with each of these people in harmony and peace.

- Do this until your love, compassion, understanding, and forgiveness are unconditional. Then give these qualities to all whom you meet.

16. Guilt and Shame

- When you feel guilty, ashamed, or embarrassed by your mistakes, visualize yourself in a spacious room filled with understanding, compassion, and forgiveness.

- Absorb these qualities.

- Practice this until your love for yourself is unconditional.

17. Resentment

- It is all too easy to get stuck in self-righteous anger and resentment for the wrongs done to us by others. Anger is seductive, attractive, magnetic, and difficult to shed. But righteous anger is not love, and it steals our peace.

- To reduce your negative ego-driven anger, go to the second floor and stay there even when other people are wrong and you are right. This is a big part of spiritual work as it involves ego reduction and soul expansion towards unconditional love. How else can you get to unconditional love unless this condition plays itself out again and again? Not getting your way is the only way.

- Righteous anger is a lower vibration of consciousness. Get to the second floor and stay there no matter what other people do. Otherwise we are filled with emotions about what other people are doing to us. This does not mean you are a doormat. Protect yourself on the outside. Reduce your ego on the inside.

18. Growing Love is Most Important

- Of course it matters what happens on the first floor, but how we respond matters even more.

- Let the story unfold on the first floor, and then spiritualize that story with second floor healing qualities.

- The greater the pain, the bigger love has to be.

- When love is strong enough, the first floor story dissolves and love is all there is.

- Painful tests recur until love is unconditional. Even then, there may still be painful tests, but you will be a skillful pain manager.

19. The Greater the Pain, the Greater the Victory

- The deepest suffering requires the deepest healing.

- The bigger the pain story on the first floor, the more work we have to do with methods and qualities to manage it skillfully.

- For example, problems can be 1--100 in severity. If you have a 1-unit problem, you need 1 unit of a healing quality to match. I am a little anxious, so a little meditation can work to calm me down.

- A 20-unit level of anxiety would require deeper and longer meditation.

- An 80-unit problem will require day-to-day, hand-to-hand combat for weeks, months, or years. Despite the long-term effort required, the payoff on bigger problems is great. The healing qualities we need to manage that pain skillfully will have to match and exceed 80 units. Big doses of peace, courage, strength, compassion, and the other qualities can then be enjoyed, shared with others, and deployed for tests to come.

20. Endure with Courage

- When we get stuck with first floor problems that will not go away, we can endure with courage while we use our willpower to practice methods and cultivate qualities. This is the work.

- First floor: accept and endure your problems with courage.

- Steps to the second floor: apply your willpower to the methods.

- Second floor: apply your willpower to cultivate the qualities.

- As you practice, the quality is growing but you may not feel it until later.

21. Lifelong Practice

- Expect bouts of unskillful pain management on the first floor of the house due to old brain grooves carrying negative thought and emotional habit patterns that take over against our will.

- Go to the second and third floor early and often, and stay there as long as you can.

- The way forward is practice. Practice is lifelong. Be patient.

22. What House

- In the beginning, we understand the goal of all first floor pain is to get us to the second floor and then the third floor of the house.

- Go to the second floor and bring the qualities down to the first floor. This may be hard at first. You may find yourself stuck on the first floor and find it difficult to get to the second floor, let alone stay there. All you experience is your painful problem.

- If you persist, however, you can get to the second floor for short periods of time and progressively stay there longer. The qualities are growing and you feel them. There is more peace, love, compassion, strength, courage, patience, and more. You feel better.

- When advanced, we stay on the second floor all the time, and the second floor qualities take over the first floor. We remain even-minded under all conditions.

- Eventually we break through the ceiling on the second floor and enter third floor superconsciousness: the peace that surpasses understanding, pure love, ecstatic joy, bliss, nirvana, God.

- With practice, superconsciousness occurs more often and lasts longer.

- Masters live in a house filled with unlimited healing qualities and higher states of consciousness. What rooms? What walls? What floor? What ceiling? What roof? What house? Only love. Pure love. No forms. Disembodied consciousness. Infinity. Eternity. Immortality. Absolute spaciousness.

- Blow off the second story ceiling with your ever-expanding compassion and love. You will see the stars, then touch them.

Points to Remember

- Healing qualities already exist on the first floor of the house, but we always need more. Go to the second floor early and often to improve your ability to manage pain skillfully. Practice when you feel good and when you feel poorly.

- An uninvited problem that we cannot eliminate creates agitation. We can reduce this agitation by giving the problem a spacious room filled with stillness, silence, and serenity.

- When life does not change, our response to it can. We can accept all problems with serenity. When we practice the methods described in this work, we create an increasingly serene space to hold our problems.

- We can bring second floor qualities to first floor tests and trials. When we focus on the qualities instead of our problems, we slowly spiritualize the entire first floor of our home. Eventually, love, compassion, understanding, courage, perseverance, and strength permeate our atmosphere.

- In the beginning, in ordinary consciousness, a problem like a big fish creates many ripples in a small pond. In higher states of consciousness, the same fish has little or no effect, as our consciousness has expanded. We have the space inside to handle anything, including death.

Affirmations

- I add love to every moment.

- I accept every problem as a guest-teacher.

- I accept all problems with serenity.

- I surround, feed, permeate, and saturate all of my problems with healing qualities.

- I burn karmic problems with love.

- Love burns karma---mine, yours, and ours.

Chapter 45

The Movie

- Our identification with the drama causes unnecessary reactivity. We can reduce this reactivity by rolling the universal healing wheel. The following exercise illustrates this principle using the movie as the metaphor.

- When we roll the wheel, the movie of life goes through four stages.

The Movie

1. Immersed in the movie

2. Spiritualize the movie

3. Watch the movie

4. What movie?

The Movie

1. Immersed in the Movie

- We are actors in a movie. When we completely identify with our role, we have the feelings of that role. This is a necessary stage. We all start here.

- Part of the story is painful. The pain story is seductive. It successfully grabs and keeps all of our attention.

- We are immersed in the pain story often without being conscious that this is happening, and even when we are conscious of it, we still can't get out.

- To change this pattern, let the story unfold. Give the pain its day in court. Let it tell the story from its point of view. But don't stay there. Move on to the next step: infuse the pain story with healing qualities.

2. Spiritualize the Movie

- Roll the wheel. Practice PMQ. Permeate the story with ever-increasing love and its associated healing qualities.

- Keep weaving, working, and massaging the pain story with love qualities.

- As we roll the wheel and the qualities grow, we begin to develop a little space between the movie and us.

3. Watch the Movie

- Now we can watch the show without being completely absorbed in it.

- We are still in the movie as a participant, but we are watching it as entertainment at the same time.

- Affirm the witness: *I watch the cosmic movie with calm detachment.*

4. What Movie?

- In advanced meditation, when love is so great it completely dissolves the story, we enter a state of pure consciousness and pure awareness.

- In this state of superconscious love, there is no form but the formless form.

- There can be no story or form in a love this strong.

- What movie?

Exercises

1. Roll the Wheel

- Practice PMQ and notice:
    a. How you rotate through the four stages: (1) immersed in the movie, (2) spiritualize the movie, (3) watch the movie, (4) what movie?
    b. How you go in and out of the drama.
    c. How sometimes you can't change anything in the movie, but you can always reduce reactivity by increasing the qualities.
    d. How the ego is slowly reduced and replaced by the qualities.
    e. How the qualities are slowly becoming unconditional, spontaneous, and automatic habits.
    f. How your mental power increases.

g. How you can ultimately face anything life throws at you with courage and strength.

Points to Remember

- The four-stage movie takes us through a process of purification, sometimes purification by fire. The ego is reduced and replaced by unconditional love.

- Recall the two levels of pain: the inevitable suffering of life and our reaction to it. The reactivity factor is huge. We get carried away. All recovery is about choosing from a variety of methods to help us respond differently and better. We learn how to step back and gain some perspective by cultivating the witness.

- Be full of love, compassion, and understanding. Be in the flow of the movie without attachment to the outcome. Stay out of the drama as much as possible. There is no control over most of it, anyway. Watch the cosmic movie with calm detachment.

Chapter 46

School

- Life is school. Pain is the teacher and stimulant for the cultivation of healing qualities and higher states of consciousness.

- There are classes, subjects, teachers, pop quizzes, and scheduled tests. When you finish a class, there are new classes. When you pass a grade, you go to the next grade.

- In the school of life, there is always another class, teacher, subject, and test. No matter how far you get, there is always more to learn.

> School keeps going until you finish off your ego and realize your higher self and Higher Power as unconditional love, compassion, understanding, forgiveness, and the other healing qualities listed in the spiritual alphabet. This is the universal lesson plan.

Classes

- There are a great variety of teachers, classes, and subjects in the school of life.

- Everyone has different classes. We get what we need.

- Some classes are required and some are elective. If we don't sign up for all the required classes at registration, the Principal of the university of life school will assign them for us.

- What class are you in? Who is the teacher? What is the subject?

- Have you taken this class before and didn't finish, or is this your first time around?

- What are the lessons?

Tests

- There will be many tests and battles on the first floor of the schoolhouse, tests of the world and tests of the body.

- The spiritual purpose of tests is to get you to the second and third floor of the house. The second floor is unlimited healing qualities, and the third floor is higher states of consciousness.

- We want to win every battle but we can't. Tests are designed to bring out our weak spots so we can make ourselves stronger. Failure and mistakes are a natural part of the process, as they show us where we need to do some work.

- The only bad mistake is the one we don't learn from. When you fall off the horse, brush off the dirt, figure out why it happened, and what you need to do differently, and get back on.

- As you go through this process of purification and sometimes purification by fire, be courageous, strong, and persevere. Be gentle, compassionate, and forgiving toward yourself. Get help from your higher self and Higher Power.

Report Card

- If life is school, is it possible to know our grade and report card? Am I in kindergarten or graduate school? Am I getting an A, B, C, D, or did I flunk?

- When we respond to tests with healing qualities, we pass the test. When we react poorly, we stay in that class and continue practicing PMQ.

- With continuous practice of PMQ, you will respond to the tests and trials of life with less reactivity and ever-increasing patience, kindness, love, understanding, and other healing qualities.

- The grade and score are less important than doing the work as best we can, learning from mistakes, and moving on. It doesn't matter if you are a beginner or advanced, if your problems are complex or severe, or the degree of your imperfections. If you do your best, you get an A.

- Some try to be on the second and third floor of the house without dealing with their problems on the first floor. This is a consequence of the spiritual ego. It is blind to our current state and makes us think we are higher than we are. Stay on the first floor and roll the wheel. You can't get where you want to go without being where you are. Just do PMQ and you will go forward and rise. You can only lay one brick at a time. The second and third floors arrive on their own schedule through grace.

Recess And Vacation

- There is scheduled recess every day for rest and relaxation, and when we finish a set of classes and pass the tests, we get a vacation.

- When the bell rings, we return to class. School is in session. There is more work to do.

- What happens when the bell rings, the teacher calls, the class starts, and we don't show up?

- What happens if we stay in the playground of life too long?

- If we don't find our way to class, does the class have a way of finding us?

Chapter 47

The Car

- The healing model described in this workbook works for persons of any persuasion: atheist, agnostic, religious, or spiritual. The only absolutely essential component is the universal healing wheel. Everything else is optional. To illustrate how this works, think about building a metaphysical car. (See illustration below)

- You can build a metaphysical car that will take you wherever you want to go on your recovery and healing journey. Even when you get stuck in a rut, it will get you out of trouble and help you move toward your destination.

- The car has three parts: a body, a wheel, and traction devices for the wheel.

- **Body**: The body of the car is atheist, agnostic, spiritual or religious. Which of these best represents you?

- **Wheel**: This is the universal healing wheel or PMQ. The wheel is for everyone.

- **Traction Devices**: Traction devices for the wheel include the stuff of religion. What gives you inspiration so you can deal with whatever shows up and not get stuck in the mud?

Metaphysical Car

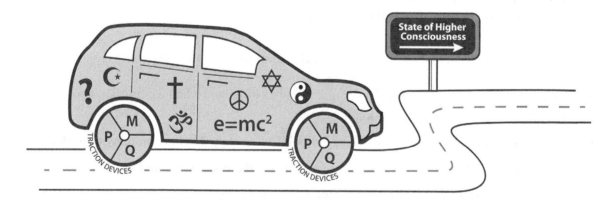

- Everyone gets a car but the design is up to you. You pick the body of the car and traction devices for the wheel. What does your car look like?

- We can park the car in the driveway or garage and take it out for a ride later. We can rent it out. We can sell it. Or, we can drive it as far as we want all the way to the Big Space. What will you do with your metaphysical car?

In the next chapter, you will study a universal healing method, including the dynamic relationship between will and grace.

Chapter 48

A Universal Healing Method

- Please review chapter 9, A Universal Healing Method, on pp. 125--140 in *Healing Power Revised*. Following is a review of this method with some additional points and pearls.

- Life is a series of tests and trials every step of the way. Tests have a deep metaphysical purpose: to bring us to a higher state of consciousness through the cultivation of healing qualities. Following is a method designed to help us fulfill this purpose. If we practice this method, we can turn the tables on our pain to make it work for rather than against us. We can turn a seeming barrier into an opportunity. We can spiritualize our problem.

- The universal method includes the universal healing wheel or PMQ and adds external action, Higher Power, will, and grace. Below you will find the ten steps for spiritualizing any problem.

Universal Healing Method

1. Define your problem. This can be any problem: physical, mental, emotional, interpersonal, or spiritual.

2. Higher Power: Ask for help from your Higher Power.

3. Outside action: Take necessary action in the external world as needed.

4. Method: For residual suffering, practice any of the twelve recommended vertical axis options.

5. Quality: Cultivate any one or a combination of healing qualities.

6. Will: Apply all of your willpower to the chosen method and quality.

7. Grace: When we do our part at maximum effort, ask for help, and endure the problem as long as it is there, grace follows.

8. Expansion of healing qualities.

9. Repeat steps 1—9.

10. Mastery: Finish the problem. Go around again with a new problem.

Exercises

1. Will

- Steps 1--3: It is our job in the healing process to define the problem, ask for help from our Higher Power, and take action in the outer world.

- Steps 4--5-: For residual suffering, we pick a method and determine the quality we need.

- Step 6: We exert maximum effort on our method and quality for as long as it takes. This means putting our whole being into the work. Review Will in *Healing Power Revised*, pp. 142--150. You will find affirmations related to will on p. 158 in *Healing Power Revised*.

- When we apply all of our willpower to our chosen method and quality, grace follows. (steps 7 and 8).

2. Grace

- Review Grace in *Healing Power Revised*, pp. 132--3.

- We have access to a vast intelligent healing power within and around us.

- We can tap into this power and get help with any type of suffering through work and grace. When we do our part at maximum effort, ask for help and endure the problem as long as it is there, grace follows.

- We can conceptualize grace coming from a conscious God of love or from healing laws of the universe that work for us when we cooperate with them. We can use whatever concept gives us inspiration and traction. The healing and transformation process works no matter how we label it.

- Grace opens the gate to the unified field of omnipotent healing energy. We have no control over the gate. The Keeper of the gate, a mysterious intelligent force or law, opens the gate for us. The gate may or may not open for elimination of disease, disability or other painful problems. However, if we do the work, the gate will always open to allow expansion of healing qualities such as peace, love, strength, courage, wisdom, and joy.

3. Will and Grace

- Will and grace work together to add another dimension of healing to the healing power equation.

- Spirit steps in when we can't help ourselves, but we cannot get this help unless we make the effort.

- The formula for success in working with any pain or problem is:

a. Ask for help from your Higher Power.

b. Take action in the outer world.

c. Apply maximum effort to your chosen method and quality.

d. Accept and endure as long as the problem remains. *I will work the problem however long or severe. I will wait for You Lord, until You appear.*

e. Grace comes on its own schedule. An Omnipotent Power responds with an answered prayer, resources, expanded healing qualities, a superconscious experience, and other phenomena.

The next chapter reviews the serenity prayer. You will study the dynamic relationship between will and surrender.

Chapter 49

The Serenity Prayer

Balancing Will and Surrender

- Sometimes we can change things in the outer world and fix the problems of the body. But we are all confronted with times when the world and our bodies give us a bad time and there is nothing we can do about it.

- When we do all the right things and it still hurts, we get frightened and discouraged. But here is the good news. When backed in a corner, when everything is stuck, we can still work a new brain groove, cultivate a healing quality, and reduce our reactivity. Often this is the only choice we have.

- We must learn to control what we can and drop the rest, and we must learn to do this under a variety of conditions: ordinary problems, major crisis, brutal realities, and even chaos. We must learn to manage it all.

- Please review chapter 10 on The Serenity Prayer in *Healing Power Revised,* pp. 141--160. You will learn about two powers: will and surrender, how they work separately and together.

- You will learn:

    a.   How to change what you can with willpower, pp. 142--150
    b.   How to accept what you cannot change, pp. 151--154
    c.   How to manage problems with both will and acceptance, pp. 154-156.

- Following is a review of these principles and some pearls and quotes from members in groups and classes.

Exercises

1. **Cultivate Willpower**

    - No matter where we are on the evolutionary ladder, we will need more willpower for those challenges and tests that are bigger than us.

    - To improve your ability to change what you can, review the following in *Healing Power Revised.*

        a.   How to increase willpower, from spark to bonfire: pp. 142--146.
        b.   Goal setting: pp. 146—150.
            - It doesn't matter how much willpower you start out with. Just set a goal and start your practice.

- Here you will find a nine-step method designed to help you quit any addiction.

- Embedded in these steps are some affirmations specifically designed to eliminate any bad habit or accomplish any goal.

- The example given is for cigarettes but you can apply these steps to any bad habit or problem.

- You will find some additional affirmations designed to help you increase your willpower on p. 158 in *Healing Power Revised*.

2. Cultivate Acceptance

- You will be given tests and challenges that are bigger than your capacity for acceptance.

- To improve your ability to accept what you cannot change, review the following in *Healing Power Revised*.

   a. Surrender, pp. 152--54
   b. School, pp. 283—86
   c. Chapter 23, Transformation of Emotion, pp. 345—357 and in this workbook on pp. 236-243

3. Will, Acceptance, and the Wisdom to Know the Difference

- For deep healing and full recovery, we need to apply will and surrender at the same time.

- We need one-pointed, calm, continuous use of our will to change what we can and to surrender and expand our healing qualities in response to what we cannot change.

- What is the right combination? How do we know whether a condition requires more or less will or surrender? Often we do not; but we can improve. Stillness is the key. When we are awake, alert, and calm, we can hear the still, small voice within, guiding us to a balanced combination of will and surrender.

- Bring in as much stillness as you can. Try meditation, contemplation, prayer, or whatever method helps you cultivate stillness.

- With sustained practice, our foundation of inner peace broadens and deepens. The mind remains calm, so we can hear the messages from that voice within. As long as we remain calm and unruffled, the Great Teacher helps us know when to act and when to remain silent.

- With time and practice, we can use will, surrender, or a combination of both in increasingly sophisticated ways, thus expanding our love and our usefulness.

Memorable Quotes from Groups and Classes

Will

- We need all of the willpower we can get and more.

- Shift gears from *I can't* to *I can*.

- Our heart and soul never asks us to be small, to play it safe. Our heart leads us only in the direction of more love, more kindness, more compassion, more understanding, and more forgiveness. To move in that direction—especially in the face of those situations that are messy and painful—can sometimes take all the fire, all the passion, all the *shvoooom* we can muster.

Surrender

- Surrender is letting go of control and being with whatever is there.

- We have to be in pain to learn how to navigate our way through it.

- It hurts no matter what, but this way it hurts the least.

- Decrease the resistance to suffering to decrease suffering.

- Sometimes I can't change anything in the outer world, but I can always roll the wheel.

- I can't change the world or you, but I can reduce reactivity by cultivating a quality.

- I surrender to the pain and God. I sit with the pain and trust God's process of purification, sometimes purification by fire.

- Your heart is a wooden bowl. With each pain and sorrow, the bowl is carved deeper, to be filled with more joy.

- Not getting my way requires courage and endurance.

Will And Surrender

- We need both acceptance and change. This is tricky because it involves opposites. But when we get this right, we get the best possible deal. We keep plugging away to change what we can in the moment and accept what we are stuck with. It still hurts, but it is the line of least resistance and the least amount of pain, since we are not reacting or adding unnecessary suffering.

- I do the footwork and let go of the rest.

- God, grant me the serenity to accept the people I cannot change, courage to change the person I can, and the wisdom to know it is me.

- We need to learn how to accept the painful conditions of our current reality that cannot be changed. When we run out of options on the horizontal axis, we can always work in the vertical axis by cultivating acceptance and associated qualities: patience, kindness, compassion, understanding, courage, strength, humility, and more.

- Through will and surrender, we can learn how to create inner space, embrace it all, and be ready for anything.

In the next chapter, we will study the ego---a very important topic for those interested in skillful pain management.

Chapter 50

Ego

Ego Building and Ego Reduction

Replacing the Ego With the Soul

- In this chapter, we will study the works of the ego: how it causes unnecessary pain for ourselves and others and what we can do about it.

- If we are to become ever-increasingly skillful pain managers, we must address the ego. It is intimately involved in pain management every step of the way.

- The ego is defined in a variety of ways depending upon the model under study. This chapter will define, clarify, and simplify the ego, an otherwise complex subject, that's difficult to grasp.

- In this chapter, we will study how the ego helps us manage our pain and how it makes it worse. The goal is to help us see how the ego works on both sides of the equation. Then we can embrace its positive contribution and begin the process of ego reduction when necessary.

- This is not an easy task, but the result is profound. We become more skillful pain managers, feel better, become better people, and may experience higher states of consciousness.

- The ego is a trickster and it is not easy to discover its tricks. It likes to operate in the dark. It keeps itself subtle, hidden. We don't even know it is operating until it is too late. One of its greatest tricks is to make us think it doesn't exist. But it does and it all too often wreaks havoc in our lives.

- It takes a long time to see how the ego functions, to learn all of its ploys. This chapter will outline some of its maneuvers.

- When we see how the ego operates, we can set up strategies to reduce its dark side, replace it with soul qualities, and restore the peace.

- You can judge for yourself whether or not this material applies to you.

- This would be a good time to review step 5 in *Healing Power Revised*, pp 56-73. Following is a review of some of that material and some additional thoughts.

- Before we get started, a word about reactivity. We are going to review how the ego, when it spins out of control, causes a high degree of unnecessary emotional reactivity. This is to be distinguished from the heightened emotions and sensitivities resulting from major mental illness: schizophrenia, bipolar disorder, PTSD, anxiety and depressive disorders, traumatic brain injury, and more. In these instances, there is a biological and/or genetic contribution to heightened reactivity that may or may not respond to the techniques recommended here.

- In the next section, you will find a description of some key principles describing the works of the ego. You will learn about the battle between the ego and the soul and how to replace the ego with soul qualities.

Ego

Key Principles

1. **CEO of Physical Plane Consciousness**

    - The ego is the chief executive officer of our physical plane consciousness. Its job is to satisfy the core drive: our need for *unlimited* peace, love, joy, and safety, more time, and no pain. It does this by establishing our place in the world of relationships, work, and recreation. This is good. We do get a portion of the peace, love, joy, and safety we crave from our relationships and activities.

    - However, most of us go too far on the horizontal axis looking for *unconditional* love and safety, which can only and must ultimately be achieved inside.

    - When we "look for love in all the wrong places," we get into trouble. The motor overheats. We develop a restless mind, overreactive emotions, bad habits, codependency, power trips, hyperactivity and more.

    - When blocked by the limitations of the physical plane, the ego counters with a variety of subtle and complex tricks as it redoubles its effort to eliminate pain and cultivate the peace, love, joy, and safety we crave. In so doing, it gets bigger and spins out of control, contributing multiple hidden layers of unnecessary suffering.

    - To counter this universal root cause of reversible pointless suffering, we have to go through a process of ego reduction and soul expansion.

    - In other words, we have to build up the ego so it can do its job of achieving that part of the love, safety, and self-esteem we can get on the physical plane, and then reduce it when it goes too far. This is a complicated and tricky maneuver. It takes time and practice. This chapter outlines some tips on how to do this difficult work.

2. **Material Consciousness: Separate, Alone, and Limited**

    - The ego gives us a distinct sense of individuality and personality. This is good. But again, the ego goes too far as it keeps us separate from our higher self, Higher Power, and creation.

    - Like a rebel monarch, the ego declares itself the sole owner and operator of consciousness. It tricks us into thinking that material consciousness is the only reality. Its greatest trick is to make us think this is all there is.

- The false god of ego blocks awareness of the soul, keeps us separate from Spirit, and prevents us from experiencing higher states of consciousness. Forcing out all experiences of higher consciousness, it would have us believe we are alone and limited.

- Our trials may be great but our greatest enemy is our ego--for it is the ego that keeps us separate from the Creator.

- With the ego in charge, we are denied access to the great omnipresent reservoir of healing power within and without.

- When the ego has its way, we would not even believe in the possibility of getting help from the Great Physician.

3. Ruler of the Universe

- The ego builds its empire on a foundation of control and power. It doesn't want to just be in charge. It wants to be the ruler of the universe.

- But we are not in charge. On the physical plane, suffering and the unknown have great power and death wins in the end.

- The ego is terrified by this arrangement and responds by secretly taking over the control rooms of the mind, emotion, desire, body, and action. It uses these tools in its desperate search for immortality and permanent peace.

- The search is in vain, however, as the ego runs into the brick wall of limitation and the inevitable suffering on the physical plane. Nevertheless, the ego does not give up its battle. It counters with an insatiable desire for recognition, success, and power. This results in excessive attention seeking, inflated self-importance, accumulation, and empire building.

- The ego behaves like a dictator, using a variety of tactics to gain power over others, including subtle manipulation and overt aggression.

- Concerned primarily with itself, the ego behaves as a greedy narcissist. *I! Me! My! Mine!*

- Territorial and self-important, it tries to manipulate others to its own ends and purposes.

- With a voracious appetite for control, it stifles dissent and ignores criticism.

4. Fear of Extinction

- Even if the ego's works give us success, power, and wealth, we are still in trouble.

- No matter how important we become, under the control of the ego we remain separate from the vast kingdom of peace within ourselves.

- Since it has no foundation, at its core the ego is insecure and fears extinction.

- Thus, it is paranoid and defensive when it does not need to be and tries to be right all of the time, even when it is wrong.

5. A Desire Making Machine

- The ego projects fantasies from its desires. It tries to get our needs met by controlling and pushing events and people.

- However, the world does not conform to our egotistical desires; and when things do not fit, we create new desires.

- Instead of working with what we have that is good, it escapes into fantasy, to what we think we want next.

- The ego, in its drive for immediate gratification, gets us into trouble with addiction and attachment. Not only do we lose preexisting strength, but also spiritual qualities cannot grow.

- The soul, on the other hand, yearns for healing and love and is willing to pay the price: work, perseverance, discipline, and self-control.

6. Superiority and Inferiority

- Self-esteem fluctuates up and down as we surf the waves of success and failure on the ego-controlled physical plane.

- When self-esteem goes too high, we feel superior, arrogant, dominant, and proud.

- When self-esteem goes too low, we experience inferiority, insecurity, anxiety, and doubt.

- The antidote to the problem of fluctuating self-esteem is the cultivation of soul esteem: unconditional love for the self, no matter what happens in the outer world.

7. Past Replays and Future Projections

- The ego is strongly attracted to the past and the future.

- While it is good to learn from the past and have hopeful plans for the future, the ego goes overboard in its replays and projections.

- We relive past hurts, resentments, and regrets, which only serve to recycle anger, depression, and guilt.

- Our projections of the future breed unnecessary fear and insecurity.

- The soul, on the other hand, is locked into the present moment when life offers up its knowledge and lessons, entertainment and joy, and opportunities to love and serve.

8. Lacks Introspection

- Because the ego lacks introspection on its own problems, it remains self-righteous while it scapegoats others.

- The ego resists change and continues to hold on to outmoded ideas.

- It leads us into the dead-end streets and dark alleys of our consciousness.
- With the ego in charge, we remain troubled, insecure, alone, and frightened.

9. Resists Change

- The ego, considering itself the king/queen of truth, denies any problems under its leadership. It sees no need for consultation.
- This sets up a fierce battle between our pain and our ego. Our pain demands that the ego get out of the way so new knowledge can flow in to save the day.
- Sensing a great and a potential humiliating defeat, the ego clings to the status quo as it fights off new ways of understanding and perception.
- The ego fights a bitter, resourceful war to the end. It resists every attempt of the soul to take over, and it does this in subtle and devious ways.
- Often we don't even know it is present and in control.
- When we discover and work to dissolve a layer of ego, another layer quietly takes over, silently waiting for an opportunity to cause trouble.
- Ego reduction is slow and difficult. However, victory is inevitable to those who persist.

Exercises

1. Following is a list of ego maneuvers that cause unnecessary pain for us. The list is long and comprehensive. Please do not be intimidated. We are not going to focus on the problems of the ego. This is the false self and only represents where we need to do some work. We are going to focus on the antidote to the ego, the soul or one hundred healing qualities adding up to love. This is the true self.

The Trickster Ego

- Accumulation: Voracious appetite for control over people, things, and events; empire building
- Aggressive
- Alone
- Attention seeking
- Attached to outcomes
- Blames: Criticizes, judges, and tries to change others.
- Change: Resists change. Stuck on outmoded ideas. Fights off new ways of understanding and perception. Defends current positions even if based on false convictions. Afraid to be wrong and afraid of change. Unable to give up its power without embarrassment and humiliation. Keeps us from seeking.
- Competes
- Control: The ego is about control. We want to be in charge.
- Criticism: Supersensitive to and ignores criticism.
- Defensive: Defends its territory even at the slightest provocation.
- Denial: Lacks introspection. Denies problems. Ignores feedback. Afraid to look within and uncover imperfections.
- Desire: Desire begets desire leading to attachments and bad habits; immediate gratification.
- Devious: Subtle and devious ways; remains hidden. Sometimes we don't even know it is present and in control.
- Dictator
- Dissent: Stifles dissent.
- Domination
- Judgmental
- Fear: Insecurity, worry, and doubt. The ego has no foundation. It fears extinction.
- Grandiosity: Do you know who I think I am?
- Greed
- Inferiority
- Jealous
- Layers: The structure of the ego is like an onion. Remove one layer; another waits.
- Identification: Identification with the physical plane, body, personality, role in the drama, desires, habits, attachments, flaws, and problems---all of which lead to the limitations of material consciousness.
- Material consciousness: As the sole owner of physical plane consciousness, the ego forces out Higher Power and higher consciousness. In material consciousness, experience is limited to the vibrational frequencies detectable by the ordinary mind and five senses.
- Manipulative
- Narcissistic

- Needy: What have you done for me lately?
- Paranoid
- Power over others
- Projection: Holding another responsible for our feelings.
- Pride
- Reactive
- Recognition: The ego strives for greatness in the world. *I want to be somebody.* It can't get enough of this external reward gratification. When it gets some, it needs more. There is an insatiable desire for recognition, success, and power.
- Rigid: It builds a rigid structure of selfish, dogmatic, overvalued thoughts, opinions, likes, and dislikes.
- Rumination: The mind gets stuck in a rut.
- Scapegoats others to protect itself from changing.
- Selfish: Concerned primarily with the self. Thinks of self more than other people. I, me, my, mine.
- Self-importance: Makes everything more important.
- Self-righteous: Tries to be right and look good all of the time. Seeks control by knowing everything.
- Self-righteous anger: One of its greatest tricks.
- Self-justification
- Separation: From others, soul, Creator, creation.
- Superiority: Arrogance, pride, domination.
- Territorial
- Winning: Has to win.
- Worry: Creates imagined calamities. Rumination. Replays.
- Other

2. Review the functions of the ego listed above.

3. Make your own list.

4. Observe how the ego plays out in your life and the lives of those around you.

5. You may be able to see other people's egos more easily than your own. It is more difficult to see how the ego operates within us, especially its more subtle aspects.

6. Be aware that you can't fix another person's ego, only your own.

7. You are the one who must decide when and how the ego is operating in your life. Become a student. It takes a long time to learn all its tricks.

8. Notice the positive and negative aspects of some ego attributes. For example, accumulation: clearly, having a good support network and possessions is a good thing. However, the ego has an insatiable desire for control over people, things, and events when it goes too far.

a. Observe how positive and negative ego attributes play in your consciousness.

b. Describe how your ego helps you and gets you into trouble.

9. Do you have to be right all of the time?

10. Are you afraid to change?

11. Do you find yourself overreacting, defending, and fighting for your current position at the expense of listening and staying open to new points of view?

12. The Ego Operates by Stealth

- The ego is always operating and it operates by stealth.

- It has multiple, subtle, powerful, invisible, hidden layers.

- We can't see it. It gets in through the back door and takes a seat in the living room quietly and imperceptibly.

- We don't even know it is in charge until there is an unhealthy reaction that comes seemingly out of nowhere. But this is a blessing in disguise, as it is now on the surface and tells you where you need to do some work.

- When you overreact, look for the ego's contribution.

- Consult the list of ego tricks on pp. 345-346. Which one or combination of these maneuvers is causing you trouble?

13. Right Size the Ego When It Gets too Big

- Emotional reactions to stressful events can be perfectly appropriate. Emotions are natural, normal, healthy, and intelligent: a rich source of information. They help us find our problems and point us in the direction of what we need to do.

- All too often however, we overreact and overreactions are a product of an inflated ego. When the ego gets too big, we add untold unnecessary pain to the equation.

- For example, a family member, friend, or colleague behaves poorly. We feel self-righteous anger. The anger is appropriate, as it helps us determine the issues and seek needed solutions. However, with the ego in charge, our reactive anger can be too big---in which case, it becomes the problem.

- We can recognize the ego's negative contributions by consulting the list of ego tricks. (See pp. 345-346) Then, through the practice of PMQ, we replace ego-induced reactive anger with understanding, non-injury, patience, forgiveness, peace, and strength.

- To determine when your response is appropriate and when the trickster ego is causing unnecessary emotional reactivity:

    1. **Ask for help**: Ego reduction is a difficult and complex task. You may need guidance from a mentor, sponsor, or professional counselor.

2. **Introspection**: The purpose of introspection is to discover what needs to change without unnecessary guilt, low self-esteem, or humiliation. Be gentle and compassionate with yourself. Remain calm and accepting. Rather than feel bad that you have problems, feel good that you have the courage to face them and the integrity to change for the better.

3. **Let the story unfold:**
   - Sit with the pain and let the story unfold.
   - Notice your heightened state of anger, fear, or any emotion.
     a. Use the healthy part of your emotion to find and solve your problems.
     b. Look for the ego's game: the source of destructive emotional overreactivity.
        - Review the list of ego tricks on pp. 345-346.
        - Mindfully be aware that the ego plays these tricks on all of us, so why not you?
        - Remember, the ego is subtle, hiding, and difficult to detect. Slow down. Take your time. Go inside. Can you hear the still, small, loving voice within? Here your conscience speaks the truth.
     c. When you do this work, there are three possible results. Only you can decide whether your emotional response is completely appropriate; partially appropriate and part ego-based; or completely ego-based.

4. **Roll the wheel**
   a. When you decide the ego has taken you up a blind alley or dead end street, practice PMQ.
   b. (P): Define the ego's trick as your painful problem.
   c. (Q): Choose a quality such as patience, kindness, humility, compassion, understanding, or forgiveness.
   d. (M): Choose any one or a combination of methods to help you grow your quality.
   e. Roll the wheel.

- With continued practice of PMQ, you will reduce and ultimately replace the negative ego with the power and wisdom of the soul's healing qualities.

- Ego reduction and soul expansion are a lifelong project. As you evolve and shift your locus of control from outside to inside, reactivity is reduced and replaced by healing qualities. In the end, at mastery, you are unconditional love itself.

14. Ego Building and Reduction

- We need both ego building and reduction throughout life---with a progressive shift toward ego reduction as we move the locus of control from outside to inside.

- Like the body, the ego needs to be fed or built up. It gets fed through its people and activities on the horizontal axis. We get love, support, and recognition from family, friends, teachers, a spouse, children, and colleagues. This is good. We need this.

- However, with its voracious appetite for recognition, success, and power, the ego eats too much and gets fat. When this happens, it needs a diet. The diet is ego reduction.

- Through mindful introspection, we can see the ego trying to get *unlimited* peace, love, joy and safety on the outside, which is impossible.

- When we see the ego is reaching out and needs to be fed from within instead, we can switch gears from the horizontal axis of people and activities to vertical axis mindfulness and meditation.

- When we practice mindfulness, meditation, and other vertical axis methods, we will find the *unlimited* peace, love, joy, and safety we crave is already inside, waiting to be tapped, free of cost.

- We need to build up the ego when self-esteem is low and reduce it when it gets too big.

15. Self-Justification of the Ego vs Insightful Wisdom of the Soul

- The ego is selfish, insecure, defensive, controlling, and self-important.

- In the face of criticism, it becomes frightened and aggressive. It will try to tell a story solely from its point of view. Self-justification is one of its greatest tricks. It does not admit mistakes.

- Since it lacks introspection on its own problems, it remains self-righteous while it treats others as scapegoats.

- The ego tends to act like a self-righteous victim, defining the faults and weaknesses of others as the source of our discomfort.

- While it may accurately discover others' faults, it is blind to its own. It may be right but this only serves to prolong our suffering. It is easy to get stuck here.

- To reverse this tendency, retreat and look within. You might review how to process emotional pain into self-knowledge in *Healing Power Revised*, pp. 351-354. Following is a brief summary of the technique presented there.

  a. Without fear, go to the deepest, darkest place in your consciousness, to those recesses needing exposure and work.
  b. Take out your inner mirror.
  c. Turn on the light of introspection.

d. Adopt an attitude of kindness, compassion, and gentleness toward yourself.

e. Remember this: feelings are intelligent. They tell you where you need to work.

f. Ask your emotional pain the following questions:

1. Why are you here?

2. What do I need to learn from you?

3. Why do I repeat the same mistakes?

4. What flaws do I have that cause pain for others and myself?

5. What do I need to learn to become a better person?

6. What work do I need to do in the external world and within myself?

16. Events, Ego, and the Perfect Peace of the Soul

- Think of three layers:

    a. Events
    b. Ego: Reaction to events
    c. Soul: The perfect peace of the soul

- The middle layer, our ego determined reactivity, is very powerful.

- We need to take away its power and give it to the soul.

- All of the methods described in this work reduce egotistical reactivity and expand the peace of the soul.

- Practice PMQ to move towards the perfect peace of the soul.

17. How Can You Tell if You Are in Your Ego or Your Soul-Spirit

- The ego has many tricks. (See pp. 345-346)

- The soul is a composite of one hundred unlimited healing qualities. (See p. 79)

- We are a complex combination of both. How can you tell which part of you is in charge? Below are a few tips.

- The ego operates on the horizontal axis where love is conditional. The soul loves unconditionally. Ask yourself, *Am I in unconditional Love, or something else?* That *something else* would be the ego.

- The ego reacts. The soul does not react. The soul is still, silent, spacious, and serene no matter what the world or body is doing.

- The ego judges and categorizes. The compassionate soul loves everyone equally without attraction or repulsion.

- The ego experiences division and separation. The soul experiences unity and oneness.

- The ego ruminates on success and failure. The soul is safe, secure, calm, watching and enjoying the show.

- The ego experiences humiliation. The soul transforms humiliation to humility.

- The ego creates superiority and inferiority. The soul breeds equality and humility.

- Can you think of some other examples?

18. Love and Service without Attachment to Outcome

- The ego is attached to outcomes. It derives its power in the battle for victory over defeat, success over failure, gain over loss, and pleasure over pain.

- When the ego takes credit for success, it puffs up; when it fails, it grieves. In either case, it maintains its territory.

- To combat the ego, practice love and service without attachment. Then, the ups and downs of life cause less reactivity.

- When motivated by the ego, we add to the separation between God and ourselves. The same act performed selflessly moves us closer to the soul-Spirit.

- Claim nothing for the self, no matter the level of personal sacrifice. The outcome belongs to a higher order, God, the universe.

19. Identification with the Ego Versus the Soul Connected to Spirit

- With the ego in charge, the central problem is one of identification.

- We experience limitation because we identify with our body, personality, and role in the drama of life.

- We think we are our desires, habits, attachments, flaws, and problems.

- We feel separate from others, creation, and the Creator.

- We accept ordinary material reality as normal.

- We believe impermanence and change have ultimate power.

- Because of these identifications, our perception and experience is limited to the vibrational frequencies detectable by the ordinary mind and five senses.

- To counter this problem of ego-identification, practice PMQ. Gradually, you will come to understand your true identity as the soul connected to the Spirit.

- As healing qualities slowly reduce and replace the ego, you will experience the ever-increasing peace, love, joy, power, and wisdom of the soul-Spirit as your true self.

20. Grandiosity of the Ego vs Humility of the Soul

- We are tiny, infinitesimal specks in an infinite universe. The ego puffs up that speck to make it look like the grandest thing that has ever happened. Confusing its little story with the whole of reality, the ego leads us into the blind alley of self-importance and arrogance.

- The ego projects its tiny speck of knowledge as the nature of reality even when information comes in to oppose that falsity. We can counter this tendency by cultivating humility, the mother of all spiritual virtues.

- You might take some time to review the chapter on humility in *Healing Power Revised*, pp. 393-405.

- When humiliation becomes humility, the ego is reduced and replaced by the soul. Discuss how this process works in your life. See *Healing Power Revised*, pp. 71-73.

21. The Three-Story House

- Using the metaphor of the three-story house (See p. 315), the ego operates on the first floor where we have all kinds of emotional reactions, sometimes helpful but often destructive.

- The second floor is the soul or unlimited healing qualities.

- The third floor is Spirit.

- On the second and third floor, there is no reactivity, only healing qualities.

- Focus your attention on the second and third floor, the soul connected to Spirit.

- At mastery, when the soul replaces the ego and merges with Spirit, your unconditional love will keep you even-minded under all conditions.

Points to Remember

- The positive side of the ego helps us establish our place in the world of people and activities. The negative side of the ego separates us from others, creation, and the Creator.

- We need to right size the ego when it gets too big or too small. We need to build the ego up when self-esteem is low and reduce it when it gets too big. Eventually, we see we are not better or worse than anyone else. This is soul equality, a good place to be, a source of strength, a place of power in the story.

- Selfishness, territoriality, self-importance, I, me, my, mine, and a host of other sly tricks of the ego---find their way into our consciousness and reap havoc in our lives.

- Ego reduction is a slow lifelong project with plenty of opportunity, day-to-day, and moment-to-moment.

- "The ego clamps on like a bull dog and won't let go." A member

- "The ego creates a lot of noise and BS!" A member

- "God comes when the instrument is empty. Empty of what? Ego. God comes when the house is full. Full of what? Love." Anonymous

- We are connected to, immersed in, and one with Spirit, but we don't know it because of the ego. The ego makes us feel separate, alone, and limited. Separation is the root cause of our trouble. Every pearl of wisdom and technique described in this work is geared to close and finally eliminate that gap, to connect the soul to Spirit, to merge with the one source of all.

- In the next chapter, you will study Omniscient Love and terror at the abyss.

Chapter 51

Omniscient Love and Terror at the Abyss

> The ultimate spiritual battle is between Omniscient
> Love and terror at the abyss.

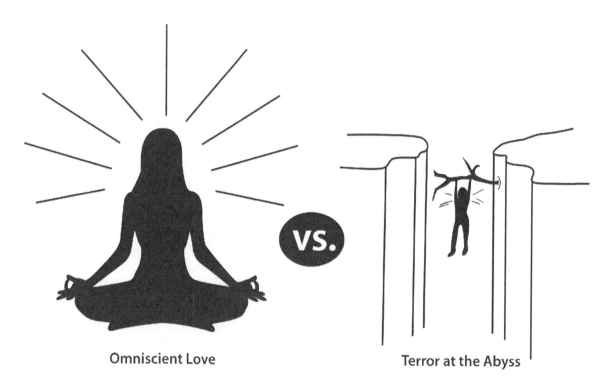

Omniscient Love   **Terror at the Abyss**

- Recall the definition of the gap-abyss: the feeling of anxiety-panic we encounter when we introspect to find and work on our problems. Fear is the number one barrier to self-healing. Even making little changes can create a panicky feeling that we might unravel to the abyss. For deep healing, we must learn how to manage the feelings in the gap-abyss.

- In the gap, we feel anxiety.

- At the abyss, we experience panic.

- Even when just in the gap, it feels like we might enter the abyss and break.

- The gap-abyss is the rate-limiting factor in growth. It occurs when we introspect and find the need to make some changes. Fear stops us from moving forward.

- Healing is like remodeling a house. We have to tear down some structure in order to rebuild. We deconstruct to reconstruct.

- When we deconstruct, it feels like God is holding us over the Grand Canyon by the scruff of the neck and asking if we trust Him. We say, "No! Put us back on land. Give us back the illusion of control and safety."

- Deconstruction feels like death. A part of us dies when we move from one spot to another but spiritual practices help us fill that seemingly empty, scary space with *a higher grade of Love*.

Fixed and Opened Belief Systems

- We can look at Omniscient Love and terror at the abyss through the lens of fixed and opened belief systems.

- In a fixed system such as orthodox religion, everything is in place. No changes are made in the system.

- In the opened system, changes are made.

- It is very difficult to go from fixed to opened beliefs. In a fixed system, everything is known and accounted for. In the opened system, there is mystery, the unknown, and the corresponding feelings of the gap-abyss.

- Some need more religious structure than others but the ultimate spiritual battle is between love and fear or---if you prefer---Omniscient Love and terror at the abyss.

- We can go to church, synagogue, or mosque, read sacred text, appreciate spiritual community and our respected spiritual leaders, but the love-vs-fear battle occurs inside the body temple. No one can do this part of the work for us. We have to fight this battle within ourselves.

- The gap-abyss is a frightening and lonely place to be. It can be dangerous if we don't learn how to manage it skillfully.

- On the other hand, facing the gap-abyss and learning how to manage the deep suffering that occurs only there, opens the door to a corresponding level of deep healing.

- What will help? In the next section, you will find some suggestions.

The Cave of Darkness
Heavy Lifting in the Gap-Abyss

- Please review chapter 27, Humility, The Way of Darkness in *Healing Power Revised*, pp. 398-400. Here you will find a description of the cave of darkness and some suggestions on how to manage it skillfully. Following are some additional ideas.

- First, we must remember a few key concepts.

  1. The dynamics of healing are the same whether our problems are tiny, small, medium, large, or huge.

  2. Sometimes we have to have more pain to have less pain.

3. Love qualities are more powerful than any painful problem.

4. The bigger the pain, the bigger the quality must be.

5. The mechanism to carry out these principles is rolling the wheel.

6. When we practice PMQ, at some point, love comes in to contain, reduce, or eliminate the pain and guide us through what is left.

- Here is the typical sequence.

Comfort zone → Problem → Gap-abyss → Roll The Wheel → Increase Love → Comfort zone → Repeat → Mastery

---

- We feel comfortable and safe. The abyss is in the living room, hiding and silent; we don't feel it.

- A problem shows up and sweeps away our illusion of safety. It points us in the direction of some work we need to do.

- We understand the need to face the unknown and the gap-abyss as this leads to the next level of power the healing qualities have to offer.

- Roll the wheel. Love burns up our problem and fills in the gap.

- When we finish this layer of work, we feel safe and comfortable again.

- Then another problem shows up. We are tested beyond our current capacity and go around again.

- It's a process. We get thrown back into a painful problem and rediscover the healing powers of the wheel.

- As we practice PMQ, the qualities are slowly moving towards unconditional, and the locus of control shifts from outside to inside.

- This sounds good---and it is---but it is not easy to do. When the anxiety at the gap transforms to terror at the abyss, it not only blows away our illusion of safety but also seemingly takes out our belief system and knowledge. Some call this the dark night of the soul, the cave of darkness, brutal reality, or a personal ground zero.

- This is a tough place to be. We don't want to be here without any tools. We need a plan to manage the powerful feelings of the abyss, so we can be as ready as possible.

- Following is an example of how PMQ works at the abyss.

1. P might be fear or terror at the abyss.

2. Q would be any one or a combination of healing qualities adding up to love. Qualities that come to mind for the abyss are acceptance, courage, strength, endurance, perseverance, patience, trust, faith, compassion, and surrender.

3. We can use our two great powers, will and thought, to cultivate these qualities when tested beyond our capacity.

4. We can fill the seemingly empty and terrifying space of the gap-abyss with love qualities by rolling the wheel.

5. No matter how rough it gets, we persist. We keep rolling the universal healing wheel and choosing the methods and qualities that work for us when pain is great.

6. We can do this whenever the abyss shows up and for however long it takes.

7. If we do this work, eventually the light of Spirit enters the cave of darkness bearing gifts of peace, love, strength, and wisdom.

8. The illusion of safety based on an external locus of control gradually shifts to the reality of safety rooted in an internal locus of control.

9. We eventually discover the absolute love and safety we seek in the outer world can only be found within.

10. At mastery, we find the ground of all-being is not terror at the abyss but the safety, security, and immortality of Omniscient Love.

11. Make the effort. Effort is progress. This is heavy lifting at the gap-abyss.

- What PMQ will work for you when suffering is at its peak at the gap-abyss?
- The next chapter is a compilation of inspirational quotes from groups and classes.

Chapter 52

Inspirational Quotes from Groups and Classes

- Insight is a spiritual step.

- When I get the right people and activities at the right dose, at the right time, I am in the rhythmical flow of things, the zone, synchronicity.

- All pain goes through the mind and the mind makes it bigger or smaller. Practice PMQ. The mind gets stronger. Then it can work to contain, reduce, or eliminate the pain.

- The omniscient blockhead, the ostentatiously intelligent person who knows everything except the one thing he really needs to know: everything that he doesn't. This is fatal. The silent killer. Thomas Friedman

- Surrender to the infinite. It determines what comes and what doesn't come.

- Saints are not patsies.

- Judgment is an energy vampire, a Venus flytrap.

- My intention is to help from now unto eternity. My way is playful, loving, and deep.

- How to receive critical feedback: "Thank you, I will take a look at that."

- Trust God, clean house, serve others.

- You already have what you're looking for.

- We all came here to be healed.

- Pain is the motivator but so is life. I want to do the right thing.

- I am not growing old. I grow old when I stop growing.

- When pain is big, it sweeps away all knowledge. There are no methods, no qualities, no wisdom, no knowledge. Just pain. There are great reservoirs of strength in our weakest moments. We must surrender to find it. The darkest hour can be just before the light. Persevere.

- Sometimes the only thing on the menu at the Brutal Reality Cafe is a big hot plate of *damned if you do* served with a side of *damned if you don't*. For most of us, this is a hard meal to swallow. Choosing to bear our suffering instead of pigging out on self-destruction often means a long wait for dessert. Fortifying ourselves with patience and faith gives us the strength to endure the wait until our reward arrives. Tim Casebeer

- Roll the wheel every moment of every day at work, home, or at play.

- Love is the religion; the universe is the book.

- The universal wheel is the physician within. Roll the wheel and you expand healing power, become a more skillful pain manager, and evolve spiritually.

- The answer is right next to the problem.

- Put on a new behavior. It's easy.

- Mind left alone goes into free-fall.

- Mystery: I love it.

- When the guitar string is too tight it will break. If it is too loose, it will not play. When just right, it plays in harmony with the earth.

- Clean out all the skeletons.

- I may not be able to change outer conditions, but I can always reduce my reactivity.

- Every time I stop thinking about myself is a spiritual experience.

- God gives me unconditional love. I give that to you.

- No matter what happens, look for Love over pain as a means of expressing creativity and evolution.

- Do Good. Avoid evil. Appreciate your lunacy. Pray for help. Buddhist slogan

- I need to receive and accept whatever comes in the movie. I need to relax into it. I need to learn how to do this on all of the stages I walk on: friends, family, work, groceries, waiting in line, public speaking, suffering, whatever shows up. Some people call this surrender.

- The list of one hundred healing qualities is like spiritual polypharmacy. We can fight with these qualities as we go through our tests and trials.

- Read the lives of the saints and masters. Then you will not be confused about the role of pain. They often suffer more than we do but they respond with patience, kindness, compassion, love, understanding and forgiveness. They are skillful pain managers.

- Jesus was a master pain manager. He said, "Father, forgive them for they know not what they do."

- Mastery is not possible for most of us at this time but we can follow the lead of the great ones.

- We can find our power in the story when we learn how to respond to suffering with healing qualities.

- We have great, unused power right here, right now. When we learn how to navigate our way through our pain skillfully, we find our power in the story.

- We see the world through a looking glass darkly. When we practice the recommended methods, we slowly clean the glass and see the world more clearly.

- The methods peel back our enormous reactivity, calm down racing thoughts, and heal ragged emotions.

- Start where you are. Use what you have. Do what you can. Arthur Ash

- The only disability in life is a bad attitude.

- For skillful pain management, you must train your mind, learn from your emotions, and curb your desires.

- Thought, will, breath, concentration: these are the tools we need for spiritual work.

- Big Love is the answer to every problem. This is yoga.

- There may need to be more pain to have less pain. When you ride the demons, they get smaller, slowly.

- Do not worship saints, but see the divine through them and then you can become that. Everyone is welcome in this school. Rumi

- I have become a stranger to myself. Rumi

- Thanks for those who disturb us, who put the Love challenge to us.

- Grow the qualities until they become unconditional, spontaneous, automatic habits. This is the way to Big Love.

- Give me the courage to face my limitations and see the sacred in myself and my work.

- Energy is given to us. Surrender is going with the flow of that energy. Fighting it causes trouble. Going with it is most beneficial. The stream is always more powerful than we are. Go with it to get it.

- When you practice PMQ, Buddha is your therapist.

- Affirmative wisdom travels from your sacred book to your head, then to your cells, and then to surrounding space and other people as healing vibrations.

- The healing power in our cells will do the work but it wouldn't mind our cooperation. We cooperate by connecting our mind with love qualities and sending those qualities to our cells and surrounding space. In this model, love is the connecting link between mind, body, and Spirit.

- In the room of stillness, the ego shrinks, healing qualities expand, and problems burn up.

- The wave is never separate from the ocean but it feels separate, isolated, alone, frightened, limited. Practice the methods to realize the connection between wave and ocean which is soul connected to Spirit. Forgetfulness of this connection is the source of our misery.

- God is exquisite love beyond words.

- God is always greater than we can think or imagine by infinity.

- The pain of regret is greater than the pain of discipline.

- When you practice affirmations, use thought, picture, and feeling to get the most power.

- When we practice PMQ, our problems are still there but we no longer identify with them and they have less power. We identify with the qualities.

- Jesus and Buddha are inside. They will cool off your hot potatoes.

- Reactivity is a spiritual power failure (SPF). The light goes out.

- Is there a love, a drawing together of any kind that is not sacred? Rumi

- Cultivate gentle spiritual strength.

- Drench your Spirit with these wisdom pearls.

- We are not just the mind and body. We are the soul connected to Spirit.

- Jesus came without a book, building, or church---only Big Love. We can melt our addictions and attachments with this love by rolling the universal healing wheel. It's all about love. Start your climb.

Chapter 53

Staging Disease and Recovery

- We can use the universal healing wheel and Spin → Float → Integrate → Liberate for staging disease and recovery.

- Following is an example of staging recovery for people who suffer from chronic severe illness.

> ### Spin → Float → Integrate → Liberate
>
> - **Spin:** This is high acuity requiring multiple visits to the emergency room, hospital, and clinics. Those in the spin zone have one or more of the following: active physical illness, mental illness, addiction, low or no income, unemployment, or homelessness. These individuals often spin between the hospital, jail, and street. There may be danger to self or others.
>
> - **Float:** With medication, housing, and financial support---mental illness, physical illness, and substance use improve. If present, symptoms are more manageable. People isolate in their rooms, watch TV, smoke, hang out, and wander aimlessly. There may be some social contact but little or no connection to meaningful social, recreational, vocational or spiritual activity. There is often no meaning and purpose.
>
> - **Integrate:** This is community integration involving people, activities, and belief systems. People get their social, recreational, vocational, and spiritual lives back.
>
> - **Liberate:** Integrate higher states of consciousness with good mental health.

Staging Recovery Using the 15 Methods

- The universal healing wheel includes fifteen methods. Some will choose none of these. Others will apply all fifteen.

- To move from spin to float to integrate, we need positive action on the horizontal axis of people, activities, and belief system.

- For deepest healing and liberation, we may need to move from fixed to opened belief systems, and add vertical axis healing options including meditation and self-knowledge. This requires managing that gap between fixed and opened belief systems, where even a little anxiety is perceived as the uninvited guest in the living room.

The Methods

Horizontal Axis

1. People

2. Activities

3. Belief system
   a. Fixed
   b. Opened

Vertical Axis

4. Affirmations

5. Habit transformation

6. Progressive muscle relaxation

7. Breathwork

8. Contemplation

9. Meditation

10. Prayer

11. Mindfulness

12. Practicing the presence of God

13. Service

14. Yoga

15. Transformation of emotion

Staging Recovery and Healing

- Level 1: No options. This individual chooses none of the fifteen methods. Some people are overwhelmed by stimulation and need to stay alone to remain stable. Others may lack initiative or energy. The illness may be too acute. There may be too much pain. This individual will remain in spin and float.

- Level 2: People and/or activities. This individual chooses people and/or activities. There is social and recreational recovery but an inability to engage in cognitive-behavioral work (belief systems) or vocational recovery. This person benefits from day programs and drop-in centers.

- Level 3: People, activities, and belief system. This individual engages with people and activities and has a belief system: traditional religion, twelve-step program, or other healing models. This includes social, vocational, recreational, and spiritual recovery. This individual remains primarily on the horizontal axis and has an external locus of control.

- Level 4: People, activities, and belief system with any one or combination of vertical axis options. There may be a need to move from a fixed to an opened belief system. The locus of control begins to shift from outside to inside.

- Level 5: As with level 4 but add transformation of emotion and meditation, the two most difficult and advanced vertical axis techniques. With the addition of these two powerful digging tools, one can remove all traces of negativity, leading to the recovery of the higher self and Higher Power as the *unlimited* peace, joy, love, and safety we crave. The locus of control is primarily inside. There is an expansion of higher states of consciousness, sometimes referred to as liberation or enlightenment.

Chapter 54

Frequently Asked Questions

- **Why do you repeat yourself?** This material is difficult. It takes time to understand. Going at it from a variety of angles and repetition helps reprogram the mind.

- **What kind of problem does this model work for?** This model works for any problem or pain. Your problem can be physical, mental, emotional, interpersonal, or spiritual. It can be tiny, small, medium, large, or huge.

- **Do I have to be in pain to practice this model?** No. Even though the universal healing wheel is PMQ or pain, method, quality, you can practice a method and quality when there is no pain. But don't worry; there will be plenty of opportunities to practice the P in PMQ.

- **How much do I have to practice PMQ before I feel better?** That depends on the size of your problem. Tiny problems can be managed easily and quickly. Big problems are locked in brain grooves that have a lot of power and will take a corresponding amount of work and time.

- **How do I work through and past this painful problem so it doesn't define me?** When we practice PMQ, we define the problem but do not focus there. We focus on love qualities, which are defined as the true self, higher self, or soul.

- **You use the word universal a lot. What does this mean?** While we are unique and require individual support, this work speaks to what we all have in common. There are universal life problems and solutions. This workbook is about universal solutions to universal problems. We study universal recovery and healing principles, methods, and qualities. Everyone has pain (P) or the inevitable suffering of life and reactivity. The methods (M) and Qualities (Q) are likewise universal. This is how we can address everyone's issues.

- **Is unconditional love or even-mindedness under all conditions repression or denial?** Spiritual talk divorced from the human condition can sometimes sound inhuman or robot-like. This work embraces the human condition and acknowledges our imperfections and the inevitability of suffering. At the same time, we can reduce unnecessary reactivity, become more loving, and help others in increasingly sophisticated ways. While we have to have pain, we can create an enlarged compassionate space to hold all.

- **I worry about ego reduction and soul expansion. Will I be boring without a personality?** You will not lose your individuality or personality. You will reduce that part of your ego that causes unnecessary pain for others and yourself. Everything else improves. You will feel better and become a better person. There will be more peace, love, joy, power, and wisdom. You may even have a superconscious experience.

- **Are there any shortcuts?** If you try to avoid pain that you need to face, you make it worse. This work is devoted to helping you face your pain and manage it skillfully. Life will still be hard but skillful pain management will give you the easiest possible ride.

CONCLUSION

Whether your problems are physical, mental, emotional, interpersonal, or spiritual, love is the answer. It doesn't matter whether your problems are tiny, small, medium, large, or huge, throw love at them. When your body gives you trouble, throw love at it. When people are difficult, throw love at them. When you regret the past, throw love at it. When you worry about the future, throw love at it. When you find yourself in the gap-abyss, the cave of darkness, or the dark night of the soul, hold on to love. Bring your love to brutal reality and serve there. Respond with love no matter what the world or your body does. Love is the great healer and the great pain manager. It is needed now more than ever. Take the love pill. Practice love until love is all there is.

About the Author

Dr. Phil Shapiro is a psychiatrist and devotee of yoga-meditation with an interest in the magnificent intelligent healing power as an antidote to the brutal realities of life. He has had a forty-five-year career as a clinician, teacher, and administrator in public psychiatry. Work has taken him from the inner city to the Alaska bush, from holistic to addiction medicine, and from the boardroom to the streets.

In 1974, he worked in one of the first interdisciplinary holistic clinics in New York City. In 1983, he became the Director of Mental Health and Developmental Disabilities for the State of Alaska. Following that, he was the Chief Medical Officer at Oregon State Hospital and then Clinical Director of Forensic Psychiatry at Western State Hospital. He has been a surveyor, reviewing quality of care in hospitals and clinics throughout the country. For the past twenty-two years, he has worked in community mental health centers.

Dr. Shapiro received his medical degree in 1969 from the University of Illinois Medical School, where he was a member of the medical honorary society, Alpha Omega Alpha. He trained in psychiatry at Albert Einstein College of Medicine, Downstate Kings County Hospital in New York City, and he received a master's degree in public health from Columbia University. Dr. Shapiro has been on the faculty of the Department of Psychiatry at Columbia University and is currently an associate clinical professor in the Department of Psychiatry at Oregon Health Sciences University.

Dr. Shapiro lives in Portland, Oregon. He works for Central City Concern, a community healing center where he teaches groups and classes about skillful pain management, expansion of healing power, and spiritual evolution.

He is happily married to Sharon Whitney, author and playwright. They have two sons and five grandchildren.

Index

I

J

K

P

R